About George

"In the NFL and other sports, when it comes to players, the word 'leader' is often overused, however George Martin truly was and still is a leader to this day. I played football with George on the New York Giants for 10 years. With the Giants, George was a leader not just in the locker room, but on and off the field as well. He was a big brother to many players, a father to others and a friend to all. Sometimes he acted like a high school guidance counselor, helping coach players on the field, but also aiding players to keep or get their personal lives in order. When I was a player, I probably took the role he played for granted, but as I look back now as a commentator and see the dynamics of NFL teams today, I realize just how important George's role was and what a shame it is that so many teams do not have a natural leader like him to fill it. I was not at all surprised when I heard George was going to walk across America to help support the rescue and recovery workers of 9/11. It was typical George and typically the way he has led his life, leading and helping others every chance he gets."

Phil Simms, Retired New York Giants Quarterback and Current Commentator, The NFL on CBS

"Anyone working on 9/11 witnessed indescribable destruction and despair, as well as tremendous acts of gallantry and heroism. Emergency workers were lauded by elected officials in the days after 9/11, but their unique needs became ensnared in red tape that extended all the way to Washington. When George Martin walked across America, every step he took and the pain from every callous that he endured was for them. George never forgot the true heroes of 9/11, and they and their families will never forget him. By any standard of measure, George is a true American hero."

Sgt. Ed Mullins, a 32-year NYPD veteran and President of the NYC Sergeants Benevolent Association

About George Martin's *a Journey for 9/11*

"By any standard, George Martin's *Journey* was a remarkable feat. The attention he brought to the plight of thousands of ailing rescue and recovery workers of Ground Zero was surely instrumental in the passage of the James L. Zadroga 9/11 Health & Compensation Act. George is a Giant of a man, and it was my honor to work alongside him to achieve justice and secure care for a vast community of selfless and courageous Americans."

U.S. Congresswoman Carolyn B. Maloney

"George Martin's *Journey* is one of the most uplifting and inspiring stories to emerge from the ashes of 9/11, and provides valuable, timeless lessons for young and old alike. In ways that extend far beyond the events of 9/11, his singular, monumental achievement for those in need teaches us about the potential of the human spirit, and about the limitlessness of what determined, caring people can accomplish."

Alice Greenwald, Executive Vice President for Programs and Director of the 9/11 Memorial Museum

"George Martin's *Journey* astounds on every level, and set a new standard for selflessness and generosity in the wake of America's national tragedy. Working relentlessly to help save and extend the lives of true heroes, his *Journey* should be admired and studied as a great act of heroism in its own right."

Jay S. Winuk, Co-founder, 9/11 National Day of Service and Remembrance, 9/11 family member, and director of communications for *a Journey for 9/11*

"George Martin ranks high among the heroic leaders who stepped forward with passion and action to make a real difference for the rescue and recovery workers of Ground Zero. From every perspective, his *Journey* was a monumental achievement. The world surely could use more like George Martin."

John Feal, Founder and President, The FealGood Foundation

About George Martin's *a Journey for 9/11*

"After 2 weeks at Ground Zero, I had something going on with my breathing. One day after a fire, it all came crashing down for me. I ended up in the hospital with smoke inhalation and was forced to retire. I had anticipated doing 30 years on the job.

Mr. Martin's Journey for 9/11 sponsored my treatment through the NY Rescue Workers Detox Program. It gave me the opportunity to open a new chapter in my life. I won't be held back by breathing issues, and it's helped me spiritually and with my family.

Me getting a chance to thank you personally is something that's not taken lightly. You've set a standard for all Americans, and I thank you for helping us through this difficult time period. I appreciate your personal dedication to getting us well and whole again. Thank you."

Greg Parr, 19-year FDNY firefighter

"There are really not enough words to describe what George did for people affected by 9/11. It wasn't just the funds he raised, although they were wonderful and we put them to good use for responders. It was more the sense that, with every step he took, more of our country and the world understood the pain this event had caused and felt the need to do something about it."

Dr. Michael Crane, Deputy Director of the Mount Sinai WTC Monitoring and Treatment Program

Just Around The Bend

My Journey for 9/11

GEORGE D. MARTIN

With
Richard Fritzky

Edited by Jim Zebora

All photos in this book were taken and contributed by teammates and friends of *a Journey for 9/11*.

Special thanks to Joe Tessitore of Significance Press, my "coach" on the field of the printed page.

First Edition

ISBN: 978-0-9886509-8-5

DEDICATION

To my faithful parents, George and Janie, to my beautiful wife of almost 40 years, Dianne, and to my loving children, Teresa, George KK, Benjamin and Aaron, the very heart of the three generations who gave rise to all of this in the first place.

Thanks to my parents for molding and shaping me and teaching me that it is only in the giving that we receive. My mother, Mrs. Janie Pearl Martin, is without question the very rock upon which the Martin family crest was established. Mom purposely girded me and my four siblings with all of the necessary wherewithal to confront and succeed against the inevitable challenges that we would face as both children and adults. We owe a tremendous debt to her boundless sacrifice, for which I and all of my siblings will be eternally grateful. Thanks, Mom.

Thanks to Dianne for always supporting and sustaining me, no matter how far outside of the box I went, and for teaching me daily that love is always the opening door. She has been, and continues to be, my enduring lover, my cherished advisor, my voice of reason, as well as my much-needed alter ego. Together we have gone through the lowest depths of despair and anguish, and we have clung tightly to one another as we miraculously rose to the heights of societal success. Amazingly, two rather naive country bumpkins, who, when the cupboard of life appeared to be bare, undauntingly clung to their faith and each other for comfort, support and guidance, and eventually, against all odds, made it through.

All the while she never left my side, nor I hers. Super Bowl championships, hall of fame honors and various awards, executive promotions, celebrity spotlights and the like, in my humble opinion, pale in comparison with having someone special by your side in good times and bad, to help navigate through the paradoxes that life has to offer. For those reasons and many more, she remains my guiding light, as well as the love of my life.

Thanks to my children for bringing profound meaning and purpose to my life and for reminding me daily that Dianne and I have managed to light four bright candles in the darkness.

George D. Martin

Just Around the Bend

CONTENTS

Just Around the Bend

FOREWARD

Like everyone else, I suppose, there are some things I know a lot about and some things I don't. For example, I don't know much about interior decorating, the migratory habits of the South American condor, nor the exact origin of the Egyptian pyramids , but I do know a lot about the business of horse racing and most recently, the finer and more interesting points of sports commentating. And, of course, I especially know a lot about running a football team -- what it takes to succeed on the field, about the kinds of players and coaches you need to be competitive, what a franchise needs to do to keep a loyal fan base, and about how tough it is to be an NFL player.

Having coached or operated five NFL teams over the course of three decades, all of which achieved some level of success, I'm comfortable saying that I know, too, what it takes for professional players to be *winners*, to *excel*. Not nearly just in terms of athletic ability. That's just a start. There are plenty of players out there with special physical gifts who never quite excel the way you think they should. Because, as we all know, success and winning is about much more than just the magical combination of athletic ability and some measure of luck. Winning in the NFL is also about guts, determination, teamwork, study, leadership, sacrifice, selflessness, endurance and passion. It's about digging down *deep* and finding a way to mentally and physically exceed whatever you thought your absolute limits are, and then extending that some more. And doing it over and over again -- down after down, series after series, quarter after quarter, game after game, season after season. The great ones, the truly *great* ones, have that fiber. They are able to get it done, to play that way. And, believe me, I've been privileged to coach my share of that rare breed.

George Martin is one of that select group. Over the course of a 14-year playing career, he was a marvel to watch on the field. He played during an era when players did their jobs without the need to call attention to themselves every time they did something well, or simply did what they were expected to do. George went about his business, day in and day out, in the most professional and determined way, generating tremendous results. He is one of a handful of guys you could just count on. And that is a coach's blessing.

I do believe that of all the players I've been privileged to coach, George may be the most underrated. His skills, work ethic, consistency and results were of the highest caliber. Now, some of him being underrated may be because he played in the shadow of several of the greatest to ever grace NFL fields, such as Harry Carson, Phil Simms and Lawrence Taylor. And maybe some of it's because he wasn't flashy about what he'd get done. But nobody, and I mean *nobody*, was more important to the success of that Super Bowl XXI Championship NY Giants team than George Martin. He was the anchor.

If you can be a leader of leaders, that was George. Sure, he made what I called "the greatest football play I've ever seen," acrobatically intercepting a pass and running 78 yards for a touchdown in a 1986 game against the Broncos. And sure, he memorably tackled John Elway in the end zone for a safety against those same Broncos in Super Bowl XXI, a singular play which set us on a course to victory. And, yes, he set the record for touchdowns by a defensive end, amassed a ton of sacks and tackles, and co-captained a defensive team that ranks with the all-time greats.

George's greatest contributions, though, were in being a *leader.* A true, true leader. He had attributes of General George S. Patton, Martin Luther King, Jr., Robert F. Kennedy and Bill Russell all rolled into one, with a storyteller's touch of Bill Cosby thrown in for good humor. Players *gravitated* to him, they *learned* from him, they were *inspired* by him and they *loved* him. George did what the great ones do – *he made his teammates better.* And that's the best thing I can say about a player.

But unlike even most great ones, George made players better *off the field* as well. He nurtured young players, having them to his home in New Jersey for holidays. He set up a model program, still widely used today, to allow players to return to school during their playing careers, to earn college credits toward graduation. For those interested, he shared his religious faith with players, as our own internal pastor. He was a model for older players looking to extend their careers. And he very effectively worked, as player rep to the League and then as president of the NFL Players Association, and then even later as the first president and executive director of the NFL Alumni Association, to improve the quality of life for thousands of players during and after their days on the field were over. The man has simply been a can-do leader, a pacesetter, a maverick all his adult life.

So when George called me in August 2007 to tell me he was going to walk across the nation, sea-to-shining-sea, for the benefit of heroes now suffering, I thought, "I don't know how, but if anyone can do it, walk all those miles for months on end at age 55, with a family at home, a job in the city, etc., it surely is George." As monumental the task he described was, I just was not surprised he intended to tackle it.

This is a man who played 14 seasons in a league where the average career is just over three years. He never suffered a serious injury playing a position where serious injuries are common, and he only missed six games over the course of those 14 seasons. *Six games.* George came *prepared* to play. He fought through pain as well as anyone I know and he had an unshakeable determination to win, to complete the job, and to do his absolute best. So I knew he would prepare well, physically and mentally, for this marathon of a walk. And I knew he would make it.

Now, I've experienced and witnessed some extraordinary things in my life. Great acts of courage. Impressive demonstrations of athleticism and endurance. Moments of true generosity and selflessness. Rarely, if ever, though, do you see *all of that wrapped into one.* But that's really what George's Journey was. A very powerful (and long!) act of physical endurance and skill, true patriotism, sacrifice and selflessness all at once.

George likes to give me credit for having taught him some things as a coach and, I suppose, as a man, on and off the field. I'm genuinely proud of that, especially coming from him. When all is said and done, among a coach's greatest pleasures is to have made a real, lasting difference in the lives of the men or women with whom he went to war. But the truth is, and I mean this with all sincerity, over the years I've probably learned as much from George as he learned from me. And that's one of the reasons I chose George among all others to introduce me in Canton, Ohio, for my induction into the Pro Football Hall of Fame in 2013. George Martin is the guy, then and now, I want in the foxhole with me.

And I'm still learning from him. I believe there are lessons for all of us in George's Journey, not only about perseverance, and caring for your fellow man, and physically pushing yourself beyond your perceived limits, but also about America itself. Amidst all the chaos in our government, and the seemingly daily social and economic challenges our nation faces and more, it's easy to forget sometimes that we truly live in the greatest country in the world, home to the most impressive people from every walk of life. George and his amazing Journey remind us in every way that the American tapestry is a work in progress but also a work of art, and singular in the history of the world. His Journey made me realize that George Martin is surely among those who make me proud to be an American.

What drives a man to walk 22 miles a day and millions of steps for almost 10 straight months? To leave his family behind to benefit other families? To endure freezing temperatures and blazing heat and rainstorms and mountain climbs and muddy streets and highway traffic, and speeding pickup trucks and wild dogs on lonely country roads? What is the make-up of a man *who so loves his country* that he chose this historic way to both enjoy its splendor and give back to those who desperately needed and deserved a helping hand?

Take a reader's walk with my friend George Martin, this Giant of a man, as he shares his Journey for 9/11 and you'll find out.

Bill Parcells

PREFACE

JUST AROUND THE BEND:
a Journey for 9/11

George D. Martin

I had criss-crossed America hundreds of times by plane and dozens of times by automobile. As an old Pacific 8 football player and a 14-season veteran of the National Football League, I often saw the United States from above and I had certainly visited our more prominent cities. I spent many a day in Los Angeles and Denver, Chicago and Dallas, Miami and New Orleans, D.C. and Philadelphia and other great cities, while my home base was the Big Apple, New York City itself. Oh, I knew the geography of America all right, but I wasn't in any way intimate with it, because I had but passed over and by and through, absorbing very little of its essence in the process.

I visited some of those cities frequently to be sure, but I was there only to practice and play, and all I'd really get to see were the hotels and the stadiums. I invariably rushed in and out of town, to and from the airport, on a team bus that invariably had dark and tinted windows. As a result, I captured only scattered images of these great American cities. And besides, pre-game we were pre-occupied with playbooks and the anticipation of battle; and post-game, beat up and bruised, we had neither the strength nor the desire to look anyway.

Nothing changed when I traded my shoulder and hip pads for a business suit. It's just that the magnificence of stadiums was traded for dreary conference rooms or great restaurants that went wholly unappreciated. You rushed by so much, but never took it in.

Since childhood, as a South Carolina farm and country boy, I had been keenly aware of America's both majestic and simple beauties, but I had never seen nor internalized them. I had never gotten up close and personal with my country, this land that I love, this land that I wanted to see and embrace. It had long been on my personal bucket list, this desire to experience and appreciate America's "amber waves of grain" and "purple mountain majesties" in person.

I had always wanted to meet the American people, too, up close and personal.

Often in my youth, I went so far as to fantasize and dream of walking along the byways and back roads, and through the hidden valleys and Great Plains of America.

*****

Then oh so much later in life, on a blue-sky, sun-drenched morning of a spectacular day, the kind of day that makes every cell within you jump for joy at the mere thought of being alive, I was reminded of this. This love of the land and need to be intimate with its people struck me again while I was walking through the suburban outskirts of Canton, Ohio, right in the American heartland. I was there to celebrate with my great friend and teammate of 14 years, Harry Carson, his induction into the Pro Football Hall of Fame.

It was August 6, 2006, and the glory of that stunning day when all of nature seemed ablaze was richly complemented by the well-deserved glory being showered upon my fellow warrior-in-the-trenches and New York Football Giants co-captain. Middle linebacker and defensive end, we were part of what appreciative fans long looked upon as the *Big Blue Wrecking Crew.*

Uninvited and out of the blue, on that Canton morning made in Heaven where all I passed seemed to be teeming with life, it just struck me, this age-old desire to see America up close and personal. And so did the thought, if not now, when? As well as the ancillary question, if not now, never? And so I reached an impulsive and sudden decision, rising up wholly from within, to explore the possibilities of literally walking from "sea to shining sea," along with the attendant thought of attaching it to a cause of noble note.

I had always wanted to meet the American people, up close and personal.

Moved by the soft wind that brushed by me and by the lush green fields that I passed and by the sun that caressed Akron and Canton, I actually promised myself to explore what might be done to bring this over-the-top and out-of-the-ordinary childhood dream to life. Immersed in nature and in what was a picturesque environment, my August 6 was the most extraordinary walk that I had ever taken up to that point, for it had inspired and breathed life into a determination to walk clear across the United States of America.

Yes, it was an extraordinary moment, but neither crazed nor delusional. Few of us ever dream of walking across America and fewer still actually do so. But dreaming and musing about doing something crazy happens every day. Most of us conjure up incredible notions every once in a while, those do-the-impossible, larger-than-life, glorious notions that we just as quickly and easily, and understandably and rationally, give the boot to when reality clicks back in.

As reality usually does!

The only real surprise was that reality didn't click back in.

This particular New York-to-California-dreaming of a notion, born on the sun-speckled outskirts of Canton, stuck in my psyche.

It was still with me the next day as I made my way back to Ringwood, New Jersey, where I lived, and back to New York City where I worked. It was still there as I spoke to my wife, Dianne, that evening and when I spoke to my colleagues at AXA Equitable later that week.

I took this dream and I immediately busied myself with trying to put wings on it so it could fly. Acting as if the extraordinary were ordinary, I almost remarkably and in short order found that both those I was responsible to at home in Ringwood and at the office in New York were basically supportive. That both my wife and four children were theoretically on board would allow me to try to place all of the necessary wheels in motion.

While there were kinks to be worked out and a great deal of planning to do, family, colleagues, and friends had all agreed that I wasn't necessarily out of my mind.

So much for reality!

*****

With Step One accomplished, it was game on and my attention was directed to Step Two, which was, of course, to give an act this large the purpose and the meaning that it warranted. Satisfying the good old country boy instinct inside was all well and good, but justifying an effort of this magnitude necessitated giving it both weight and substance.

It helped that I was no stranger to causes, large and small, and that the labels community-minded and charitable and humanitarian had generously been attached to me.

I had long tried to be the real deal.

Influenced by a father who taught me to leave behind something better than what I found, I had tried to be one of life's givers rather than takers. I believe, in my gut, that we are born to be our brothers' and sisters' keepers and that we all owe a duty to one another. The phrase, "We shall all pass this way but once," should be front and center in our lives, and the Golden Rule is golden for a reason. Decency and goodness and charity should burn within each of us.

While never looking for accolades or tributes or plaques, I have garnered a truckload of them, because goodness always gives way to goodness and people will go to extraordinary lengths to thank someone for doing what they ought to be doing anyway. To serve is to be blessed, to have your cup filled with grace. It is the one tonic that satisfies the soul.

Perhaps those that mean the most to me, however, were the receipt of the Byron Whizzer White Award, which is given annually to the one National Football League player who best extends himself to service people and community, and the Heisman Humanitarian Award.

"We shall all pass this way but once" should be front and center in our lives, and the Golden Rule is golden for a reason. Decency and goodness and charity should burn within each of us.

As to the cause, I first thought about my own Minority Athletes Networking Etc., Inc., or "MAN," a New York metropolitan organization that I co-founded to help provide young minority athletes in inner cities an educational, social and personal boost. Although the work that MAN does is both laudable and formidable, I determined that there was a need to define a cause that was more national in scope.

To do so, I needed to look no further than outside my own office window to be reminded of the events of September 11, 2001, when the World Trade Center towers collapsed and nearly 3,000 Americans perished – and the heart of a nation cried out, and the whole world mourned.

That was my inspiration. All it took was a simple glance out the window, a glance that stirred up the memory of those awful feelings that live forever in the depths and recesses of one's mind, heart and soul.

Two faces among the many who died that day immediately came to mind. There was young Christian DeSimone, a childhood friend of my sons', a light-up-your-life kid upon whom the sun just seemed to shine. Well loved, there is a frequently visited personal memorial to him at the Ringwood Library. The second face was of the son of a friend of mine at AXA's MONY subsidiary, Victor Ugolyn, whom destiny and fate placed right at the impact point of the second plane. The even harsher impact of this inconceivable tragedy was the sense of pervading loss that was for so long and so heavily worn by his family and those who loved him. Tangible, personal, immediate, it cut all who knew them like a knife.

So thoughts about the tragedy of 9/11 quickly focused me upon the contemporary plight of the first responders to that horrific event. They were, in greater and greater numbers, developing severe respiratory ailments that were linked to their service at Ground Zero in that dark smoke cloud during those dark days. At the time, Washington was turning a deaf ear to that plight and so many were being left out in the cold by a system that was full of holes. In coming to their aid, there was, I believed and hoped, indeed a cause that the whole nation could rally around.

In serving the first responders, there was a cause worthy of walking across America!

And so, *a Journey for 9/11* was born. Great resolve, great purpose, and great passion would be attached to it.

Influenced by a father who taught me to leave something better behind than what he found, I had tried to be one of life's givers rather than takers.

As the former captain and defensive end of the Super Bowl champion New York Football Giants, I had lived a dream, but more importantly, I remained a dreamer of dreams and *a Journey for 9/11* was to be the greatest of them.

I was responsible to many people as a father, husband, and the then-Vice President of Sports Marketing and Programming at AXA Equitable, but Dianne and my children blessed my madness and I engineered a generous leave of absence from AXA. I then quickly pulled together a veritable legion of accomplished friends to lend support.

Bill Parcells, my former coach, who would later make the contribution that put us over $1 million raised, mightily influenced *a Journey for 9/11* from the moment it was conceived. What Parcells taught me about planning for every conceivable contingency, and strategizing and organizing and executing and following through, had become ingrained in me. I knew that it was incumbent upon us to prepare for this walk across America the same way that he once prepared us to face the Dallas Cowboys.

This required developing our own rules for the mission, establishing a board of directors and an engaged team, creating procedures to assure safety and control, and both implementing and adhering to a schedule that would be honored. As it happened, we would guard our flanks by gauging what was happening on the road up ahead, by having a trailer car to communicate and guide and respond to any eventuality, by having constant security, and by insisting upon no iPods, no earphones, no music, and no distractions of any kind. Not while walking!

So disciplined were we to be that every morning on the road began with a 6:00 a.m. meeting. That's 6:00 A.M. – and rule No. 1 was that no tardiness would be tolerated.

After all, Bill Parcells and tardiness did not get along well together.

Now don't get me wrong. We weren't militant. We were just prepared, and being prepared didn't keep us from stopping to smell the roses or enjoying and appreciating the people and the places that we passed by. It only made it easier for us to welcome and be touched by the wonder and magnitude of all the "stop-you-dead-in-your-tracks" sights that we encountered. There was a grace that was showered upon us each and every day. It could have been fostered by the heart of a single person passed on the road or met in a restaurant, or it could have been inspired by any of a thousand different occasions that touched our hearts.

Now, *Journey* certainly wasn't always easy, and there were days when 20 to 25 miles vexed both body and spirit, but the wonder of it was that we had the pleasure and the honor of meeting goodness over and over and over again. Around that next bend or over that next hill, goodness was invariably waiting to embrace us. In that goodness, there was a grace so rich and thick that it was as if we were being physically immersed in what was a spiritual blessing.

And there were extraordinary days when we were just overwhelmed by the goodness of the American people, who, in the end, made each and every step that we took worthwhile.

There were no ordinary days on *Journey.*

I was going to fulfill a wide-eyed dream and get to scratch off the most improbable item on my bucket list.

*****

In this book, I intend to place you inside *a Journey for 9/11* and bring you on the road with myself and my team, so you too can see and feel what we saw and felt. We want you to embrace the heart and soul of America just as we did. We want you to get up close and personal with your country just as we did. In doing so, we believe that you will be powerfully moved and inspired by the inherent goodness of your brother and sister Americans.

Given an economy that still refuses to grow enough jobs and politics that is all too mean and intransigent and a world that is all too jaded and cynical, there is a hope and a promise in these pages that is sorely needed, and maybe even a belief that longs to be reclaimed. Our *Journey* didn't exist in a vacuum and while it began on September 16, 2007, and ended on June 21, 2008, it is still living in that it continues to impact and change lives today as it is revisited and celebrated. Inside *Journey,* the determination to make a difference is far more powerful than any angst or despair, and the goodness and grace of Americans is ever so much bigger than the mean-spiritedness of its rhetoric.

Here in this story, the charity, generosity, humility and goodness that is the strength of America is on parade.

And the *Journey* is appropriately and meaningfully framed by my own story – from my South Carolina childhood on a sharecropper's farm – to my days on the field and the court both at Armijo High and the University of Oregon – to 14 years in the defensive trenches for the Giants – to my love for Dianne and our family – and to all that has colored my life.

There is many a story to tell and I'm confident that both the tales and the legends and the aspirations will get to you.

Join us on *a Journey for 9/11*, on a not-so-elusive search for the best of America and Americans, and for that which continues to make the United States of America a "shining city on a hill."

What its leaders may lack, its people still have in abundance.

1 – IN THE BEGINNING

From Greenville, South Carolina to Fairfield, California

A few minutes after 7:00 a.m. on September 16, 2007, and perhaps 1,000 steps into a journey that would eventually count more than 5 million, I stopped for a moment mid-span on the George Washington Bridge, halfway between New York and New Jersey, over a Hudson River glistening in the early morning sun, to see America as I had always hoped to see it.

Below me rushed the mysterious waters of the continually changing Hudson River. To the west rose 200 million years of enduring substance in the New Jersey Palisades. But to the south, where two massive towers of steel and glass once challenged the lower Manhattan sky, something was broken, and a haunting emptiness loomed.

It was to the brave souls who rushed into that emptiness six years earlier, and spent days searching for survivors, weeks putting out the flames, and months breathing air filled with toxins as they sought to resurrect our American spirit, that I dedicated those first 1,000 steps and the millions more to come. America had given me amazing opportunities over my first 54 years, enabling my decision to embark on this long walk from New York to San Diego, more than 3,000 miles and 9½ months in duration, to raise money for their care. For those opportunities, and for the chance to give something back, I am profoundly grateful.

This walk was for me, too. From my youngest days and earliest memories I have always been curious about my world, my country, and the people who inhabit it. Behind each face, beyond each horizon and inside every building façade there is a story that I want to know. I believe they all play a vital role in realizing the American Dream.

So, after growing up black in the Jim Crow South, working hard the way my parents taught me, and achieving more than I could have imagined – including winning the Super Bowl one January Sunday in 1987 – I set forth on the most monumental task I have ever undertaken, one that would give honor to those who sacrificed so much for us on 9/11 and in the dark days that followed. I understood that everything that had gone before in my life was preparation for this *Journey*, which was set in motion on February 16, 1953, the day George and Janie Martin gave birth to their second child, George Dwight Martin – me.

*****

I had the humblest of beginnings. The rural home where I grew up was on the outskirts of what is today's far more cosmopolitan Greenville, South Carolina. The Greenville that I knew, however, was little more than the simple farm we lived on, our one little country store, the gas station, that smallest of luncheonettes, the clapboard Baptist church where we worshiped and sang hymns – although I didn't quite know what worship was in those days – and the dirt that was both under foot and in the very air we breathed on the farm. On those hot and humid summer days that dirt threatened to choke me.

Today's Greenville boasts of an outdoor skating rink and amphitheaters, a busy downtown, and walking trails, while mine boasted only of broad fields of crops, the animals in the yard, and the rocks that we dared to throw, counter to the puritanical rules that were part and parcel of our poverty.

Of Greenville, I have always maintained that "it wasn't exactly nowhere, but you could, sure as hell, see nowhere from there."

We didn't even get TV – a 9-inch black and white Philco with an antenna three times its size and an always-fuzzy picture that became our only window to the outside world – until we made our first move to Savannah, Georgia.

Of Greenville, I have always said that "it wasn't exactly nowhere, but you could, sure as hell, see nowhere from there."

In my earliest days, our entire universe was rural to the bone and Southern Baptist to the bone, and somewhere between the farm and church we lived our lives. We prayed loud and we sang loud, for when it came to the Lord, we were taught to hold nothing back.

There was no football or basketball or baseball or even a 25-cent Spaldeen in my childhood – just rocks. There was no paternal or maternal interest in our play. Why, play itself was neither blessed nor nurtured, because my parents, I fear, were all too focused on just surviving.

Their eye was on the prize, and that meant keeping food in our bellies and a roof overhead. So there was neither Monopoly nor Parcheesi, neither Candy Land nor Clue in our childhood – just rocks and dung. In Greenville, there was a great deal of room in which to run and play, but there was nothing to play with. That was okay, because back in those days, the days of Greenville and its hot sun and thick dust, my siblings and I had no knowledge that such things even existed.

That would, of course, begin to change when the little 9-inch black and white 9-inch Philco made its way into our household and our lives later in the early '60s in Savannah.

The truth is, as children in Greenville, we played no sports or games because recreational activities were frowned upon altogether by my well-meaning but hard-steeled parents, who deemed such pursuits a waste of time and energy and purpose.

Even being caught throwing a rock was cause for reprimand and punishment, should the reprimand not suffice; but throw them we did, and reprimanded and punished we were. The truth is that all we had to fall back upon were the rocks, the animals on the farm, our own imaginations and each other. The 'we' included my older sister and mentor to me like no other, Brenda; my younger sister, Helen; my baby sister Lori; and my younger brother, Doug. Like me, Doug, despite having no balls to play with in our earliest days, would one day play in the National Football League. I had my 14 seasons with the New York Football Giants and he played 10 with the Minnesota Vikings.

The five of us were tight in our growing up, as we always fell back upon each other. Separated by nine years only, Brenda was two years older than me, Helen two years younger than me, and Doug five years younger, but two years older than baby sister Lori. It was the five of us and the trust and faith that we had in each other that was the primary force in our lives. Our parents guarded our flanks, but it was Brenda who led us. She was the smartest, the fastest and the most protective. My parents were either working or exhausted and it was left to Brenda to tuck us in and quash our fears. If we were hungry and there wasn't enough food, we always got Brenda's.

The truth is that all we had to fall back upon were the rocks, the animals on the farm, our own imaginations and each other. We didn't have any toys and we never played catch.

That's the sum and substance of a beginning – as well as the sum and substance of Greenville. I was the dirt-poor son of a sharecropper who worked two jobs, and of a homemaker who ironed the clothes of others; the dirt-poor son of parents who busted themselves so that we could subsist in poverty, just one toe over the line.

More than 50 years later, the four of us remain close, despite sadly losing our baby sister Lori a few years ago, because what was sharpened and steeled there in the harshness of our youth was built for a lifetime. Poverty and want and sacrifice also have gifts to give and legacies to leave.

Beyond the sharecropping, my namesake and father was a civil servant who worked for the military in a maintenance and janitorial capacity, originally at Hunter Air Force Base; and my Mom, Janie, was a domestic who cleaned homes and took in ironing. Of course, she was much more than the woman who stood silent before the ironing board in the night, and she, her hardworking husband, and often my grandparents as well, came together to maintain a productive farm.

They were good and faithful people who worked hard to provide for us and who certainly passed on spiritual virtues that rooted and took greater hold as time passed.

If we were hungry and there wasn't enough food, we always got Brenda's.

But our lives were entirely devoid of the extras or accents or exclamation points. As I look back, there was simply no color in my childhood.

My parents put it all on the line for us, but the truth is that they instilled no dreams and extended no sense of worldliness or high purpose and achievement, and there was nothing warm or fuzzy in their way of being. They weren't the kissing or hugging or "I love you" or smothering-snuggling types, and the hard truth is that I learned more from what they did not do than from what they did. The good news was that where they left off, my nurturing sister Brenda began.

I know that it might be hard to believe, but as far back as I can remember, in what I garnered from my parents, I looked to the opposite or the antithesis. The lesson of so much of what they passed down to me and my siblings was discovered in what they could not give us and, most certainly, in what they could not do.

At times, in simply thinking about them then, I can become consumed by an almost palpable, even harsh angst, for no matter how grown nor how old, the child we once were never stops longing. Yes, there is that something deep inside that goes on longing and wishing for gifts that never were imparted. It's just the way it is – there are some regrets that just sit like cold stones in the depths of our souls.

It is certainly not about anger, nor is it about bitterness. Neither is it about a need to forgive, for I know that my Dad and Mom did the best they could under difficult circumstances. They worked hard, but as children it was we who stood up, like young men and women, and accepted the coldness and the lack of color in our lives while reaching out to find the joy in each other.

There was just no time, and so we were never told just how unique or special we were or that we had the wherewithal, in us, to move mountains. We found that out ourselves.

It's just the way it is – there are some regrets that just sit like cold stones in the depths of our souls.

I love my parents still. I always have and I always will, for there was good in them, but the simple truth is that my parents were human, puritanical and limited. The vagaries of life, the demands of life, as it were, had sucked that very life out of them.

When my Dad died, his legacy went to the grave with him, and that simple yet so powerful word, love, had almost tragically and certainly sadly never been voiced or expressed by him until he stared his own end in the face. It is the never fully realizing or knowing him that hurts, the having no knowledge of his childhood, or of the hopes and dormant dreams that may have been buried inside. In large measure, who he was went with him to the grave and it was never expressed, which is why I was so determined to fully live and to do the opposite.

As to my Dad's passing, there indeed were blessings that surrounded it, but there was and there remains an abiding sense of regret.

*****

I did enjoy a close and nurturing relationship with my maternal grandmother, Cora Terry, but I never knew my maternal grandfather. On Dad's side, there was Benny Lee and Catherine, who lived immediately south of us in a town called Due West, which was, you guessed it, due west of Greenville. There's something to be said for the fact that Dianne and I named our second son Benjamin, for Benny Lee was a good man and everything you could want in a paternal grandfather.

Beyond our grandparents, we had extended family all over Abenville County, South Carolina.

The extended family did come together to help teach us Martin children what was considered life's most important and primary lesson, one that was entirely spiritual and religious in nature. At the youngest of ages, we were introduced to a "Higher Being" to whom we owed our very lives. There were also characters like Noah and Moses and Job – and there were prodigal sons and sowers of seeds – and there was Lazarus and Mary Magdalene – and, most importantly, a wooden cross and blood-spattered nails and that empty tomb with the displaced rock.

In church, I discovered the all-important gift of humility in the clear and simple realization that life was ever so much bigger than me. Living, as I did, where the eastern branch of the Bible Belt was most solidly rooted to the ground, how could I not be impacted by faith?

For the record, without complaint or reservation, that impact remains one of the cornerstones or foundations of my life.

It remains the richest of blessings.

With apologies for the repetition, we were indeed rural to the bone by virtue of our location and life's happenstance, but we were Baptist to the bone by virtue of parental will.

Our segregated, all African-American congregation, was animated and loud and determined to get the Lord's attention.

In church, I discovered the all-important gift of humility in the clear and simple realization that life was ever so much bigger than me.

And get his attention we most certainly did. In the midst of our always rollicking praise, I was inevitably struck by something that effected a quiet, life-affirming change, by an awakening in me and the beginning of what transpired into an abiding personal relationship with my God.

Suffice it to say that it has always been in me. Of the presence of God in my life, there has been no doubt.

At a young age, I also learned something extraordinary about the perception, and perspective, of my church. In life outside the church, you see, my Dad commanded little status or respect, as he was a civil service janitor at night and a sharecropper by day – and sharecroppers, after all, didn't even own the land they worked on, but rather worked, in a subsidiary and sometimes degraded status, for those who did. Yet in church, on Sundays, my Dad was a deacon and a leader. In church, within those off-white clapboards and red bricks, I was, as a little boy, just bowled over by the respect and even deferential treatment my Dad was receiving.

"By God, my Dad was a leader, so I could be one too," I thought.

That was truly my first life's brush with the very concept of leadership. Why, even a poor sharecropper or janitor or dirt-poor son of a sharecropper could be a leader? And wasn't that something worth dwelling upon? It was duly noted within, filed accordingly, and there was something about it that inspired and empowered me as I grew, yet I never focused upon it until much later.

Our segregated, all African-American congregation, was animated and loud and determined to get the Lord's attention.

*****

There were two other impactful experiences in the earliest of my days, in Greenville, that an "Oh, so very young" me internalized.

So much so that they motivated me forever!

The first was simply a line that my Mom repeated over and over again, reflecting her considered opinion of the human condition, an opinion or view that should ultimately be labeled as "softly critical," in that there was no mean-spiritedness in it.

"Common sense," she'd say, "is an uncommon commodity."

It was indeed a simple, thoughtful and memorable observation – *"Common sense is an uncommon commodity."* Whether directly or indirectly, my Mom kept sharing, almost painstakingly sharing, the concept that thought and consideration were to be valued, and in repeating this line as often as she did, whenever anything went awry or someone did something stupid, she was saying that thought and consideration, simply thinking something through, were critically important in life.

Why, even a poor sharecropper or janitor or dirt-poor son of a sharecropper could be a leader? And wasn't that something worth dwelling upon?

One might argue that to place a premium on thinking is to herald the obvious, but I didn't look upon it that way, as my Mom's "*Common sense is an uncommon commodity*" helped to frame the deliberateness and thoughtfulness and careful consideration that has been part and parcel of my own way of being in the world.

For rarely, as you'll see, have I been victimized by impulsiveness.

It is important to note, by the way, that my Mom, Janie, had no more than a 6th grade education, while my Dad, George, actually had only a 3rd grade education, so what knowledge they had was largely gained through experience. They learned how to live by living it, and were, of course, constrained by the limits of their education. They would necessarily go only so far in life – only as far as hard and back-breaking work would take them.

"Common sense," she'd say, "is an uncommon commodity."

I also realized and noted that.

Where it hurt, I think, was only in that their own lack of education devalued the very way they looked upon education generally. As a result, we were not motivated by our parents to achieve or excel. We were not told to do well in school or to work hard or even to do our homework. Many forces would come together to teach me otherwise, but among them was that basic "opposite or antithesis of" component that I had purposefully formulated, so long ago, in charting a course that was different from that of my parents.

I am, therefore, a great believer in the importance and value of education, and one of the most important things I did while playing for the New York Football Giants was to return to school to complete my education at Fairleigh Dickinson University and become the first in my family to earn a college degree.

There were some great people who inspired me along the way, but I can honestly say that it was personal will alone that largely drove me from the very beginning, as my parents were simply missing from the equation.

*****

The second experience was a simple encounter that I just happened to witness, out in the fields, between my Dad and a white man in the still-Jim Crow South of the '50s. I don't recall and likely was never aware of the details, but it was the conversational substance of the encounter that stuck.

It was not the action, but rather the words.

Simply, the white man's tractor had broken down and my Dad diagnosed the problem and helped him to get it running again, upon which the white man said, "Why, George! You a real smart man, George."

That was it – "You a real smart man, George" – a supreme compliment coming from a white man, who said it as if it were completely unexpected or implausible that such wisdom could come from a black man.

After all, black men were deemed ignorant and "less than" whites in the pre-Civil Rights movement, Jim Crow South.

Oh, I was well aware of the bias and bigotry in the man's tone of voice, but that was commonplace and to be expected in the world we walked in then, and so I, like my Dad no doubt, put that aside.

It was rather the affirmation by this man that my Dad was smart that stayed with me. After all, if my Dad was smart, then so too might I be. Even a bigoted, biased white man praised my Dad and said that he was smart, because he was grateful for my Dad's help.

The odds of a South Carolina white man praising a black man back then were extremely unlikely, which only suggested how smart my Dad had to be.

I had heard him say this, all right, and healthily assumed that I was smart too.

After all, all black men were then deemed ignorant and "less than" in the pre-Civil Rights movement, Jim Crow South.

The truth is, I could find life affirmations in the oddest nooks and crannies and once I found them, they stuck. As to the "who I am and what made me" stuff, this genuinely matters. Just give me a reason to believe, and I'll hang onto it and ride with it forever!

*****

Before 1959 gave way to 1960 and I reached the tender age of 7, our family made its first major move from the wide open spaces of Greenville, South Carolina, to the near metropolis of Savannah, Georgia. As a move, it was truly a culture shock of monumental proportions and simply mind-boggling, because we had lived in this incestuous way in Greenville, always falling back on ourselves and the relationships in our immediate and extended families.

But Savannah, why *everything* was in Savannah and it was all new. Savannah was traffic and movies and cars and congestion and other people and gangs and mischief. Savannah was opportunity and trouble and excitement, and our band of country bumpkins wasn't quite ready for the prime-time performances that living there demanded of us.

My initial experiences in Savannah would vacillate from having once fed farm animals to now running with a street gang, from behaving like an altar boy to nearly being laid out on an altar myself, from chasing pet dogs and treeing squirrels to dodging police and chasing girls. For me, Savannah quickly became a regular smorgasbord of young juvenile degeneracy.

Even at the tender age of 8 or 9 years, my haunting memories of that city are replete with words like jungle and prison and trouble and delinquency, and had fate not intervened, I was on a fast track to either a maximum security cellblock or to the grave.

Probably sensing the dangers, Dad quickly moved the family for a second time to the outskirts of suburban Savannah and away from the immediate decadence.

We then took up residence in a plain, quaint, four-room bungalow on Bonaventure Road directly across the street from a casket company, which always served as a subtle reminder to me that my future could still take a turn for the worse at any moment.

There can be no doubt, however, that this second move created a better balance between our Greenville country roots and the not-so-civilized city that we had quickly and somewhat rudely been introduced to.

On Bonaventure Road, I also was returned to the biblical fire and brimstone of church and to "Baptist peacekeeping sentinels" on almost every corner of the neighborhood, who reported any misbehavior to all in authority through the use of that brand new Bell Telephone "Party Line" technology.

The truth is, I could find life affirmations in the oddest nooks and crannies and once I found them, they stuck. As to the "who I am and what made me' stuff," this genuinely matters. Just give me a reason to believe, and I'll hang on to it and ride with it forever!

One month before, I had been running the streets stealing sodas and candy bars, and the next I was in a place where I couldn't tell my younger sister, Helen, to "shut up" without it being reported to the local universe. What a difference a few miles can make in life!

All places and all situations teach, and still a child on the outskirts of Savannah, Georgia, I did have the makeup of one who was always willing and ready and waiting to be taught, ready and waiting to take in and internalize lessons that could make a difference and foster a strength of character that just might sustain a good life. I had an open mind and heart and soul, and from the very beginning I would stockpile memories and experiences and words that would sharpen me, as a man needs to be sharpened, if he is to truly live.

Such life lessons could come from both the most obvious and the most unlikely of sources.

One formidable piece of my "life's lessons learned" puzzle was fashioned by a hardworking, kind-hearted and older gentleman who lived a few doors down from us. A contractor, Mr. Russell offered me my very first paying job as a "clean-up boy" at the age of 10 in the summer of 1963. It required me to get up very early in the morning, which was problematic, to meet Mr. Russell at his house, to travel to the job site, and to then pick up and dump whatever construction debris had been discarded.

While it wasn't exactly brain surgery, I quickly discovered that hard manual labor wasn't my cup of tea, and after three days I told Mr. Russell, "Thanks, but no thanks."

Mr. Russell, who I only later learned had this reputation of helping young boys stay off the street, told me to come by his house over the weekend to "settle up." At the time, I had no idea what that meant and I prepared myself for an angry tongue lashing at the very least, but that is not what came to pass. I received only Mr. Russell's trademark kindness and the cash wages that were, for the very first time in my life, placed in the palms of my hands, leaving me with a keen understanding of and appreciation for the cavernous depths of my mistake.

I was completely shocked and blown away.

Wow, cash! Real cash, the likes of which I had never before seen!

It was a seminal moment in my life, the moment when I first realized that kindness and simple, honest, hard work can be rewarded so kindly and lucratively. I decided, then and there, that this was the path to follow and I would never look back or second guess myself as to the direction I would go.

I would work and I would earn and I would do good like Mr. Russell.

Moments before the first steps of *A Journey for 9/11*, I am joined by distinguished members of the Port Authority Police Department, which lost 37 officers that fateful day. On the far left is my friend and former teammate Harry Carson; NYPD Sergeants Benevolent Association President Ed Mullins stands third from the right; and at the end is Beau Dietl, who generously donated security for the walk.

The enthusiastic students and teachers at Friendship Public Charter School in Washington, D.C., made it an inspiring stop on the *Journey*.

In just a moment, through the goodness of Mr. Russell, I learned the value of hard work. I learned that service to others will be rewarded. And I would, I thought, in my life, work as hard as it took to build a good life.

Any skeptics out there can be assured that I still speak of this today, with a passion that will leave you thinking that it might only have happened yesterday. In a very real way that's because I act as if it just did. And the truth is that I feel it just did, because I keep this memory of Mr. Russell so close.

Heroes in life don't necessarily have to save the planet. All they have to do is help save you, and Mr. Russell's goodness did just that, since rather than reprimand, he welcomed the prodigal back home.

*****

There is a kind of tortured memory about the Sol C. Johnson Elementary School in Savannah, a memory that might have been written off by most, but one from which I extracted a most unlikely positive.

In telling it, please understand that even in a segregated, "poor black" school, there were social distinctions and pecking orders. There were, for instance, in the vernacular of the day, dark-skinned negroes who were probably poor themselves, and dark-skinned "poor" negroes who were dirt poor. And we, Greenville imports, were dark skinned and dirt poor, and, whenever you mixed country breeding and poverty, the clothes were likely to be a tad more dirty and hygiene was certainly not all it could be.

Sure, Brown v. Board of Education had already been won and the Supreme Court of the United States, in a decision written by Chief Justice Earl Warren, had determined that "separate but equal" institutions were inherently unequal. There was change in the offing, but the segregated South had dug its teeth in to resist and to fight the final battle of the Great American Civil War.

Told that change and integration had to be implemented "*with all deliberate speed,*" they were however in no rush to do anything of the kind in Savannah, Georgia. General Sherman may have claimed it as a Christmas present for President Lincoln in 1864, but Savannah was, nearly 100 years later, still standing up in the name of southern bigotry.

In the Deep South, it would take decades of struggle to move the "Segregation today, segregation tomorrow, segregation forever" crowd out of the way. So Sol C. Johnson remained proudly segregated in the late '50s and early '60s when I attended.

But to be segregated wasn't quite enough, as the school itself further segregated those deemed deserving from the undeserving like me. Even in a racist society that treated African-Americans as second-class citizens, the second-class leaders themselves practiced their own form of Social Darwinism.

Sure, Brown v. Board of Education had already been won and the Supreme Court of the United States, in a decision written by Chief Justice Earl Warren, had determined that separate but equal institutions were inherently unequal. There was change in the offing, but the segregated South had dug its teeth in to resist and to fight the final battle of the Great American Civil War.

The memory I have is of an altercation in which another boy got cut and for which I got blamed. It was not true, but the word of the boy's older sister carried more weight than mine, because my own dirt-poor status somehow devalued my word.

My teacher's name was Miss Green and she took pleasure in beating me with a ruler – and her anger, why it truly seemed to be almost personal. With a kind of disdain, while whacking me with the ruler, she blurted out "How could you, George Martin, get second-highest score in this class!"

Recently subjected to a day of standardized testing, her anger fueled the only report I ever received about the results. In fact, I'm quite sure that were it not for the emotional outburst, propelled by the beating, not even that bit of back-handed good news ever would have been shared with me.

So afterwards, it was neither the injustice nor the welts that bothered me. In fact, I always looked upon it as the best beating I ever got. After all, I had been informed that I must be smart, as my biased teacher had so tellingly conveyed her refusal to accept the fact that I did better than her better-dressed, better-cleansed class favorites.

So there you have it – a white man, with a repaired tractor, told my Dad that he was smart, and Miss Green, in a wholly unintentional and obscene way, told me that I was smart, and my Mom turned to me one day and said, "Boy, where do you learn all those big words from?" Yes, that, the all of that and the nurturing of the idea, deep inside, that I was capable of being whatever I wanted to be in life, the nurturing of the idea that I had the smarts to be something more, helped set me on my life's journey.

Long before I knew that I was capable of playing sports at the highest of levels, I, like the Tin Man in *The Wizard of Oz,* knew that I had a brain. "Oh joy! Rapture!" he said and I knew exactly what he meant, and that helps to make one very big difference in life.

Today, interestingly, while they are still called the *Atom Smashers*, there is only a Sol C. Johnson High School in Savannah, long integrated and considered among the best high schools in the nation, a million light years removed from the school I attended; and ever so much more worthy of its namesake, the founder of *The Savannah Tribune*, the oldest newspaper in America that once targeted and served an underserved African-American population.

In my roots, by the way, there is this keen appreciation for what it means to be the target of bigotry and injustice – and injustice also teaches.

So, I learned that I never wanted to lay that elitist crap on anyone else. Knowing what it was to be demeaned and looked down upon, I knew, as it happened to me, that I could never do the same to another human being. I learned, as a child, that my life would rather be enriched by helping people feel special and good about themselves. I learned, as a child, that goodness, simple goodness, has to be at the heart of any life well lived.

These yin-and-yang, "tension-of-opposites" lessons, as to both prejudice and bigotry experienced and my parents' limitations, run deep inside me.

In my roots, by the way, there is this keen appreciation for what it means to be the target of bigotry and injustice – and injustice also teaches.

Other pre-teen Savannah lessons came from the old 9-inch, black-and-white Philco. Watching family TV shows, I wondered what planet they lived on, because it certainly wasn't mine. I couldn't begin to imagine a world where you wore clean clothes, ate a hot breakfast, and talked to your Dad every day to resolve problems, but I could dream about it.

But it was easy to imagine myself as the hero in the adventure shows who always did great deeds, saved people, and never wanted the accolades. I was ready to sign up for that gig any day.

*****

After my life's lessons in Savannah, we took off in an overloaded station wagon for Fairfield, California, to Dad's new assignment at Travis Air Force Base, an entrée to a brave new world. By then, I believe that I had already laid claim to many of the key aptitudes and values that would come to define me.

For good, bad or indifferent, I believed that I was capable, even smart, and I well knew that I could compete, although I did not yet know how.

I genuinely valued hard work and I was deliberate and considerate, and, out of harsh bias, I had taken the road less traveled to discover the values of goodness and kindness and humility. And my spirituality and Christianity were already morphing into something more, into a force that would be paramount in my life, into a faith and love that would color every aspect of it.

I valued education and knowledge and unlike my own parents, I would hug often and love openly and live a more fully human life.

Then too, there was that brush-with-leadership moment that would drive me, as a young boy and throughout all phases of my life, to lead and not to satisfy ego, but rather to serve and to make a difference.

I had heard that line about saving one and so saving the world. Well, I knew not how nor when, but I knew that and I was determined, somehow – some way – someday, to give living expression to it.

I valued education and knowledge and unlike my own parents, I would hug often and love openly and live a more fully human life

2 – CALIFORNIA DREAMING

Where 1042 Pierce meets Armijo High

As we move on to California, it is time to get to know my sister and earliest mentor, Brenda, much better. Two years older, she called me Dwight, as all my siblings did and continue to do. My first role model, she loved school and so did I, and she excelled at athletics and so would I. On that first compass of mine, it was Brenda who was "True North," the one whose example I would follow. She was the first to believe in me and she always had my back, and when there was not enough to go around, she gave me hers.

If there was a star in my formative years, it was Brenda, and her handwriting is all over this part of my story. As to who and what I would become, she in my late grade school and high school years impacted me mightily.

So, first there is Brenda, but there were two other points of impact to take note of as well: the first an event and the second a perspective. The event was the death of President John F. Kennedy in November 1963, an assassination that tugged at the heartstrings of every single American. I remember coming home from school to find my Mom sobbing. She told me what had happened and in my youthful ignorance I asked about her obvious grief , "Why, Mom, did you know him?" Then glued to the TV over that weekend, like the rest of America, I was moved by a little boy's salute and riderless horses and the haunting sound of "Taps," and all this talk about the passions and contributions of a lost president and promises unfulfilled.

My Mom's tears and that weekend were, in the 10th year of my life, my first inspiration to look beyond my own insulated world. It was a potent social and civic wake-up call, the call to involve and participate and engage.

John Fitzgerald Kennedy left me with that desire, and from that moving weekend on I took more notice of both my country and my world. Maybe not enough at times, but at least I had determined to try.

*****

The perspective I took from Savannah, I never let go of the sheer beauty of it, the beauty of the homes that survived the Civil War and were reclaimed in the antebellum South. There was something about the stately Gone with the Wind homes with rich, lush, rolling green lawns and floral tapestries, with gardens and landscapes that were works of art, that mesmerized and warmed the soul! Obviously, I was neither of them nor privy to them, but I still saw them and what I freely took from them is exactly what Mr. Gerald O'Hara talks to Katie Scarlett O'Hara about in the opening scene of Gone with the Wind, the "love of the land."

"It is the only thing that stays the same, the only thing that remains," he says. "And one day, this love of the land will get to you."

Although it was anything but mine, Savannah and the love of the land got to me, and to this day I look forward to stealing a few hours in my own land – my own garden – my own dirt. I use my hands to do my part to nurture the wonder that the Earth has to offer and to fashion my own floral tapestries. And oh, what peace is found in simply planting some flowers, in manicuring the lawn, in planting a tree, and in doing the handiwork of Heaven.

*****

But I digress, and we must move on to Fairfield, California.

From the back window of our beat-up but roadworthy Chevy station wagon filled with a family of southern hicks, a greater and unimagined world literally opened up before me. Wide-eyed and open-mouthed, I took America in and it was spectacular, and our ride to California became a life-altering and exciting adventure.

I simply couldn't get enough of it and I wanted to know and take it all in, and I was frustrated only by our lack of information.

Thoreau, in Walden, writes of going to the forest to "suck the marrow out of life," because he didn't want to discover, when he came to die, that he had not lived. Our cross-country trip was not unlike that for me. I wanted to fill myself up with all that we passed by. I wanted to know the history, the way of life, the people, and the larger-than-life stories that just might be worthy of the land itself.

I was an American who just wanted to take America in, and so it was, to me, a very special journey and experience.

In a very real way, *a Journey for 9/11,* which I'd been unknowingly preparing for since birth began right then and there. While a lifetime was to be lived before it would happen and more than 40 years were to pass, Journey was spiritually born there and at that moment – this powerful, consuming desire to slow life down and walk across America to become more intimate with this land. The dream of the *Journey* was born then, when I was only 10 years old.

Deferred for more than 40 years, there would be a new epiphany, an awakening of that dream, on a beautiful, stunning morning outside Canton, Ohio, where I was celebrating the entry of my great friend, Harry Carson, into the Pro Football Hall of Fame. On August 6, 2006, the embers of what was but a childish notion were stirred and lit – and we'll dive into the thorny details of it all a bit later.

*****

Arriving in Fairfield was not unlike a human being's sudden transport from the Earth to Mars. We weren't just moving from Georgia to California, from East Coast to West, but literally to a new land, a new country, and a new world. Out of a still-segregated last stand of the Jim Crow South to an integrated, almost-cosmopolitan Fairfield.

Practically, physically and spiritually, Fairfield was just different. On one hand, we were lifted from using an outhouse into a home that was still small but with an actual indoor toilet; and on the other hand, the surprise of surprises was that our neighbors were white and they lived right next door rather than miles away.

An indoor toilet and white neighbors! The world we dirt-poor South Carolinians knew had suddenly turned upside down and inside out.

The changes were staggering, and so too were the opportunities. Now don't get me wrong, Fairfield still wore its bigotry with prominence, and had its challenges and preclusions, but it was indeed, in oh so many ways, a brave new world. It had, for instance, a "Welcome to Fairfield" sign – with a "Let's Keep Fairfield White" sign adjoining it – and the town of then 38,000 was indeed a bastion of hot-mouthed rednecks who liked to spew their venom, but they were largely all talk. And their children were far more open than they.

We discovered stores of all types that we could actually walk to, convenience stores rather than general stores, and a strange new thing called a "laundromat." Above all, there was this thing called "sports" that tall, strong, somewhat burly types like myself were just naturally, with Brenda's help, lured into. Balls of all types and sizes, round and oval, large and small, were available to us, as we left the recreational world of throwing rocks behind.

As to arriving in Fairfield, it was not unlike a human being's sudden transport from the Earth to Mars. We weren't just moving from Georgia to California, from East Coast to West, but literally to a new land, a new country, and a new world. Out of a still-segregated, last stand of the Jim Crow South to an integrated, almost-cosmopolitan Fairfield.

A track star, Brenda could run like the wind and my influential older sister became the first athlete that I wanted to emulate.

A few years after we arrived, we made another, equally revolutionary move within Fairfield, one to 1042 Pierce Street – the one that represented our "moving on up" to the big time. 1042 Pierce came with running water and central heating and all of the modern conveniences and amenities. I remember thinking it was our ticket to the land of perfect homes and perfect lives a wholly imperfect me had already been introduced to on TV. 1042 Pierce had an actual lawn with a real fence. Now it may not have been worthy of the Savannah antebellum palaces, but it was to be ours, and that was staggering enough.

At the time, my parents were still living by their longstanding motto that children were to be seen and not heard (nor given a lot of information), so we were unaware but would later learn that our parents had to run the institutional racist gauntlet of redlining in order to land 1042 Pierce. They had bobbed and weaved with the "That's not available to you" and "It's way out of your price range" and "Someone else's bid is higher" web of excuses or rationales for two years before finally succeeding.

It boggles the mind, but the truth is, in an America that has already elected an African-American president, there are neighborhoods where redlining, the practice of institutionally excluding minorities from living there, still happens.

*****

While I believe our parents, and especially our grandmother, carried the fears and codes of the Deep South with them into Fairfield, we, their children, were not similarly bound.

So we freely immersed ourselves into its more open environment, its more modern culture, and its people. And for the most part, our white neighbors proved to be friendly and I found no impediments or problems making white friends for the first time in my life.

Our elders also had a hard time shaking the taboos of the Deep South while we did not. One point of great concern, however, was my having any association with white girls. Good God, where we had come from, many a black boy had been hung for crossing that line.

To be sure, Gregory Peck had won his Academy Award for his moving portrayal of Atticus Finch in *To Kill a Mockingbird* just before we got to California, and so there was the assumption, in a growing, more liberal and open America, that we had come a long way, baby. But the central plot of that great movie, in which a black man had the temerity to come to the aid of a white woman, was, to my parents, still as much a living, working reality as was Atticus Finch's belief in justice.

Our elders had a hard time shaking the taboos of the Deep South while we did not.

One point of great concern, however, was my having any association with white girls. Good God, where we had come from, many a black boy had been hung for crossing that line.

When it came to girls, I was cautious at first, but Steve Baracosa, my very first white friend; Roslyn Motes, whom he would later marry while still in high school; Lynn McNamee, whose father was a card-carrying redneck and racial separatist; and myself just happened to become an innocent foursome, and we forged a real, close-knit relationship – living, as it were, in stark contrast to anything our parents were capable of imagining or, more importantly, accepting. As Steve and Roslyn paired off, that left Lynn and me together a lot, and while there were honest feelings, we had been affected enough, I believe, not to cross the black-white line.

But our friendships long lingered, and I learned that friendship is not something that comes and goes, but rather, lasts.

Others who became especially important to me were Eddie Murchi (white) and then Alden Holt (black). Eddie and I would spend a lot of time beating up on his younger brothers, Roland and my younger brother, Doug, and generally creating mayhem, while Alden became my soul mate upon entering high school. Alden, a military transfer, not unlike us, was my very first black friend in Fairfield – my "homeboy" – and we were truly an "Odd Couple.'" When we first met, I was well beyond 6 foot already and Alden was 4 foot nothing. But we were inseparable.

As I think about the lot of my Fairfield friends, the pre-Dianne characters who held me up and stood by me and taught me and made me laugh, I do so very fondly and gratefully, because each and every friend, I believe, leaves a lasting imprint on the soul. True friends, as they were, cannot help but make you stronger and better and more capable of achieving your dreams. Steve, Eddie, Roslyn, Lynn and Alden – especially Alden – were rich blessings, and in that youthful greening and springtime of our lives, in those rough-hewn early teenage years, we gave each other life.

I remain grateful to them all for their friendship and for the confidence that they helped instill in me.

*****

As to sports, upon arriving in Fairfield, I really had no clue, but I soon discovered that I could dribble the round ball, put it through the hoop, and stand my ground with anyone under the boards, and that I could toss that weird-looking oblong ball with the best of them. Only the smaller, hard one that you used gloves to catch presented a problem for me. All it took was one low throw from Steve Baracosa that hit me right in the place where no boy ever wants to be hit to cure me of any desire to play that game.

The pigskin and the leather were far more accommodating.

Entering 7th grade in Fairfield, I attended an integrated school for the first time, Dover Elementary, which was directly across the street from Fairfield High School, and there I was quickly exposed for the first time as well to organized athletics. I immediately began playing football, which was soon to be followed by basketball.

And as fairy tale-like as it sounds, my first team, for which I was the wide receiver, went on to an undefeated season.

I won that position after making an improbable and spectacular catch on the very first day of practice. I put it into overdrive to snag a long pass that was overthrown by our quarterback, Bruce Martin, an Asian-American who had one hell of an arm. Returning to the huddle upon making that catch, he yelled, "Way to go, Sticky Fingers!" and that name stuck with me throughout grammar school and into high school.

It was later complemented by the nickname "Medic" that Brenda says I won because I "didn't like to get hit" and because I "applied academics and smarts" to the game of football.

Needless to say, I liked them both.

Steve, Eddie, Roslyn, Lynn, and Alden – especially Alden – were rich blessings and in that youthful greening and springtime of our lives, in those rough-hewn early teenage years, we gave each other life.

But what stuck with me more was my impression of Bruce himself, because he, like me, was a minority who had clearly earned respect both athletically and academically. As the only two minorities on the team, we made a great quarterback-receiver combination and I looked up to him. He, with no apparent or visible problems stemming from his ethnic heritage, had become class president and a high achiever who seemed to be accepted as white in a white world. His color made no difference at all.

You can imagine how that resonated with me, and while I'm leaping ahead here, it had everything to do with my later becoming the president of the student body and student council of Armijo High School.

I excelled in sports in high school – well, I was a mediocre tennis player, though a High School All-American in football – but I think I took as much pride in my student government activity and my involvement across the board and being designated an Outstanding Teenager of America as I did in catching the football or dunking the basketball.

We had a pretty good basketball team, for which I averaged more than 20 points per game; and our football team won no titles, yet I was still pleased to be its Most Valuable Player. But phases like this in a life go by in a blur, and it's the memory of those who help shape you forever that you take away and carry with you.

First, there was Ed Hopkins, my basketball coach, who had a profound impact on me.

He was the first white man who treated me as if I were part of his family, and he always introduced me as his son. Now, we're talking about the years 1968, when Martin Luther King was killed, through 1971, years that were dominated politically by the Vietnam War.

While I was conflicted in so many ways about the war and politics and race, Coach Hopkins reached through it all to teach me about human nature and human potential and being one's best. He reached through it to teach me about leadership, which had everything to do with realizing potential and playing unselfishly, but most importantly, and this was where the rubber met the road, about elevating others. I simply had never thought about that before.

He taught me that leadership was ultimately about taking others higher, about helping everyone else on the team reach their potential. A man who lived the Golden Rule to the fullest, Coach Hopkins was just a beautiful man who also instilled in me the idea that I could be really good and that I should look beyond high school and think scholarship.

Hopkins' work with me was solidified by Bob Miller, a running backs and receivers coach who came to Armijo High via the National Football League. Now, as they say, he may only have been there for a cup of coffee, but still, he had been to the football mecca and he knew what it was to perform at the highest of levels. This – to me – sports deity pulled me aside and told me that I had the potential to reach "far beyond this mediocrity" and to earn a scholarship, and even to ascend to the mecca myself.

Coach Hopkins reached through it all to teach me about human nature and human potential and being one's best. He reached through it to teach me about leadership, which had everything to do with realizing potential and playing unselfishly, but most importantly, and this was where the rubber met the road, about elevating others. I simply had never thought about that before.

What was more, he told me that I had an obligation to succeed, not merely for me, but for my team, my community, my younger brother, Doug, for everyone at Armijo High. Not to fulfill that obligation, he said, would be a complete cop-out. Like Coach Hopkins, Coach Miller taught me, in the clearest of terms, that each is obligated to help those around him rise up. When I look back upon my high school career, it is not about the number of touchdowns and other records set, nor is it about the honors and accolades received, it is rather about the company and presence of those two men and the gifts that they gave and the lessons that they taught.

For while I had always been a dreamer, it was they who made me a believer!

*****

If you recall, in Sol C. Johnson School, a Miss Green detested my social class and so detested me, but at Armijo High, beyond Hopkins and Miller, I also had a science teacher, a Mr. Green, who believed in me and lit the academic fires underneath me.

One day, after football season, he said, “OK, Mr. Martin, no more exceptions, the season is over and it’s time for you to wake up now.” From that day forward, Mr. Green was relentlessly on my case. He was on me and he, thank God, just didn’t let up.

He helped me to grow and to be proper and to conduct myself like a man and to better interact with and respect others. He would regularly stress what it meant to be a professional and relentlessly urged me not to abuse my IQ. He pushed me to get better grades and assumed the parental role in that regard. He prodded me upwards and did the remarkable. He turned me into a student and made me so very much want to achieve.

He also got on that leadership bandwagon and taught me that what leaders achieve is always earned and never given.

But what was more, he told me that I had an obligation to succeed, not merely for me, but for my team, my community, my younger brother, Doug, for everyone at Armijo High. Not to fulfill that obligation, he said, would be a complete cop-out.

There is one other mentor worthy of much more than a mention, Omar Herbert Smith, otherwise known as “Red” Smith, my boss. My Dad found the job with him for me, as an assistant in his shoe repair shop, which I took to like a duck to water.

His was actually a traveling shoe repair practice that eventually had me traveling all over the region or managing his shop in Fairfield at Travis Air Force Base on my own for considerable periods of time. My point simply is that we were busy and we worked and we produced and I did well with him. But while working on the shoes together or as we wound down after a long day, we'd talk about every imaginable subject, and at the end of the day I started to realize that he, too, was sharing his life's lessons and teaching me.

It could be about what went into making decisions or about maturing and trusting and building and molding oneself, or about different value systems and philosophies, or about his own upbringing and what he thought of God. Suffice it to say, Red Smith, once a professional wrestler and a certified character, was an exceptionally wise man who taught me more about life and goodness and purpose than the overwhelming majority of my teachers did.

There when I needed them, in a fragile and formative time in my life, were Hopkins, Miller, Smith and Green, and they helped make all the difference for me. There would be others like them later in life, such as Bill Parcells and David Jurist and Ken Vehrkens, to help mold and shape me, but were it not for this remarkable Armijo High and Fairfield team, those who followed would likely have had no specimen of value to work with.

*****

Before we get to my recruiting experiences, and then back-door into the tangential topics of fishing and church, before finishing with the pre-eminent topic of this book beyond *a Journey for 9/11* itself – my Dianne – it struck me that I should first talk a bit about what life was like during my high school years.

Oh, it was one helluva difficult time – civil rights and Vietnam and a people who were at such odds with their government, it was difficult all right. None of it was lost on me at the time.

Like everyone else, I counted the body bags on the evening news and we all questioned the morality of the conflict and tried to understand the mindset of the Viet Cong and there was so much doubt; but still, there was this part of me that wanted to join and serve and own my part of what so many had sacrificed themselves for. But then I also was moved by Muhammad Ali's protest and struggle and by the disproportionate price that African-Americans were paying there.

And still, I struggled with it all. Why them? Why not me?

I saw what the Black Panthers, as close as San Francisco, were doing and I could not agree or sympathize with their tactics, but I understood their arguments. In the spirit of Martin Luther King, however, I could not help but look upon violence itself – any violence – as evil.

Like everyone else, I counted the body bags on the evening news.

Then, at the big Armijo High-Fairfield High intercity football game during my senior year, there was a semi-riot in Fairfield of all places, and I watched as a group of young African-Americans tried to break the windshield of a car with a white woman and her children inside. I'll never forget the look on that poor woman's face. I'll never forget her innocence, her perplexed eyes or her incredible fear. I remember thinking that she had absolutely nothing to do with their anger and that it was all about her being in the wrong place at the wrong moment. Much like the unsuspecting truck driver who was attacked after the Rodney King Verdict was announced, none of that made any sense to me. Absolutely none of it!

The marauding attackers were, thank God, chased off and the woman and her children left safely and peace was restored, but the disquiet and confusion lived on in me. I could not free myself from the issues of race or war. Just like you, no doubt, I still can't, as our weary world takes its toll.

And while some may have come to look upon me as a warrior on the football field, I learned that day, in that parking lot after the game, just how strong were my non-violent instincts and my passionate distaste for the blindness and ignorance of racism in all of its forms.

I could not free myself from the issues of race or war. Just like you, no doubt, I still can't, as our weary world takes its toll.

Fortunately for me, at the time, two coaches and one great teacher and an old pro wrestler kept me on the straight and narrow, and pushed me inexorably forward toward a scholarship and college and a chance and hope for something larger in life.

As to the recruiting experience, I was highly recruited for football, while basketball was my first love. Schools like Berkeley, Washington, Montana, UCLA, Oregon and even West Point were most interested; beyond that, I was what they called "under the radar." I ruled Montana out when I visited there on a gorgeous, "Big Sky" Montana day of 80 degrees, only to wake up to 18 inches of snow the next morning. Then, I ruled Berkeley out, which was right in my backyard, because it was the hotbed of the "hippie-yippie" drug culture at the time and that just wasn't my thing.

In the end, it came down to UCLA or Oregon and maybe Washington, because I found it difficult to commit to six years in the United States Army after graduation. But had the years required been less, I could well have found myself at West Point. Now, both Washington and Oregon appealed because of that old "love of the land" part of me, because you just couldn't get two more beautiful settings.

Oregon especially appeared to me to be non-pretentious, and the people there seemed natural and down to earth. There I met the great Olympic runner, Steve Prefontaine, who would die tragically some four years later. I was so impressed because here he was, a national icon, and he seemed to have nothing better to do than speak to me about his love of Oregon. He left a lasting impression on me as a good and kind man.

I could not free myself from the issues of race or war. Just like you, no doubt, I still can't, as our weary world takes its toll.

On the other hand, my visit to UCLA couldn't have left me colder.

They, at the time, were the epitome of pretentiousness – all spit polish and glitz and "Jumping Jack Flash." I already had found the woman I wanted in my life, but they wanted to pair me up while I was there and I was introduced to their great party scene where the smell of aromatic marijuana filled the air. As to the pairing up, gimme a break, and thanks, but no thanks! As to the marijuana, I make no judgments, but it just wasn't and never has been for me. As to the party scene, they chose the wrong method to sell me on UCLA!

But to top it all off, I was taken into their sacred basketball arena, where the great "Wizard of Westwood" himself, the greatest and most revered coach in the history of collegiate basketball, stood right in front of me. I was taken into John Wooden's presence because, while being recruited for football, they were well aware of my desire to continue playing basketball. There he was. I could have reached out and touched him, but he didn't even bother to acknowledge me. Now, maybe he had just gotten bad news or he was pre-occupied with something pressing or he was just told "no" by a targeted recruit for the first time in history, but as a non-targeted recruit, he had no time for me – not even a second, not even a quick shake of the hands, nothing.

There I was in the inner sanctum of the game I loved, in the shadow of its Holy Grail, but there was no interest in me. Wooden left, and completely ignored, so did I.

Prefontaine or Wooden, it was no contest. Oregon, it had to be.

*****

As to my Dianne story, I fell in love with her as a freshman in Armijo High, some 45 years ago. But the story actually begins with that same big sister of mine, Brenda, for Dianne's sister, Ruth, was best friends with Brenda.

You'll find me waxing poetically about leadership quite often in this book, but suffice it to say that my older sister was the quintessential, natural-born leader. Brenda was fearless, and she was the Martin family's greatest natural athlete and greatest asset. At Armijo High, she cleared the path for all Martins to follow. As they say in the vernacular, Brenda just "didn't take any shit from anybody." No time! No way!

Dianne was upper-class in every way – she was a sophomore and I a freshman – but through the great grace of God, she decided to choose an underclassman – me – at the Annual Sadie Hawkins Dance, where the girls get to pick their guys. I remember the setting, the decorations, the lighting, and the storm that rose up in me when her lips touched my cheek. I was smitten and I was smitten forever.

As a result of what transpired that evening, of course, no one on this planet has a greater appreciation for dear old Sadie Hawkins than I.

Yes, the relationship was classic. Dianne was a cheerleader and a member of the band and I tried always to be her football hero, and we walked to school together and we regularly stopped at Snowman's Burger Joint after school and I had the honor of walking her home, every day, day after day. We'd go to the mall in Concord and we'd go to church together every Sunday morning, and we'd be a part of all things Armijo High and Fairfield, and contributed time to charitable events together.

Dianne was upper-class in every way – she was a sophomore and I a freshman – but through the great grace of God, she decided to choose a lower-classman – me – at the Annual Sadie Hawkins Dance, where the girls get to pick their guys. I remember the setting, the decorations, the lighting, and the storm that rose up in me when her lips touched my cheek. I was smitten and I was smitten forever.

If there was an event for young people, we were in, but the event of events was her Senior Prom. It was one of the most magical nights of my life. It was my first plane ride and my first overnight and my first trip to Disneyland, and the night and the attractions and the lights and the feel of the woman whose hand was in mine rendered it spectacular.

Together back then, by the way, we'd enjoy the Motown sounds and Stevie Wonder and Chicago and Three Dog Night and The Mamas and The Papas. Today, it's largely smooth jazz and fusion, but I saved all of the 45 rpm records purchased during the days of our high school romance.

Because the romance endures!

Of course, we were young then and immature and some would say that we moved too quickly, and there might be reason to call me jealous, even obsessed with Dianne, because I was. From the moment I met her I knew, and I can say that our love has withstood the test of time as we now celebrate 40 years of marriage.

So the truth was that I just couldn't leave for Oregon without sanctifying and assuring what was ours, so I spent my vast fortune of fifty bucks on one very affordable, "poor man's" diamond ring and she said "yes" and the earth moved, and I was free to go to college with her promise sealed in my heart.

As you will learn shortly, that was not enough. I still couldn't rest.

*****

Before moving on to Oregon, I want to share a couple of other thoughts with you, about religion – and about my family's second religion, fishing.

I had a grandmother, Mrs. Cora as she was known to most (on my mother's side), who raised 12 children and largely fished to feed them, because the cupboard was bare and to her, fishing was just another way of praying. You'd set the bait, string the line or cast, and then commune with God as you'd wait for the nibbles on your earthworm or dough ball.

Not so saintly, fishing was truly my Dad's mistress and passion, for which California's plentiful waterways and creeks and lakes were a lurid land of plenty, a veritable Godsend to one who once had to satisfy himself with Greenville's muddy Ash Moe's Creek.

Fishing, in the Deep South, had been a necessary means of putting food on the table. My grandmother and grandfather took the fishing tradition very seriously, i.e., they genuinely believed that talking could disturb or keep the fish away, so talking was taboo.

In large measure, it was rules like that which cured me of any desire to make fishing a key component of my life, though my brother has. Yes, my brother Doug sure was different than me, as he inherited Dad's passion – lock, stock, and barrel, he inherited it – and that love was passed down to his family and to my own boys. Consequently, we, as a family, have canoed and boated on the most serene, revered and beautiful fishing holes or lakes or creeks in North America with our poles in hand and earth worms in our pockets.

For the record, I witnessed far too much mouth-watering cornbread getting rolled into balls for the fish to have any tolerance for it myself.

My Dad, I thought, would rather feed the fish than us.

*****

We actually were one of the founding families of Mount Calvary Baptist Church in Fairfield. That's right, George Martin Sr. was one of the founding members as well as a deacon, along with Reverend Lee and Reverend Bell, who was later disgraced and left the church after a rather messy and public affair that led to his divorce.

All we Martin children were members of the choir and we dutifully participated in Sunday School services as well. Being emigrants from the southern Bible Belt as we were, it was our practice to attend church on a regular basis, while our Californian counterparts were much more free and easy with their attendance. But make no mistake about it, for Brenda, Doug, Lori, Helen and me, it was a virtual command performance.

My parents may have taken little interest in our schooling or our grades, but our attendance at church and being right with the Lord was commanded by them.

At Mount Calvary, my younger middle sister, Helen, was not only a member of the choir, but she also played the piano in a very accomplished fashion. We were extremely active there and it was in that church where I was originally baptized. Many years later, both my Benjamin and George were also baptized at Mount Calvary, although its location had changed by then.

While still in high school, however, Dianne and I flexed our own theological muscles and moved to Rev. Joseph B. Davis' Saint Stephen's Baptist Church. We broke with my parents in both a literal and figurative sense. There, at Saint Stephen's, we went on to become leaders in the youth program, volunteers in community endeavors and Sunday school teachers. While my connection there became disjointed and limited by life at Oregon and with the Giants, this role was still sustained many years into my Giants life in the off- season.

*****

There is more. There is always more, as each day is filled with thousands of thoughts and hundreds of movements and dozens of conversations and dozens of prayers, and always a dream or two deferred and a new one set in motion.

But we must move on to Oregon and then to the Giants, just to get to the *Journey*, which after all is what this is all about. And there, who I become and who I am will be fully manifested.

3 – ON TO OREGON

And the Not-So Mighty Ducks

In August 1971, I reluctantly headed north to the University of Oregon for my first collegiate football camp. The reluctance, of course, had everything to do with leaving Dianne and not necessarily the difficult days that awaited me, and while I had been blessed at Armijo High School with MVPs and High School All-American accolades and class presidencies, there was something about me that just wasn't quite ready for independence or prime time, much less collegiate stardom.

I had long been transported into the cosmopolitan environs of Fairfield, California, but I was still a good old country boy from the dirt of Greenville, South Carolina, at heart.

Romantically and spiritually, I was also so invested in Dianne that the mere act of separating myself from her was literally and palpably depressing. The loneliness, with its attendant gaping holes and heartsickness, struck and broke me before I even got to the beautiful city of Eugene and the equally beautiful campus of the University of Oregon.

In high school, my course had been charted for me and everything imaginable just came together or seemed to fall into place – a great girl, great friends, great achievements, grades that were if not great at least good enough, acceptance, and even a measure of stardom. Looking down from above, I had it all in high school.

I had been blessed. And maybe even spoiled!

For while there were heights yet to reach and awards to be made worthy of in days to come, nothing ever came as easy for me as it did in high school.

And while I was to take two major steps forward at Oregon, steps that would be critical to my development, steps that would, in many ways, determine the path that I would follow and contribute mightily to the maturation of my character, one part of Oregon was sadly to be the black hole of my life's story.

I loved the University, which produced then and continues to produce today a goodly number of NFL star players. In fact, I was on an Oregon Ducks team that included future San Diego Chargers quarterback and Hall of Famer Dan Fouts, future NFL All-Pro wide receiver Ahmad Rashad, and future Patriots and 49ers tight end Russ Francis. "Fantasy" football didn't really take off until I was nearing retirement, but we Oregon alums in the '70s and '80s would have made quite a fantasy team.

I played well enough on the field at Oregon to remain a contender, but the larger world hardly noticed and I accomplished little there – outside of surviving and holding my own as a football player – to be proud of. There were few victories, no glory, little to celebrate, great angst, too many encounters with injustice, and too much anger welling up inside to enable me to feel good about myself.

And teammate to teammate, despite personal loyalties and hard edged bonds of affection, we failed each other – failed to hold each other up, failed to be the best that we could be.

But with a four-year football scholarship in tow, I rode north in that summer of 1971 toward a brave new world and life, though one that at the time was especially cloudy. Yes, there was a measure of expectation and natural excitement, but there would be no friends waiting and no support system to rely upon. At the outset, I doubted everything from whether or not I'd have what it took to play in the Pacific 8 or the NCAA to whether or not my Art Education major was a good fit.

And teammate to teammate, despite personal loyalties and hard edged bonds of affection, we failed each other – failed to hold each other up, failed to be the best that we could be.

In actuality, Fairfield, California, halfway between Sacramento and San Francisco and just 20 miles from the fertile Napa Valley. Eugene, Oregon, which lay in the equally fertile Willamette Valley between the snow-speckled Cascade Mountains to the east and the dazzling rock crags, low-lying mountains and tall timbers of the Pacific Coast to the west, was but a 500-mile, 8-hour run straight up or down Interstate 5. As trips go, it wasn't that long at all and it could easily be accomplished in a day, but it may as well have been on the opposite end of the universe to me. That is exactly what it felt like, as each mile north further separated me from my family, my friends, and most especially, my fiancé.

*****

It wouldn't take me too long to rectify that, as Dianne and I, against the advice and will of my parents and others, would get married during my junior year. My parents' purported righteous opposition was so strong that they did not come to the small civil service we arranged in Vacaville (locally known as Cowtown, California), just 10 miles north of Fairfield. And that's the kind of gut punch that leaves a sore and nagging hole that lasts.

Outside of the fact that Dianne and I got to affirm our love and commit our lives to each other on that bright "*California Dreaming*" day of March 22, 1974, before a Vacaville justice of the peace, there was nothing particularly special about the ceremony. That is, of course, besides her. A good friend of mine and high school teammate, Alan Grant, stood in as my best man and about 14 family members and friends also stood with us. The only member of my family who attended was Brenda, whose close friendship with Dianne's sister Ruth had brought her to me originally. So it was largely a Smith affair, as Dianne's fellow Smiths were there to witness her assuming the name of Martin.

Interestingly, the whole excursion home from Eugene to quickly marry and then just as quickly return with my stunning bride and our beautiful little girl, Teresa, happened only because a very close friend, University of Oregon teammate and mentor about two years my senior, Tom Graham, had made it possible with his no-questions-asked and no-strings-attached loan of $500. That paid for the travel, the gas, the U-

Haul rental, the flowers, the small reception, the justice of the peace, the license, and a day of wining and dining my bride.

The honeymoon and all of the extras were put off for another day.

Fortunately, having heard me pine about Dianne once too often, Tom just knew that it was the moment for me to call the question, the one that Dianne had answered affirmatively more than a year and a half before. So he simply slipped me the $500 and said it was time – time for that $50 engagement ring to work its magic!

"Time it was and what a time it was – a time of innocence, a time of consequences," Simon and Garfunkel sang, and so it was – the best decision I ever made, the best action I ever took. I was the luckiest!

So a U-Haul packed with the trappings of Dianne's life, her Volkswagen bug, my bride and me and our Teresa headed north on Interstate 5 to Eugene, where we would be housed in the Westmoreland Dormitory for married students.

It was done and I was forever and happily married.

*****

As to the Oregon years, outside of affirming the importance of my friendship and relationship with Greg Milton and Tom Graham, and my active association with the University's Fellowship of Christian Athletes (FCA), there was nothing beyond my marriage to Dianne that was quite so important or worthy of reporting to you. I'll share some thoughts momentarily on the FCA, but first, my collegiate days on the gridiron:

The truth is that I carry too many bitter memories of the football program then at Oregon, so much so that there's much I don't choose or want to remember. I do not fondly reminisce about my days at Autzen Stadium.

Of course, the first two years I played basketball as well as football, because I liked basketball more, but it took too much out of me and after two seasons of two sports, all it got me was a prominent place on academic probation. And that's academic probation at a *"Your education comes first, wink – wink,"* Division 1, "*As goes our football team, so goes the university*" institution.

Without exploring the fine details, all I'm trying to say is that they had my back during the football season, for they were indirectly, via scholarship, paying me to play football, but not necessarily during the basketball season, because they had made no financial investment in my playing "'round ball." The ethics enveloping the role our colleges play as the amateur underbelly of the National Football League and the National Basketball Association is its own insidious story, and while I could share my own chapter and verse about it, that is not what I am after here, other than to say there is much about it that saddens and sometimes sickens.

Oregon's lack of interest in my basketball career ultimately didn't matter, because as a 6'4" back-up center who already had his fill of being manhandled by 6'10" rivals night after night, I resigned myself to the fact that the NBA was never going to come calling.

If I had any future in sports – and there were certainly no guarantees and plenty of unanswered questions – it was in football.

While I was at Oregon, we had a defense that was twice good enough to be ranked the best in the Pacific 8 Conference. We had players with great mobility and dexterity, and on paper we looked halfway decent.

We also had some truly exceptional players like Dan Fouts, who went on to become a Pro Football Hall of Famer and arguably one of the game's all-time greatest quarterbacks. Then, too, there was Russell Francis, another Hall of Famer and a superb tight end – maybe one of the few in the nation better than me. The problem for me was that Russ was on my own team and so dropped me into oblivion on the draft depth charts. While I was still a tight end, I had the misfortune of playing behind Francis on offense, so pro scouts saw much more of me at defensive end. As to great players, I cannot forget my mentor, Tom Graham, who was as good as any other linebacker in his day. He was a fierce competitor with all the skills and, in a fairer world, he too would have been a Hall of Famer.

*****

I know the old line, "Let the past bury its dead," and that if you have nothing good to say, keep the commentary to yourself. That, of course, presents an ethical problem for me, because I have nothing good to say about our coaching, nothing whatsoever, and yet I have much to say that rightfully needs to be said.

The ethics enveloping the role our colleges play as the amateur underbelly of the National Football League and the National Basketball Association is its own insidious story.

So maybe I can cross the ethical divide by being brief and temperate, if not kind. I was in Dick Enright's head-coaching hands for my first two years and in Don Read's for the next two, and while Don Read managed to grab the brass ring and win the laurels with Montana a decade later, he led us into the throes of an unprecedented 14-game losing streak and a 66–0 beating by our archrival, the Washington Huskies.

That disaster topped off the six wins in two seasons under Enright. Dick Enright rather remarkably believed that he could turn Fouts, one of the best pocket passers the game had ever seen, into an option quarterback. For two years, he abused Fouts and insisted on utilizing the option. But the option can only work if the quarterback has speed, real speed, the one and only commodity missing from Fouts' considerable arsenal.

He couldn't run – he just couldn't – and Enright insisted that he do so. Consequently, we had a great weapon that was so underutilized.

No, underutilized just isn't strong enough. He was brutalized!

So, there were mean and lean and bitterly frustrating days on the field of Autzen Stadium on the banks of the Willamette River in the early '70s. It sat just under 42,000 then, although it has been renovated of late and now seats some 54,000.

Historically proclaimed as one of the loudest stadiums in the nation, fans made little noise generated over the course of my days there.

And there was little for Donald Duck, the longstanding face of our Oregon "Mighty" Ducks (the original Mighty Ducks) football team to cheer about. Walt Disney himself had, in a handshake agreement in 1947, awarded Oregon the right to showcase Donald as their own.

Our sports ethics code was – get ready for this – referred to as *The Code of Conduck.* I kid you not. I take such codes seriously and I expect my coaches to do the same. I'm thinking about baseline notions like honor and goodness and integrity and honesty and fair play.

But all of the above and more were all too often missing!

First of all, there was what we referred to as the "Minimus Rule" that required all NCAA coaching staffs, in the wake of the Civil Rights movement, to have their token black coach. Always in a subservient or tertiary position and typically with little or no impact on game-day decisions, this coach's one prominent position was in the staff picture that was taken for display in all publications. And then there was the unspoken but widely practiced rule that, "*Those blacks really can't play positions where they have to use their minds and/or make decisions.*" They certainly could never be trusted to play quarterback or middle linebacker.

Yes, I played, as did Tom Graham, at middle linebacker of all places, as did many other African-American teammates, but many others who should have did not. The Civil Rights movement had forced paradigm shifts and everywhere real change was in the air, but there was, as there always are, vestiges of resistance. I saw lightly veiled racism affect our team constantly and I spoke up and I battled, and consequently, outside of the joy of having Dianne to hold me up and hug me through it all, and the honor of having friends like Tom Graham, Greg Milton and others, the greater University of Oregon football experience was, for me, sadly tempered by harsh urgencies.

As I look back, I don't think that I would have stayed in the Oregon program for as long as I did were it not for Greg and Tom. Greg's friendship kept me balanced and sound. Whenever I'd get ready to fly off somewhere over something, it was he who generally pulled me back to Earth and kept me grounded. Dianne will be the first to tell you that it was almost as if she discovered two husbands upon her arrival in Eugene, as Greg's daily routine and mine were one and the same. Fortunately, he followed our lead and got married himself during my junior year, which more than likely helped save my marriage, since Dianne must have been exasperated by Greg's constant presence.

As for Tom, he and his wife, Marilyn, proved to be a spiritual force for Dianne and me. Two years my senior, he both advised and inspired. It was he who urged me to become involved with the FCA and its Bible studies classes, prayer meetings and ethical workshops, which reaffirmed and crystallized my faith. In the clubhouse and on the field, I felt embattled and unsettled and all too often angry, but with the Fellowship, I grabbed hold of the goodness and patience and resiliency and inner strength that would help me overcome.

At the Fellowship, in prayer, I realized that I might not be able to change the world that I lived in day after day, but I damn well could keep that world from changing me. So, true to myself, I persevered in large measure because of Tom's influence. If I didn't make a meeting, he'd come after me and reel me in, and whenever I doubted what was in me or what I was worth, he helped me to believe in myself.

When he was drafted by the Denver Broncos in the third round in 1973, we had a conversation in which he assured me that I too was going to make it, but not if I gave up on myself. He told me that nothing would disappoint him more if I didn't make it. The thought of letting him down was almost too much to bear, so he, in large measure, drove me in my final years, drove me to becoming that "by the skin of my teeth," 11th-round pick by the New York Giants.

And oh what pleasant surprises were to follow!

At the Fellowship, in prayer, I realized that I might not be able to change the world that I lived in day after day, but I damn well could keep that world from changing me.

Such was my relationship with Greg and Tom that they were built to last and our families have been conjoined over the years. We mourned when Greg lost his wife Sandra, or Sammy as I called her, a couple of years ago a mere three years shy of their 40th wedding anniversary and we grieved with Tom and Marilyn when they recently lost their son, Jason, to cancer. After surviving a kidney transplant, a gift from his Mom, he tragically succumbed to his disease. Like Job, they were mightily tested, but Jason and his parents truly believed that he had been saved from the beginning and that death had no dominion over him.

Both healed and redeemed, they remain at peace. “There is a joy unspeakable that Jason knew,” said Tom, “That gives us such comfort.”

*****

In the interest of letting you hear another voice from time to time, I will ask a few friends and peers to speak with you directly. I begin by asking Tom Graham if he wouldn’t mind commenting on some of the issues that I have related:

On inviting me into the Fellowship

“Oh, what interesting meetings we had when George arrived. He wasn’t shy about speaking his mind. And he was so easy to gravitate to – what I call ‘easy pickings.’ I liked him from the start and was struck by the notion that I had no one to counsel or guide me when I first arrived, so why not try and be there for him. After that, we spent time with each other every day. We became brothers.”

On their competitive spirit

“One day, we were going to have this friendly, pick-up basketball game. Nothing serious! But George, he took the gloves off and showed no mercy, as if his life depended upon humiliating me on that court. That was fair warning as far as I was concerned, so when we met on a sunny Sunday afternoon, Chargers versus Giants special teams, I tried to take his head off, which I think shocked him. On the field, the buddies and friends gloves were off.”

On George and Dianne

“My wife had a son, Philip, when I married her, so when George talked to me about Dianne and Teresa, I finally sat him down and said, ‘George, can you love Teresa as if she is your own? Because if you know that you can, it’s time.’ Our situations mirrored each other’s, so I knew. As to the $500, I don’t even remember it, so I’m sure that I was just glad to do it. He became Uncle George to my children, and me, Uncle

Tommy, to his, and no one calls me Tommy except George and my brother, Duncan."

On the University of Oregon and the football program

"Here, George and I have different philosophies. We saw things differently and so had different experiences. I had no problem at Oregon and I loved the University of Oregon. When George saw someone being mistreated, it was as if he too was being mistreated. If someone got hurt, he got hurt. If he saw an injustice, he carried it with him. There's not a lot of demand for individuals like that in football, where they want you to be part of the herd."

"Now I'm a fighter too, but George and I just chose different battles. I'd let go where he would not. I also was willing to give a lot more to God than George was.

"George is a deep guy. There's more to him than people see, and I guess he really put shoe leather to that in deciding to walk across America for another cause. Now, he may have a thick skin, but he gets hurt and he got hurt a lot at Oregon."

On the Hall of Fame

"That's just George's love doing the talking. And he's probably the only one saying it. I was a very good football player, but I was no Hall of Famer. That's the province of the greats, like his fellow warrior, Harry Carson. But I'll take his wanting to place me on Mount Rushmore, which speaks to our Hall of Fame relationship, and not to any Hall of Fame career of mine."

*****

Tom Graham's son, Daniel, played for the New England Patriots, Denver Broncos, Tennessee Titans and New Orleans Saints, and our families continue to enjoy occasional respites together, highlighted by a recent fishing trip that resulted in a Curt Gowdy moment for Tom's brother Duncan and me when we caught the "mother-load."

In thinking about Tom and looking to close this out, there's a confession that I should make. I wept when he departed Oregon for his new life with the Denver Broncos. I did, because he was that close and that important to me.

Without him, I truly don't know what would have become of me, as it was his pep talks and his always having my back that saved me for football during my dark days at Oregon.

I'll never forget his return for graduate study after his first season in the NFL. How he let me have it! *He told me that I was too nice a guy to play the game, that I wasn't mean enough for football, and that it was long past time for me to learn that becoming angry and playing the game of football go hand in hand.* I was never as upset with him as I was then, but I heard every word, retained every word, and acted upon his word to improve my game and catch the last train that was taking the boys on the bubble to the big leagues.

*****

Oregon was incomplete for me, but Tom helped me realize that it was ultimately not about football, rather about the man that I wanted to be, and that if the man I wanted to be was interested in a shot in the NFL, it meant playing like a champion on a losing football team. It meant doing all that I could to elevate the game of those playing with me. And that's what I tried to do.

In no way, shape or form would I have done so were it not for Tom Graham. I would not be the man I became were it not for Tom Graham.

In truth, while I'll delve into the Giants days in the next chapter, I celebrated the $6,000 bonus that I received from the New York Football Giants like it was a one-time win, figuring that my 11th round draft status would lead me back to Fairfield, California, after the 110 players invited to camp gave way to the 55 leaving camp. I gave $3,000 to my Dad, as I'm a believer that a child's good fortune should be shared with his parents, and there was $3,000 for Dianne to return to Fairfield with. At the time, after four years of counting nickels and dimes on campus, $3,000 was a veritable fortune.

*****

In a nutshell, my University of Oregon experience revolved around my Dianne and our Teresa, my devotion to God and my commitment to the Fellowship of Christian Athletes, my wrestling with a very broken football program, and my becoming a better football player in spite of it.

Before closing, it's only fair to point out that everything about Oregon is different today, and that you don't reach the heights their program has of late without shooting straight and tapping all the talent available, which was not the case when I was there.

Eugene, Oregon, also is a slice of heaven. Nestled between the beauty of the Cascade Range and the magnificence of the Oregon coast, it is further defined by the convergence of the Willamette and McKenzie Rivers, and by a sea of parks and trails, and bikeways and public gardens, and festivals and fairs that make it one of the most livable cities on the continent.

Lewis and Clark explored the Willamette, which is today designated as one of only 14 American Heritage Rivers, as well as the Willamette Valley, a breathtaking agricultural tapestry that marked the end of the famous Oregon Trail.

As destiny would have it, the sport to be celebrated when I was at Oregon was actually track and field. In fact, when I was there, a great champion by the name of Steve Prefontaine was leaving an indelible imprint on both the University of Oregon and the city of Eugene, which forever after the Prefontaine days would be associated with running and jogging.

Even Nike, which was founded and once headquartered in Eugene by his coach, Bill Bowerman, prior to relocating to Beaverton, was to some degree an outgrowth of what Prefontaine wrought. While my team was regularly losing, his cross-country team brought home three consecutive national championships, and the only year they missed was when they devoted themselves to the Olympics instead.

Prefontaine, at Oregon, became a national icon, and along with friends like Frank Shorter and Bill Rodgers, world-class and champion marathoners who trained with him in Eugene, they rendered it a runner's haven.

His tragic death in an auto accident in Eugene in May of 1975 occurred not long after I was drafted and being summoned to a new life. His death stunned the University, the city of Eugene, and runners worldwide. Having known him briefly and having long appreciated his passion and drive, his death stunned me, too.

It forced me to dwell upon the seeming unfairness, upon the vagaries of chance and fate, and, of course, upon the precious gift of a next day and a next year. In fact, Steve Prefontaine, the undisputed champion of the University of Oregon, spoke loudly to us all.

In what is still a runner's city, there are endless miles of trails to run on and riverside parks to run through – and there is *Pre's* Trail and *Pre's* Race and *Pre* memorials and *Pre* parks and the fabulous DeFazio Pedestrian Bridge. Spiritually, he abides – going out hard, pushing all others, and demanding the very best of himself and everyone else in the race.

Reminding us to *Pre*-pare, at all times, to devote our very best to what we do.

For me, the next stop was to be Pace University, at a camp, in the summer of 1975, where the New York Football Giants would be making a lot of judgment calls, not the least of which was whether or not I had the ability to play the game of football with the big boys.

4 – TO BE A GIANT AMONG MEN

'Way to go, Rook!'

About so much more than football, my career with the New York Football Giants meant the world to me. While different players moved in and moved out, we remained a family always, a unique brotherhood of men. In welcoming my teammates who had no place to be on Thanksgiving, Dianne and I bore witness to the fact that each and every Giant was indeed family to us. We started this tradition in my first year with the team and carried it through my 14 seasons. As Thanksgiving is among the most family-oriented and personal of holidays, I believe this spoke volumes.

We loved one another, and that more than any one thing is what turns a bunch of disparate football players into a team. On the New York Football Giants, that more than anything else turned a bunch of losers into Super Bowl champions. And my Dianne's willingness to turn our Thanksgivings into a Giants family affair was a great component of our bonding experience.

Make no mistake about it, in the NFL you go to war each week – and I do mean war. It is only when you truly stand as one that you win. We loved one another, we had one another's backs, we believed in one another, and so the confetti rained down upon us from above in Pasadena and we cried in thanksgiving for our brothers who had turned ordinary football players into the game's elite – into the best of the best.

In the end, my career went by in what felt like the blink of an eye, but I managed to achieve something very rare indeed. Through the great grace of God, I played 14 consecutive seasons in the National Football League, a proving ground where a player usually lasts no more than 3 to 4 years on average. I also had the atypical pleasure of playing for one team only, the great Wellington Mara's New York Football Giants.

Blessed with good health, I somewhat remarkably missed only 6 games over the course of those 14 seasons.

During my first six seasons, as the players who remained grew closer and the missing pieces were slowly added, it was hard to hold our heads up high. From a competitive vantage point, those were lean years indeed. Six straight losing seasons, with no more than six wins in any given year, was about as tough as it gets for a team. Professionally, it was merely a continuation of my college experience by other means. To put it into perspective – and lifelong Giants fans will certainly appreciate this – I was on the sideline that infamous November 19 when our then-quarterback, "Paterson Plank" Joe Pisarcik, laid down "*The Fumble*" that rocked the football universe and put the exclamation point on our team's sad days of ineptitude.

Those also were the years when season ticket holders did the unimaginable and went so far as to burn their tickets in protest in front of Giants Stadium.

As it was, I served one season with the "Mad Dutchman," Bill Arnsparger, as head coach, followed by three seasons with John McVay, and another four with Ray Perkins. Under Perkins, things began to turn around, and then, finally and most happily, I spent my last six seasons in the arms of one the game's greatest coaches, Bill Parcells.

If you hang around long enough, it is said that you eventually get lucky. Our turnaround, football historians note, began with the hiring in 1979 of General Manager George Young, a tough and gruff old-schooler who had been reared with the Baltimore Colts, Miami Dolphins and long associated with the immortal Don Shula. George's hiring was born out of a very public and contentious feud between owners Wellington Mara and his younger nephew, Tim Mara, in which the NFL itself eventually had to intercede. The compromise thankfully was the hiring of a general manager to right the ship. Upon arriving in the New Jersey Meadowlands, he often said that the secret to winning football games was taking 11 of the biggest, strongest and fastest men you could find and getting them angrier than your opponent's biggest, strongest and fastest men. As a result, we did get our first taste of victory in 1981 under Coach Perkins, with a 9-7 winning record and a brief playoff run.

Upon arriving in the New Jersey Meadowlands, George Young often said that the secret to winning football games was taking 11 of the biggest, strongest and fastest men you could find and getting them angrier than your opponent's biggest, strongest and fastest men.

We actually enjoyed a December 27 wild-card victory over the Philadelphia Eagles before falling to the 49ers in the division series, and the taste of what it might be like to truly be good and to make a real run was finally in our heads and hearts. Once there, I can tell you, it's an awfully hard taste to lose. Once you win, getting better and improving and rising up to that place where you can be among the game's elite begin to haunt you. The truth is, though, that it likely would never have happened for us had George Young not brought in Coach Bill Parcells to assume the head coaching position, because not until Coach Parcells arrived in 1983 did we really get serious and get down to business.

As rough-hewn and harsh as he could be, it was Coach Parcells who by corollary taught us, amid teaching us a lot about football, that it was ultimately about loving one another, which is what it means to become a real team. Nineteen eighty-three, somewhat understandably, wound up being a terrible year as he cleaned house and retained only the true believers. But in 1984, his second season, the inept Giants of the '70s disappeared and we actually started to become accustomed to winning.

It is also important to note that with Bill Parcells a great staff was assembled. Bill Belichick, today's renowned head coach of the New England Patriots, most notably for me was brought in as defensive coordinator. It is fair to say that he had everything to do with turning our motley defensive crew into the celebrated "*Big Blue Wrecking Crew*" that would be toasted by Giants fans throughout the late '80s and early '90s. I was, therefore, privileged to play under not one, but two, of the game's greatest coaches during my final six years.

And not to be forgotten, today's Giants Head Coach Tom Coughlin, the one who bested his old colleague in the 46th Super Bowl, Bill Belichick, was part of that same staff. It's just that as an assistant offensive coach, he had no on-field or direct interaction with me.

Our success would culminate in 1986 with a great, franchise record 14-2 run and our 39-20 Super Bowl victory on January 25 over John Elway and the Denver Broncos in Pasadena, California, a phenomenon that I'll have much to share about a bit later. And while there was a post-Super Bowl work stoppage and letdown that would impact the 1987 season, we got back on the winning track with a solid 10-6 1988 run, one that would prove to be my last.

The team I left after that 1988 season was primed to contend, and many of my teammates would go on to celebrate another victory against the Buffalo Bills in Super Bowl XXV in 1991.

Having seen all too many veteran football players, some of the toughest men on earth, collapse in tears upon being cut in training camp or even in mid-season, I was determined to cut the Giants' front office off at the pass and go out on my own volition and lay down my No. 75 *Defensive End* jersey at the time that I thought best. While the pundits suggest that I may have had another season or two in me, I called the question and retired after 14 seasons.

Having seen all too many veteran football players, some of the toughest men on earth, collapse in tears upon being cut in training camp or even in mid-season, I determined to cut the Giants' front office off at the pass and go out on my own volition and lay down my No. 75 Defensive End jersey at the time that I thought best.

I was proud to step down along with my great friend and fellow warrior on the field, Harry Carson, who after 13 seasons at middle linebacker was also ready. It was a bittersweet to be sure, but there definitely were no doubts.

We were pros and we weren't ever going to subject ourselves to the infamous summons of, "Coach wants to see you – and bring your playbook," or the words, "We're sorry, but it's time for us to go in a different direction." Remember, even to this day, guaranteed contracts are only for the immortals, so to be cut, with what was more than likely a non-guaranteed contract, meant that your pay was going to stop immediately, whenever they pulled the plug.

So Harry, who was soon to be inducted into the Hall of Fame, and I planned to and did, in fact, exit gracefully together with the honor we had earned intact. At the time, I left having recorded 96 quarterback sacks, and having scored the most points and most touchdowns of any defensive lineman in NFL history, which was seven.

*****

Telling It Like It Is

Whenever I speak to students, something that I've done thousands of times, I always tell it like it is. To that end I profess the following disclaimer. That my personal perspective is born out of a "old-school" experience and mentality, and that by today's account and standards it might assuredly be considered passé.

They assume that playing the game must be – just has to be – about having fun. We football players are, they think, the lucky ones who get to play for a living a game that kids love to play for fun, rather than work in a steamy factory or a dull office. And how can that *not* be fun? The operative term, after all, is play, and play – well, that's just what kids do with their toys, isn't it?

We play a game!

In fact, the toy that we play with is gift-wrapped every Christmas for many thousands of kids with starry-eyed dreams of getting to do just what we do. An oblong pig-skinned football, it is the tool of a trade that has long been associated with fun and play. They get those footballs, put jerseys on with the names of their favorite players, and then toss the balls around in their backyards while pretending to be those very players.

I feel a duty to give them a dose of reality. First, I tell those students to keep their eye on the prize, which is their education, because as great a star as they may be at River Dell or Bergen Catholic or DeWitt Clinton High School, few indeed thread through the eye of the needle into the pros.

Only a precious and fortunate few.

But those who do – and this is the second point – will quite possibly sacrifice their limbs and their vital organs and their very quality of life in order to play the game. Those fortunate few will play with pain and they will bleed and they will bruise their kidneys concuss their brains, and there's the occasional frostbite when they play at 20 degrees below in Green Bay. Chronic hip and knee and neck and back injuries will give way to agony, and there is a long-term price exacted even by those like me who avoided the injury curse during their playing days.

The game is not fun.

I did not play for fun. I played because I was a professional and it was my vocation. To you a game or sport, and to me a job or career.

More often than not, what took place on the field was agony. Sure there was joy, and often great joy, in victory and pride in achievement and honor in having done your job so well that you relieved the pressure on the backs of the 10 other men on the field with you. There was something wonderful about being a part of a team. In battle, there is a fierce loyalty and affection and love shared. Given the chance, you will sacrifice yourself for your brothers. Team means everything to you and you will celebrate and hold up your teammates whenever and however you can.

And in all of this, there is joy to be found.

We took our Thanksgivings out onto the field with us.

But every single play is also a violent collision, and every violent hit you take takes its toll, and it is remembered forever. In yesterday's players, it is there in that hip or knee replacement, there in the chronic pains and headaches, there in harsh, progressive diseases like Parkinson's and maybe even in the early onslaught of Alzheimer's.

I am among the rare and lucky ones. I still have my knees, neither of which have ever seen the surgeon's scalpel, and the game gave me more than I ever expected and I enjoy a great lifestyle because of the game. The game blessed me, but I took hits that exact pain to this very day, and the overwhelming majority of those I played with have residual ailments as a result of their Sundays at 1:00 p.m. and their Mondays at 9:00 p.m. before the 75,000 or so with them in the stadium and the untold millions watching on national TV.

No, fun just never sounded right to me. A measure of joy, yes! But joy is the byproduct of so much more than fun.

I am among the lucky ones. I still have my knees and the game gave me more than I ever expected and I enjoy a great lifestyle because of the game. The game blessed me, but I took hits that exact pain to this very day.

There was much that was good about the game, but none of it was fun, unless you were among the sadistic element that shouldn't be in football to begin with. I must admit that I met quite a few of the sadists over my 14 years, but with such a lack of appreciation for the game and such a lack of respect for their opponents, none of them truly belonged there. The headhunters who'd look to physically maim their opponents didn't belong on the field then and nor do they now.

In sum, football was a vocation, and for 14 years it was my chosen vocation. I was a professional athlete in the NFL who was paid to WORK at the game of football. I gave it my best and I honored and was honored by the hundreds of men who I worked with, and while there were times to both smile and laugh, that word "fun" was just never in the equation.

Love, yes, but fun, no!

Afterthought or Long Shot?

Consider this: I was the 262nd overall pick drafted by the New York Football Giants in the 11th round of the 1975 National Football League draft. The 11th round smacked of two telling thoughts – afterthought and long shot.

While I had played collegiate football at an elite level, I was a natural tight end who just happened to play at Oregon with another tight end who would prove to be one of the greatest to ever play that position in the NFL, Russell Francis. I got lost in the shuffle behind Russ, who was drafted in the first round by the Patriots. On the board as a both tight end and a defensive end didn't help me, because what was noted first was that I was a second-string tight end, which compromised the scouts' and coaches' look at my proven ability on the defensive side of the ball.

So the 11th round it was. Not exactly a ringing endorsement. When I left Dianne in California, where I was enjoying playing basketball in a church summer league, I said that I was sure I'd be back in no more than a couple of weeks. Off to what I assumed would be my first and last training camp with the New York Football Giants at Pace University in Pleasantville, New York, I honestly did not expect to be there for very long at all.

I had received my $6,000 signing bonus, and that, I assumed, just might have to be reward enough, and it was then, to be sure, a great sum of money. Looking forward, my salary, if I made the team, was projected at $18,000, so the $500 per week training camp reimbursement was greater still. Having never made more than $300 per week before, I was walking in tall cotton with that training camp money. The longer I stuck, the better off we were going to be financially.

So yes, I was not a great believer and my tearful separation from Dianne was, I believed, to be short-lived.

But on the other side of the coin, deep inside, I possessed an inordinate amount of pride in my ability to play this game on the highest of levels, a pride that had been validated and affirmed by coaches and teammates throughout the course of my high school and collegiate careers. It wasn't as if there was one single, earth-shattering epiphany, but there had been hundreds of little epiphanies. I had been told, again and again, that "it was expected of me" to try my hand in the NFL, and that "they'd be shocked or surprised if I didn't." And to top it off and most telling, Tom Graham, my mentor, who was then playing for the San Diego Chargers, told me that "I'll be disappointed in you if you don't play pro football, because God has given you the gifts to do so."

But on the other side of the coin, deep inside, I possessed an inordinate amount of pride in my ability to play this game on the highest of levels, a pride that had been validated and affirmed by coaches and teammates throughout the course of my high school and collegiate careers.

However much I feigned indifference and assured those in my then immediate life that I'd soon be back in Fairfield to take my place on the church's basketball team, my competitive instincts came to the fore and I intended to fight for a place on the New York Football Giants, who, however late, at least had the courtesy to draft me.

Training camps are the worst, and especially the prehistoric ones that were prevalent back in the day. In ours, 110 men were going to fight for 55 positions, so 55 incredibly talented athletes were going to be bitterly disappointed. In camp, machismo and testosterone and ego were going to run amuck and you would be engaged in combat as a damned gladiator day after day. Like children, you were separated from your family in what was, in so many ways, a living hell. It was not pleasant and there were no guarantees, and old veterans would fight to hang on and young bucks would fight to ascend.

The last few days were always particularly brutal. That was the time for great disappointment and sudden tears. Whenever you divide 55 by 110, half the hopeful are gone, and egos and dreams both large and small are destined to be slain. And no matter how many years you had under your belt, there were no assurances for most in training camp, unless you were a Lawrence Taylor, Phil Simms or Harry Carson.

As it happened, good fortune smiled on me in that first camp. Without the need to mention names, the guy they had drafted a year earlier to be their next star defensive end out of Nebraska – who allegedly had all the credentials – turned out to be an overweight and out of shape failure who simply wasn't prepared. Then too, the guy who wore No. 75 before me no longer seemed able to even hit the sled in that camp. Third and most importantly, they kept pitting me against Al Simpson, an offensive lineman and their No. 2 draft choice, the one they had invested a great deal of both time and money in. As a result, I was volunteered after each and every practice to compete against Al in order to improve his game.

Now it wasn't even about me at first, because their eyes were always trained on Simpson. Our competition was all about him, but here's the rub, it was I, in larger part due to may basketball abilities, who just kept getting better and better.

The competition between Simpson and myself was making me better and better! It was Miss Green all over again as history was repeating itself. Here it was that I was being singled out and effectively being punished, and as fate would have it, I was the one being rewarded in the end.

Eventually they noticed!

I played by the rules. I accepted my place on the bottom rung of the social pecking order of the Giants food chain. I neither rebelled against the rookie hazing nor sought any notoriety. I'd be happy to look like the young, inexperienced fool that I was, rather than open up my mouth and remove whatever doubt there may have been. Because I accepted the fact that rookies are nobody, I was, in the end, accepted.

However much I hated that first training camp, and subsequently all others since, I found myself elated, in the end, to be standing among the 55 who were still on the inside.

So suddenly, much to our great surprise, there was Dianne arriving at LaGuardia Airport for the first time. She met with a real estate agent and we wound up renting a sweet little summer cottage by a Lake in South Salem, New York, near Brewster and within easy striking distance of Pleasantville, where we would practice, and Shea Stadium in Queens where we would play. My Giants – and oh what a ring that had to it – were then nomadic itinerants. The year before, they had played at the Yale Bowl in New Haven, and the next year, 1976, we would be christening our new Giants Stadium in the Meadowlands.

Nomads ourselves, the Martin family was laying its first claim to a bi-coastal existence.

Unbelievable!

Putting that dress Giants uniform on for the first time was an extraordinary and totally unbelievable experience. I know it was only preseason, but that run out of the tunnel and onto a field was also pure magic and joy.

My first game was under the lights in Foxboro and I can remember just standing on the field, mesmerized by the splendor, by the colors, by the lights, by the noise of the crowd. It was as if I was standing on a vast stage and everything seemed to be moving at the speed of light. I kept mulling it over. I am in the National Football League. I am a professional football player. I am a Giant. I have made it to the big stage. I said it to myself again and again, as if I didn't quite believe it.

At the same time, I was moved and overjoyed and in almost shocked disbelief. Everyone is familiar with *Friday Night Lights.* Well, I was under the Foxboro Lights and they were so bright and the spotlight was on each and every one of us, standing there in the fishbowl, dazed and amazed. I retreated to the safety of the sideline, where I was going to be able to take in the spectacle of my very first pro football game as an NFL player – spectator, or so I thought.

But as luck, or fate, would have it, before the first quarter had even ended, they were calling my name to go in at right defensive end. I remember hearing it in slow motion, because I didn't believe it. Such a thing just could not be! I could literally hear my heart beating, thinking this just had to be a mistake. First quarter, first game, and they're calling on me, 11th-round-and-262nd-pick, me. Jack Gregory was hurt and I was in and that was that, and nobody had ever stopped to tell me that I was second string, for fear of my running or hiding, I guess.

I don't even recall what happened on the first play, but through some grace, I managed to sack the quarterback on the second play and I was suddenly back in time, all present and accounted for, in the land of athletic utopia and ready to be noticed. And yes, magical words were spoken by John Mendenhall, the cornerstone of the Giants defensive front and most-respected member of the team – "*Way to go, rook. About time we got somebody who we can play with here.*" That was said just as Pat Hughes, veteran linebacker, reached over to fasten my chinstrap. He uttered not a word, but his veteran gesture and welcoming smile of acceptance spoke volumes. In a moment, in an almost magical moment, I make a play and the veterans let me know that I'm one of them and that they have my back. DAMN!, it just doesn't get any better in life than that … ever!

My first game was under the lights in Foxboro and I can remember just standing on the field, mesmerized by the splendor, by the colors, by the lights, by the noise of the crowd. It was as if I was standing on a vast stage and everything seemed to be moving at the speed of light. I kept mulling it over, again and again. I am in the National Football League. I am a professional football player. I am a Giant. I have made it to the big stage. I said it to myself, again and again, as if I didn't quite believe it.

Ten feet tall and flying high, I told myself then and there that I could never let these guys down.

Before every snap thereafter, I'd think of the duty I owed to those standing on that line with me.

In that same moment, I took the starting left-side (or strong-side) defensive end position, a position that I would hold onto for 14 years. In fact, when Jack Gregory got healthy, he never came home to the strong side, but rather took over on the right or weak side and we played together.

In that moment, I had made it and I got to run out on that field for the next 14 seasons as a Giant. Almost paternalistic, the veterans made me feel at home and I struggled and worked to be worthy of being among them, for I had much to learn.

Mendenhall, Lockhart, Gregory, Stienke, Hughes, my team fathers – I loved them and to disappoint them was simply unacceptable to me.

But then too, it was tough settling into that world and getting to a place where I felt as if I truly belonged. I had to keep on earning it – I could be out of favor with a coach, there could be trade rumors, there were no guaranteed contracts. So you had to accept each day as it came and stay humble and take nothing for granted and keep working hard. That is exactly what I did.

But it wasn't until 5 or 6 years later when I finally felt that I belonged and that I had earned my place.

And after 14 years, there had been a ton of magic moments, and what was achieved cannot be encapsulated into a few years or a few special games. All of them mattered! Each play mattered!

By My Side

The period in which I played encompassed the careers of quarterback Phil Simms and linebacker Lawrence Taylor, two of the most accomplished players in Giants team history. Simms was drafted to little fanfare from little Morehead State University in 1979, and struggled in his initial seasons before becoming a Pro Bowl quarterback. LT was the second selection in the 1981 Draft and, in contrast to Simms, was an immediate success, winning the league's Defensive Player of the Year Award as a rookie. The team's success in the period in which I played was also nobly aided by running back Joe Morris, tight end Mark Bavaro and Hall of Fame linebacker Harry Carson.

Quarterbacks in my lean years included Craig Morton, Norm Snead and Joe Pisarcik, but finally there was Phil Simms, who also had a lean beginning before coming into his own, along with his able understudies, Scott Brunner, Jeff Rutledge and Jeff Hofstetler.

But as misery loves company, those I first grew close to in training camp and thereafter were my fellow rookies and underlings. While most have names that do not loom large in football lore and legend, they certainly loom large with me. And what the fans often fail to see is that for every one player who goes on to stardom, there are 10 to 20 others who give their all, try valiantly and serve a role for a year or two, and then fade away. Names like Dvorak, Colbert, Powers, Buggs, Brooks, etc.

Football also can be cruel and unforgiving to many, because coming on up there is an annual, unlimited supply of even faster and stronger men than you from whom to choose.

The rookie friends who intimately shared my misery included running backs and kick receivers and punt returners Rondy Colbert and Danny

Buggs. Rondy, out of Lamar College in Texas, had a three-season run, and Danny, who was forever known as the "West Virginia Flash," had four seasons with the Giants and Redskins. A prolific scorer in college, Danny remarkably put points on the board every fifth time he touched the ball in his senior year. They were great guys and my best friends during my dog days with the Giants.

Others who were close to me included Bobby Brooks, a cornerback who had lasted two years; Clyde Powers , a strong safety who had a limited run with the Giants but was still in football as recently as last season as an executive with the Colts; Marsh White, another running back out of Arkansas who played only one season with the Giants; and there was Rick Dvorak, with whom I formed a special attachment and unholy alliance. Drafted as a defensive end only a year before me in the 3rd round, he had a near four-year run with the Giants. A Kansas farmer out of redneck country, we were the unlikeliest of pairings, but how we enjoyed each other, and are friends even to this day.

And what the fans often fail to see is that for every one player who goes on to stardom, there are 10 to 20 others who give their all, try valiantly and serve a role for a year or two, and then fade away.

So Dianne and I established our team-building Thanksgiving tradition during my first season and continued through all 14 of them. We didn't like the thought of any teammates eating room service on Thanksgiving, so anyone on the team who was without an invite elsewhere was invited to the Martin home. On that great holiday, we just couldn't stomach the idea of guys being lonely or homesick. And God bless Dianne, who was so open to this annual invasion.

The first year included all of those in the paragraphs above, as well as others. The wives, of whom there were few at the time, weren't exactly the gourmet cooks that they were later to become. As good old southern boys, cornbread stuffing is an absolute must on Thanksgiving, but oh how that was butchered in year one by Rondy's wife. She still hasn't been entirely forgiven.

"George Martin taught the New York Giants what it meant to be a family. He was our leader and he pulled us together. He was the unofficial player-coach."
Joe Morris - Running Back

Note that in keeping with the transient nature of the game, just one among the entire array of my *misery-loves-company* rookie teammates got to a fourth year on the field. The rest concluded their careers in only two or three seasons. One, I believe, hung on in the Canadian Football League for a brief time.

Giants fans will well recognize the following handful of players, who were drafted a year or two before me. This group included Dave Jennings, a phenomenal punter, who for years was, interestingly and in all likelihood, our greatest offensive weapon (Dave so sadly and prematurely passed away just this past year); Brian Kelley, a middle linebacker, who was a strong leader and coach on the field, and while maybe not the most talented, certainly the smartest player. He simply never made a mental mistake. Doug Kotar, a passionate running back who was a country boy from Kentucky, was the face of our offense in the lean years, someone who dove, crawled and scratched for the extra yard. His death to cancer shortly after his retirement left the entire Giants team and Giants family numb. Doug Van Horn, an offensive lineman, spent a lot of time with me, teaching me how to read counts and what not to do. A relentless teacher, he effected subtle changes in my stance. I called him "Magic" because he always knew where I was going prior to the snap of the ball.

Beyond John Mendenhall and Pat Hughes, another veteran who had a tremendous impact upon me was the highly respected free safety Spider Lockhart, who had a great reputation and a huge heart. He was a historic legend when I arrived, yet when I first saw him, he looked so undersized and so skinny. Spider was small and bow-legged and I thought that maybe he had just been worn down, only to be told that he had always played the game as a bantam weight.

He was an up-close-and-personal living example of the fact that "*It ain't the size of the dog in the fight, but rather size of the fight in the dog*." I played with him for only one season, but he inspired in the kind of way that stays with you. Like Doug Kotar, Spider also succumbed to cancer 10 years after he retired, on July 9, 1986. In what was the greatest Giants season ever, culminating in the 1987 Super Bowl victory, we wore a spider insignia on our uniform in his honor. Spider was indeed the angel on our shoulders who helped carry us home to the "promised land" that year. Thank you, my friend.

He was an up-close-and-personal living example of the fact that "It ain't the size of the dog in the fight, but rather the size of the fight in the dog."

We also lost John Toggle to cancer and Troy Archer to an automobile accident, so we, as a team, most assuredly took our life's hits, but there were other kinds of hits that were far more subtle, though just as deadly and affecting. What hit others too hard was stardom or the disease of the spotlight, allowing the adulation to get too up close and personal and leading to broken relationships and broken families. I saw what the party scene robbed from so many of my teammates, who for a time let fame separate them from that which mattered the most in their lives. Sometimes tainted by booze and sometimes by drugs and sometimes by burning the candle at both ends, but always by fame, that fickle friend.

There was nothing worse than watching a teammate who you cared about following a self-destructive path that would lead him to lose the battle of life. You would try to get to them, try to intervene, try to make a difference, but no matter, a grown man will make his own decisions and his own mistakes. And all that was left for you to do was often to simply pray, as so many, far too often, attempted to turn out the lights of the Big Apple.

You prayed because they were yours and you loved them.

Soul Mates

If I tried to say a word or two about all of my teammates, that would be a book in itself, but I would let myself down if I didn't mention a bit about those who especially helped me to love this unusual vocation of mine.

I loved Phil Simms' ability to overcome adversity. I can still hear that crescendo of boos building up when they announced his entry into a game. He took it all and he proved them wrong and he reached heights that no Giants quarterback ever had. But he was always just one of the guys, who would roll up his sleeves for a teammate both then and now. There was no greater honor for me than joining Phil and Harry Carson at midfield for the coin toss. To be a captain was one thing, but to serve as a co-captain with those immortals was altogether uplifting. Part of the *Crunch Bunch* of Carson, Brian Kelley, Brad Van Pelt and Lawrence Taylor, one of the greatest quartets of linebackers in football history, Harry was my gladiator, the one I drew inspiration from, and as close to a perfect athlete as I knew.

I'll never forget little Joe Morris, our spirited running back, placing his hands on my shoulder right before the team prayer in the locker room of the '87 Super Bowl. He emphatically said to me, "*You and Harry don't have to worry today. We're going to win this thing for you.*" In his face, I could see how committed to victory he was as he quietly and confidently walked away and readied himself for battle. I could see it and he hugged me and I was stunned and numb. His commitment was that palpable and that fierce. I still see Joe a lot socially and on the charitable circuit and I look at him and shake my head as I recall the incredible power that he brought to a running game. Again, let it be said, in the end "*It's all about the size of the fight in the dog.*"

"You are only as good as the people you surround yourself with. That's why I stayed close to George and tried to follow his example. Every inch a professional, he did more than anyone else to help me become one."

Perry Williams - Cornerback

Perry Williams was a great cornerback and a brother on the field, but I most respect what he has done with his life as an educator after the playing stopped. He took the very best of his teammates and applied the same to his life. Curtis McGriff and I were soul mates, opposite ends of the same cob of corn, in that he extended my career by splitting time with me. I'd play the passing downs and he the run downs. He possesses a great heart and a great spirit. Then, there was our Rambo, Mark Bavaro, and I mean that literally, because he could carry more men on his back than Rambo could take out with his machine gun.

I had the privilege of working with a young Karl Nelson after practice to improve his game, and what an investment that proved to be. But again, it's the man and not just the player, however great, because Karl gives back more than anyone I know. He is unconditionally generous, and having beaten cancer twice – I think because the Good Lord recognizes how much we need him – he remains the first to say yes to any charitable endeavor. ALWAYS yes.

If anyone were ever to do a sitcom revolving around the quintessential comic in an NFL locker room, it would have to be a take-off on Jim Burt, our nose tackle, who was the "straw that stirred the drink" in our locker room. He was the best troublemaker, practical joker and comic I ever met in a football uniform. And the beat, as to the greatness of my teammates, goes on and on, with Carl Banks and Pepper Johnson and Stephen Baker "The Touchdown Maker," and Phil McConkey and Maurice Carthon and Sean Landeta and Bart Oates and the legendary and prolific O.J. Anderson, and all the rest. In retrospect, the list of notable colleagues seems endless spanning the sum of my 14-year career.

When in my mind I retrace my steps, and I go back and I stand on the sidelines or in a huddle on the field, or lay among a twisted pile of fragile and limited but so very brave men after the whistle blows, and I look around, upon scene after scene, however bright and clear or murky, I am stunned. Stunned to have been among them, to have been in the game with them and so very blessed to have for so long been one of their defensive ends!

Having played with greatness against no small measure of greatness, the music of that song reverberates in my head – "And I know that I am, I am, I am the luckiest," indeed.

Some Celebrated Moments

My seven NFL touchdowns came on three interception returns, two fumble returns/recoveries, one lateral return from Brian Kelly following a blocked field goal, and one offensive pass reception against the Dallas Cowboys, which I have never been officially credited for, in 1980, while lining up as a tight end. It is a little-known fact that back in the days when teams rarely went with anything more than a single tight end set, I was, for most of my career, the third-string tight end, largely utilized for blocking purposes.

Every play that goes well sits in its own special place in the repository of memory, but there are only a special handful of plays that you wear on your sleeves forever. And when your time on the field is devoted to preventing the other team from putting points on the board, you are likely to especially celebrate those precious few opportunities when *you* were able to put points on that board. As it happened, the Good Lord smiled upon me in allowing me to hold for quite some time the record for the most points ever scored by a defensive lineman.

I retrace my steps and I go back and I stand on the sidelines or in a huddle on the field or lay among a twisted pile of fragile and limited but so very brave men after the whistle blows, and I look around upon scene after scene, however bright and clear or murky, and I am stunned. Stunned to have been among them, to have been in the game with them and so very blessed to have for so long been one of their defensive ends!

On October 1, 1978, at Atlanta's Fulton County Stadium, lightning struck for me for the first time – and here's the irony, Brian Kelley, one of our linebackers, did all of the work and I got credited with an 83-yard blocked field goal return. Brian recovered the ball, took it back some 76 yards on his own, and lateraled it to me from the 6 or 7 yard line as he was about to be tackled. I carried it in from there and got tackled by what felt like our entire team in the end zone.

While it was not unlike the Scarecrow's "joy and rapture" moment, there are, in all honesty, no words to adequately describe what it's like to be in the end zone with the ball tucked under your arm. You hold it so tight and determined to never let it go – which is why I still have it.

As it happened, Brian had played rugby in the past and it was his tremendous rugby instincts that took over, leading him to lateral to me and to literally give me his glory.

On November 9, 1980, something particularly unusual came to pass. Phil Simms hit me in the end zone with a 4-yard touchdown pass. There I was, playing what was actually my favorite and even natural position, in a three tight end set. Back in my formative football days, I was the receiver with the "sticky hands" at tight end. I went to Oregon as a tight end, but was converted to defensive end and ultimately drafted by the Giants for the defense.

So what even the most avid fans didn't realize was that I was the third-string tight end on the Giants depth chart for the better part of my career. On that particular afternoon against the Cowboys, they made the assumption that I was clearly out of position and lined up for blocking purposes only. The Cowboys made the drastic mistake of going "no cover" on me, "Sticky Fingers" Martin, legendary Armijo High School tight end that I was. Phil threw a perfect strike, and my old tight end skills didn't disappoint as I corralled the ball. By the way, I don't think that I would have ever lived it down had I missed.

Then, on November 24, 1985, at Busch Stadium against the Saint Louis Cardinals, I had one of those energizing moments of glory and joined my offensive teammates Mark Bavaro, Lionel Manuel and George Adams in the end zone that day. I read screen pass all the way and veered to my left. I had the running back marked and the quarterback was telegraphing it. The timing was perfect and as I picked the ball off, the only question was whether or not I could race downfield for 56 unobstructed yards without falling over. But it was clear sailing all the way, a 56-yard, 4th-quarter interception return.

Not long ago, when serving as president of the National Football League Alumni Association, I was at an event out west, and someone called me over to introduce me, just to say hello to his companion. The companion was John Elway, the great former quarterback of the Denver Broncos, and it was easy to tell that this person was a good friend of Elway's and could get away with ribbing him. "John," he slyly said, "you know, the greatest pass I ever saw you complete was to this guy right here, George Martin." Truth be told, it may well have been, and it was certainly the greatest pass play that I was ever involved in.

Deep in our own territory, my first instinct was to lateral to someone faster than me, which included all 10 of my team mates, the 11 Denver Broncos, and most of the refs.

The date was November 23, 1986, at Giants Stadium, when we played the Denver Broncos during what was to be our Super Bowl run. This guy was giving Elway a pretty hard time, but John just good-naturedly laughed it off. Of course, while that's not something I'd ever try to rub in his face, it was fun standing by as someone else kindly did it for me.

It was, without doubt, the play of plays in my football career. The offensive lineman was trying to cut my legs and I rejected his move, picked up the pass soaring over my head, jumped up, batted it in the air, and then reached out to catch my own deflection. Deep in our own territory, my first instinct was to lateral to someone faster than me, which included all 10 of my teammates, the 11 Denver Broncos, and most of the refs. Elway himself had a shot at me near the left sideline, but I bowled by him and pushed him out of bounds and then Harry made a great block.

Then that "*I will not be denied*" rush came over me, and like a man possessed I went thundering down that sideline breaking tackles, hurdling tacklers, and finally, with the help of a critical block by Mark Collins that some "*immerse yourself into the game*" analysts deemed a clip, I panted breathlessly into the end zone.

The fact was that I truly couldn't breathe with the entire team on top of me, but I prodded myself free, held that ball high in the air, and raced off the field. Out of the corner of my eye, I saw Coach Parcells screaming and urging us to get the hell off the field before being penalized for excessive celebration. The funny thing was that I got off, but my teammates were still in the end zone carrying on, much to the dismay of our head coach, whose passionate pleadings were finally noticed and belatedly obeyed by all.

It was such a great return that even the refs were inclined to give us a pass on the end zone shenanigans, I'm sure!

A 78-yard interception return, it could never get any better than that, and it indeed was a sight to see on replay. I am proud of the fact that it is heralded as one of the greatest plays in both Giants and NFL history, and even more proud of the fact that Bill Parcells, for whom I have the highest respect, dubbed it "The greatest football play that I've ever seen."

That's high praise indeed, coming from the man who most epitomizes to you what's good about the game in the first place.

What isn't widely known about this particular play is that there in the stands that day was my father, George Sr., to witness this event of a lifetime, the greatest play that his son ever made. I proudly gave that game ball away, and it rested for many years prominently displayed on Dad's mantle for all to see, was cherished by both father and son, even up until his death.

A sidebar comes to mind here, for we eked out a victory against Denver in the regular season, but went on to beat them going away in the Super Bowl. I give so much of the credit for that to our then defensive coordinator, Bill Belichick.

Give him two cracks at an opponent and that opponent was destined to pay. His schemes, his adjustments, his fine nuances were so insightful and spot-on. Truly, if there is, as I've suggested, any such thing as a football genius, in the defensive context, Bill Belichick was and is absolutely that genius. He would make adjustments that just boggled your mind, because he had just this intuitive sense of how to make either slight or major moves that would wreak havoc on the offense. Consequently, we spent as much time in the classroom as we did on the field preparing for that game of games on January 25, 1987, on the game's greatest stage, the Super Bowl in Pasadena, California. And there, somewhere between Neil Diamond's National Anthem and the "Salute to Hollywood" halftime show, I had another moment in the sun.

To play in a Super Bowl is indescribable. It is the event of events and no stage is bigger. People are so drawn to it the sociologists point out that even crime statistics go down. As a player, all the yin-yang, push-pull feelings that preoccupy you before any ordinary game just escalate. You are grabbed by that inexhaustible desire to turn the tide and be the one who helps deliver the victory, and at the same time, by that ever-present and utterly obnoxious fear of making the critical mistake.

Someone, after all, is destined to make a critical mistake.

It is late in the 2nd quarter and we're down 10-7, but Denver is backed up near their own goal line. We caught a break on 2nd down and 10, as a short pass was ruled incomplete. It was, fortuitously for us, a bad call, leaving them with a "no doubt about it," 3rd down and 10, long-pass situation. That permitted us defensive ends to put our racing shoes on and go for it. But as it happened, Erik Howard, a rookie right defensive tackle came into the lineup, so I just played a mind game, loudly yelling to Erik, "*Inside or outside, whatever I call, do the opposite. Do the opposite.*" Right before the snap, I scream "*Outside!*" and sure enough, the off lineman bites on inside. Completely duped, I veer outside and he's left standing in his tracks as I blow by him. I'm on top of Elway before he has an opportunity to react. Behind the goal line!

Two points! A safety in the Super Bowl! A game changer and momentum swing! 10-7 becomes 10-9 and those 2 points are the first of the consecutive 26 points that we will put on the board in the second half. But all the rest was, as they say, window dressing.

"Because George and I battled through the lean and harsh years together, the Super Bowl victory just meant more to us. We were brothers, and my brother George never got the credit that he deserved, for it was he who kept our team together. He opened his home to all the players, he counseled, he guided, he led. And everyone on the New York Giants looked up to him. In their hearts, every player wanted to be George Martin."

Harry Carson - Middle Linebacker

I had thought before the game, a game that loomed so big in my mind, that losing it might leave me with a temporary desire to jump out of a seventh-floor window. So while all was going well, I studied my teammates and our unique positions on the field and the colors in the stands and the larger-than-life atmosphere of it all in a way I never had before, and yet I longed for there to be an end.

I smelled, tasted, and wanted the victory to be signed, sealed, and delivered.

When the final whistle blew, signaling the end of a 39-20 game, a game in which Phil Simms had been near perfect, I remember that my first instinct was to find and hug Harry, which I did, but then I was caught in the whirlwind of pandemonium's blur, immersed in a sea of Giants blue. There was a high tide of cheers and tears and laughter. There were these mighty, deep, painstaking exhales of relief, as if years of hard work and pain and agonized effort were being released in a single, momentous breath.

There you were in a place that most never reach – grateful and relieved and blessed and joyous and overwhelmed in that unimaginable, indiscernible place. What carried me away at first was the pride that I had in and the love that I felt for my teammates, these fellow warriors, without whom I would never have gotten to this stage or these heights.

The affection and emotion were so thick that you could have cut them with a knife. At the same time, we were enveloped by a hot sun and cleansed by a cold waterfall. And then the mind turned to all those great men who once played the game with us and who never got to enjoy what we were now enjoying. There before me I saw big John Mendenhall and Brian Kelley and Brad Van Pelt and Pat Hughes and Spider Lockhart and Doug Kotar and so many others who so deserved this. I dwelled on those friends who never got to this wonderful place where I and my 1986 teammates had arrived, and I longed to share this with them, to give it to them.

It was they, after all, who made me capable of this in the first place. It was they who had made me better. Didn't they too own a piece of this? And didn't Dianne and her Thanksgivings?

I tell you, without the slightest exaggeration, in winning the Super Bowl, you run a gauntlet of emotions, as you are battered and tossed and turned by overwhelming and almost inexplicable feelings.

You are a Super Bowl champion. You are as happy as anyone can get in this game. And yet, the unprecedented happiness is laced with tears of joy and pride and honor and even sadness.

I could not sleep. I would not sleep. Why on Earth would I ever let go of this exhilaration? That was until sometime the next afternoon, when, gripped by exhaustion, I finally allowed my eyes to close.

In The Service Of Your Fellow Man

When I talk to students, I like to talk about the leader that is inside each and every one of us, waiting to be called upon, waiting to deliver. Whether or not anyone considers themselves a leader, leadership is, however unwittingly, at some time thrust upon us all.

Some just pick up the mantle. Others wait to be called.

For me, I was blessed with great mentors and role models, from junior football league quarterbacks to coaches who cared, to Tom Graham, to Frank Gifford, and later in my career but most importantly, to Bill Parcells.

In calling me a deep thinker or an individual who didn't long to run with the herd or a battler for what's right or for justice, Tom Graham was nurturing those very qualities in me. Tom helped me to realize that the all of life ought to be lived on higher ground, and that there are tried and true verities and philosophies and Christian attributes and values that you can never sever from the life you live.

In my faith, we believe that the spirit of God lives in all of us, and, to be sure, I found Him in Tom.

In later coming to know Frank Gifford, one of the most revered players in Giants history, I found the fellow Giant who I would most like to emulate. Dignified and respectful of others and gentle with the world and of neither boast nor brag, he carried a decency and a goodness with him always and so he too was a mentor.

Both provided me with direction and reminded me to always be true to who I was. True to God and true to my teammates, I came to the

Giants as one who would never – could never – embarrass either his colleagues or himself.

But later I learned so very much more from Bill Parcells about how it is that you instill the best of yourself in others. Bill was a master organizer and a team-builder, who could take the disparate talents of the multitude and meld them seamlessly together. He had the inspirational and motivational skills that could both affirm and bring out the very best in people. So he, too, became as much mentor as he was head coach to me.

Years ago while still a player, Coach told me that should he ever go into the Hall of Fame he wanted me to introduce him, and true to his word, I had the great honor of standing at his side on August 3, 2013, as Bill Parcells entered the Pro Football Hall of Fame in Canton, Ohio. What a thrill it was to stand with him and to introduce him and to humbly bask in a deserved glory that was all his. It was the Super Bowl all over again.

So yes, there were these great people in my life, some who truly nurtured me and personally invested in me, and others, who by their standing and their way of being, gave me something to aspire to. But I have learned that everyone has something to teach you. All you have to do is be open to it.

One of the first leadership positions that I assumed on the Giants was that of chapel leader. The great gift my parents did pass on to me was my faith and I practiced it avidly, as a Christian athlete, always. As such, I was just never part of the "letting off steam," bar-hopping party scene. There was a cathartic moment during my rookie season when a few of us were attending church services and I threw $20 in a collection plate. Afterwards, a teammate kidded me about the larger bill I gave. He asked, "Why, George?" I answered by asking how much he spent buying drinks the night before. Somehow, because of that simple incident, my teammates started looking at me a bit differently, and the mantle of spiritual leader was first unofficially and later officially tossed my way.

As chapel leader I engaged a local minister or priest to join us prior to each game, conducted a Biblical service before each game, and set up weekly bible study classes either before or after practice. We began the tradition of gathering on field to pray together after every game. In the spirit of Christian brotherhood that outweighed our roles as on-field combatants, we invited our opponents to join us for that on-field prayer. Over the years, many, to my delight, did so.

It turns out that one leadership position can easily and naturally lead to others, which was certainly the case for me.

All it took for me to become Giants' team representative to the National Football League Players Association was my taking self-interest and learning the facts surrounding labor issues that had a profound impact upon us all as well as our families. There was a work stoppage in my rookie year and there were all these profound, unresolved issues, and iconic players were everywhere scared as hell. I inadvertently became the team's information and knowledge repository and veterans began looking to me for answers. My simply having taken an interest in the issues resulted in my team thrusting me into the midst of it all on their behalf – besides, it was a common fear that such a position was the kiss of death should labor conflicts begin to escalate.

They were looking for both information and for help, and they trusted me to provide it.

As I and others discovered, the players had long been taking the path of least resistance and there was much to responsibly fight for. I became immersed in those battles during my playing days. I had been dubbed a spiritual leader who could be entrusted with player negotiations and so I became team representative to the Players Association and later a member of its Executive Committee, and finally, from 1986 through 1988, my final years as a player, president of the Players Association itself. In '87, when I was president, there was another work stoppage and my legacy was leading the battle for the players to garner 55 percent of the NFL's gross revenues, which set in motion the achievement of today's players in garnering 75 percent of that gross. We helped pave the way for tuition and degree completion programs, for sustaining health benefits, for drug counseling services, and a variety of other benefits and services.

The truth is that we fought the battles that provide the foundation of all that today's players enjoy.

As for me, I should note that there is little doubt that the sustaining relationships nurtured during my Players Association days have everything to do with the roles that I play today.

The heart of what is now never-ending community involvement on my part was thrust upon me then by Ed Croke, a great community relations executive in the Giants' front office for many years. He couldn't have come after me at a worse time. It was just after two-a-days on one of those oppressive near-110-degree practice days when all you wanted to do was to lay down beside an air conditioner.

He approached me with a loud and clear, "*George, you're our community representative!*" No I wasn't, I wanted to say. I was the chapel leader and the team representative and here was Ed Croke intentionally morphing my standing as a leader into yet another role. That took a bit of nerve, but even more faith in his trust in my willingness to do the right thing. He quickly explained that a prominent player on the Jets had unintentionally let down this group of parents from Hackensack Medical Center (today's Hackensack University Medical Center) who had children with cancer.

And lo and behold, as fate would have it, they were here and would I be kind enough to simply meet with them.

Instead of saying that I desperately needed to rest, I wrapped my mind around parents, kids and cancer, and said of course I would. So there was that first meeting, my "yes," and the rest was history.

Thus began an association with the phenomenal Tomorrow's Children's Foundation and Fund of Hackensack University Medical Center, an innovative battler and leader in the fight against pediatric cancer. My adopted charity, I became the honorary president and a spokesman, and out of it came a wide array of love affairs with remarkable children, two terms of service as a trustee of Hackensack University Medical Center, and a lifetime relationship with a great friend who was the first to hire me and give me an opportunity when my Giants playing days ended.

Then I got wooed into the DARE project in New Jersey, the effort to keep primary school children from being lured into the illusive and abusive world of drugs. I received my Gold Shield from Governor Tom

Kean for my efforts and was later inducted into the New Jersey Legion of Honor.

Then there was a phone call, a life-altering phone call, that I made to a Dean Kenneth T. Vehrkens at Fairleigh Dickinson University, who was doing exciting things with bringing the University into the workplace. Since most professional football players leave college upon being drafted and fail to complete their education, there was a need to initiate a degree completion program so we war-torn players could have something to rely on when our careers were over.

In fact, 75 percent of all professional football players at the time did not have college degrees.

Ken Vehrkens responded beautifully and crafted a program that would have us attend structured classes at FDU campuses in Hackensack and Teaneck on off-days during our playing season, as well as during the off-season. There also was a mandatory community outreach component of the degree completion program. The initial class of 15 active Giants players included Harry Carson, Perry Williams, my wife Dianne and myself.

Instead of saying that I desperately needed to rest, I wrapped my mind around parents, kids, and cancer and said, of course, I would. So there was that first meeting, my "yes," and the rest was history.

Fairleigh Dickinson's program eventually became the template for a program now sponsored by the National Football League itself.

It should be noted that all of the people involved in these many programs and efforts later became important players in *a Journey for 9/11.* Giving always gives way to more giving. It is the natural order of things.

We did our best to look after players in trouble and created unofficial "big brother" efforts, but there's only so much you can do to render someone, who is not very interested, respectable. However, we managed to initiate a Giants EAP, or employee assistance program, and there were near-constant opportunities for me to play a role as a facilitator in literally everything from drug counseling to marriage counseling to spousal abuse intervention.

As much was given to me, in both accolades and honors as a pro football veteran, I believed that much more was required of me. You have to keep earning it. You just never stop having to earn it. Leadership, therefore, isn't so much a specific role or status; it rather becomes a way of life as you respond to whatever the call of duty demands.

The single most important thread I see running throughout my life is that we are ultimately responsible for one another. We are our brothers' and our sisters' keepers. We must own each other's pain and bear each other's burdens or we will suffer the consequences of never fully living.

I simply accepted everything that being a true Giant demanded of me.

You have got to keep earning it. You just never stop having to earn it. Leadership, therefore, isn't so much a specific role or status. It rather becomes a way of life as you respond to whatever the call of duty demands.

My 14 years playing football for the New York Football Giants were my life's epicenter, my alpha and omega. No matter what I do in the days ahead, it will have figuratively begun and ended there, for it is those 14 years that color the all of my days.

With no small measure of pride, there will come a day when I sit down with my grandchildren and say, "I played with the great Lawrence Taylor, the greatest defensive player in football history, and Mark Bavaro and Phil Simms and Harry Carson. I played against the likes of Roger Staubach and Fran Tarkenton and Warren Moon and Earl Campbell. I played with and against the iconic players of a remarkable era."

I will tell them that I did my best for my team both on and off the field, and that I always forged ahead, never allowing myself to become mired in defeat, but always looking to and believing in the next day and the next game.

And when they ask me what I most loved about it, I will say, "Playing in and winning the Super Bowl."

And when they ask me what I hated the most about it, I will say, "Take your pick. Either training camp or the pain! But then again, neither were they mutually exclusive."

As to the values, there was that very notion of team, team, team, and loyalty and camaraderie and devotion. There was what it was to be "*brothers in arms*" and "*all for one and one for all.*" There was the loving each other.

As to sustaining yourself for all that it demanded, there were but two words – family and music. Just think Diana Ross and "*Ain't No Mountain High Enough.*"

With no small measure of pride, there will come a day when I sit down with my grandchildren and say, "I played with the great Lawrence Taylor, the greatest defensive player in football history, and Mark Bavaro and Phil Simms and Harry Carson. I played against the likes of Roger Staubach and Fran Tarkenton and Warren Moon and Earl Campbell. I played with and against the iconic players of a remarkable era."

What do I miss most about it? The Thanksgivings of my playing days, those crazy Thanksgivings with a bunch of wide-eyed rookies and grizzled veterans, those Thanksgivings where we learned just who we were and what we could become, which was, after all and forever, a family.

But in many ways, football was just the beginning.

5 – THE EPIPHANY

Oh, what a morning it was!

I loved the Adventures of Huckleberry Finn and Tom Sawyer, because they carried me back to a bygone era that inexplicably aroused the wonders of a young boy's wild imagination.

Tales like these stimulate the explorer, the Louis and Clark in all of us – or, at least, that is definitively the case for one George Dwight Martin.

I have always been a sucker for stories of adventure.

To read about Frederick Cook and his Arctic explorations of 1908 – even if he didn't reach the North Pole – along with the challenges that he and his expedition faced, is, to me, more provocative than double espresso cappuccino from Starbucks. There is an explorer who lives in each of us, and at one point or another we all have compiled our "bucket lists" of adventures or dreams that we would like to fulfill before the inevitable occurs.

For the better part of my life, mine included walking across America. It was a dream that was born when I was still a child in Greenville, South Carolina, and it was crystallized as I rode in that rickety old station wagon across the country when we boldly moved to California. Some 40 years later, it came back to stare me in the face.

August 4, 2006, marked the date of the Pro Football Hall of Fame's Annual Enshrinement Ceremony. A stellar group of NFL greats were to receive the honor of honors, entry into the Hall of Fame itself. The 2006 notables included the likes of Troy Aikman of the Dallas Cowboys; Warren Moon of the Houston Oilers; Reggie White of both the Packers and Eagles; Rayfield Wright of the Cowboys; John Madden, legendary sports commentator and coach; and Harry Donald Carson, my great friend and fellow warrior with the New York Football Giants.

There had been more than a bit of controversy swirling around Harry's long road to induction, as the well-deserving nine-time Pro Bowler was inexplicably passed over year after year by the sportswriters. Many of those who played both with and against him joined the crusade, vehemently fighting for justice and his induction. So it became our solemn duty to be there to celebrate with him when Harry's moment in the sun finally came. Among his crusaders that day, I intended to stand front and center, lending the support of a loyal teammate and lifelong friend.

There in Canton, Ohio, the home of the Pro Football Hall of Fame, hordes of families, fans, friends and football loyalists annually and eagerly descend upon this quaint, middle-American city.

It is, in fact, so unlike the cities where most National Football League teams actually play.

Quaint, livable, walkable, Canton is true small town.

There is no sprawling urban development, no high-rise structures stretching into the heavens, no wide array of cultured museums, and no major airport to handle the ballooning population that migrates there on this annual pilgrimage. It smacks of Norman Rockwell's America, and there celebrities and commoners alike gather around the local hangout of Taggart's Ice Cream parlor to wolf down those deliciously famous "Bittner" milk shakes. They reminisce about spectacular NFL moments and they get up close and personal with the stars of the game.

In Canton, each year on this occasion, there is an unpretentious, no-holds-barred interaction between fans and their celebrated football luminaries, and for my money, it just doesn't get any better.

It is said that 90 percent of Canton's indigenous population actually turns out for the festivities each year. Armed with an array of autograph pads and memorabilia and equipped with lawn chairs of every design and color, they strategically spread out along the annual parade route. They also demonstrate an overt and genuine appreciation for the inductees, who make Canton, Ohio, their home for that one glorious week each year.

With Canton's limited hotel accommodations, my wife Dianne and I decided to find a place to stay on the outskirts of the city, comfortably removed from the hustle and bustle and the occasional over-exuberance that accompanies many Hall of Fame activities. We settled in the neighboring town of Akron, just outside of Cleveland.

Early on, we also determined to drive ourselves rather than fly to an airport several counties away, only to then backtrack by rented automobile to our eventual destination. Arriving the day before the induction ceremony would afford Dianne and me the opportunity to take in the flavor of the event while preparing for the weekend's exciting activities.

After settling in at the local Marriott just off the main highway and making phone calls to some of my many colleagues who were in the area for the induction, Dianne and I had dinner with my very own Lee Reeves and his girlfriend, Flora DeJesus, who had accompanied us on the trip. Little did any of us realize at the time just how often this scene would be replicated again and again once *a Journey for 9/11* got under way.

I decided to turn in early that night so I could get my workout regimen in equally early the next morning. It was an opportunity to unwind from the long but pleasant eight-hour drive from our home in northern New Jersey, providing a welcome, soothing, and solitary retreat for my own personal satisfaction.

I had really grown accustomed to exercising on the road, as traveling was an inherent part of my post-NFL career DNA. I'd had the tremendous pleasure of traveling to all 50 states in my lifetime, and jogging or walking along the highways and byways of this great country was an adventure that I always looked forward to. To me, it was an added dimension to experiencing the essence of the town, city or region.

So whether it was the scenic countryside of California's Napa Valley, the picturesque mountain foothills of Denver, the white sandy beaches of Mexico, the seductive vineyards of France, or merely a pleasant stroll around the Wanaque Reservoir in Ringwood, New Jersey, I had always made it a point to get out and about to maintain both physical and spiritual fitness.

Canton and Akron were to be no exception.

My workout regimen itself consisted of a minimum, fast paced four-mile walk along diverse terrain. Given the circumstances, I would occasionally stretch it to 6 miles or so. Walking these days had become the exercise of choice, since I had successfully survived 14 grueling NFL seasons of trench warfare as a defensive lineman. As a result, I no longer felt the need to subject my body to further abuse by running or jogging, as I had done far too much abusing in my younger life.

Those high-impact workouts were no longer warranted, needed - or advisable.

On the day of the induction itself, I dutifully embarked upon my customary exercise ritual to usher in the morning and maintain my svelte 265-pound frame. But what normally would have been a one-hour, four-mile excursion turned out to be anything but normal, as the revelation of a lifetime was surprisingly made known to me.

I awakened as usual in the predawn hours and quietly pulled myself away from the king-size bed so as not to disturb the Mrs., then took a steaming hot shower and briefly stretched in what had become my standard operating procedure. Quickly pulling on my signature black stretch leotards and my size 14 New Balances, and taking the usual handful of vitamins with a large glass of apple juice, I was ready to hit the road.

I consider each day of my life another victory for the distinguished 50-plus crowd.

As the cloak of darkness gradually surrendered to the dawning of the new day, this particular morning for some inexplicable reason felt strangely but wonderfully different! It was one of those unforgettable days that magically seem to make life itself stand still. It would prove a day to be forever remembered.

The morning air was refreshingly crisp, but would quickly give way to the anticipated 90 sweltering degrees. The aggravating mechanical clutter of the 21st century had not yet begun to rattle and an intoxicating, aromatic bouquet with faint traces of wild jasmine, lilac and honeysuckle gently permeated the atmosphere. High overhead a beautiful eagle soared majestically along the rolling waves of cloud-cover. Without so much as moving a single muscle, the magnificent bird reigned over all that it surveyed.

The trees nestled along the hillside seemed to be rising as giant immovable sentinels, patiently standing guard over the valley below. I pictured their massive interlocking root system, formed over countless centuries, bearing witness to all that connects and binds the natural world together. The lush countryside tapestry, which was cloaked in a dense blanket of evergreen foliage, stood in stark contrast to the tranquil, rich blue of the early morning skyline.

I began my morning's journey swiftly proceeding along my pre-selected route, and our hotel quickly faded into the distance behind me. As my pace quickened and my strides lengthened, I spotted a dated and worn, turn-of-the-century bridge that spanned a briskly running yet meandering stream rhythmically flowing into the river basin. It was, no doubt, one of the many converging tributaries originating from the nearby hillside.

All along the pathway of my increasingly impromptu trail, a cadre of nature's creatures, including field crickets, toad-frogs and a wide array of birds, formed a chorus-like symphony of sound, music to the ears of a devout country boy like me. Beautiful bumble bees meticulously went about their daily business of gathering and spreading pollen on behalf of the natural community they served. The marvelously orchestrated and unified work of bees and ants forever amazes me. Such astonishing creatures have an inherent work ethic that can teach us all.

Nearby there was a dazzling gathering of summer butterflies, who fluttered by indiscriminately, fashioning a magnificent palette of colors that would have impressed Michelangelo himself.

With such an astonishing array of wildlife teeming about, my senses were pleasantly invaded, and it all gave way to a tangible state of euphoria. This Disney-like trail proved to be an idyllic indulgence and I could have just kept on walking, spellbound, forever. Each and every effortless and enjoyable step yielded utter delight and I felt not a hint of fatigue or weariness.

Oh, what a morning it was!

To this very moment, everything about that morning remains etched into the deepest recesses of my memory, forever ensconced as "The Most Perfect Summer Morning – Ever."

As I walked, my pre-planned exercise route morphed into something that was largely uncharted, because I so relished the opportunity of discovering new and unexplored sights. The chance to observe a scene or vista that you have never witnessed before is like an unopened Christmas present. To see how the breaking dawn gradually erases the shadowy images tucked along a hillside is, to me, spell-binding – as is seeing the early morning dew lift gracefully back into the atmosphere before suddenly evaporating – as is witnessing a billowing fog roll gingerly downward off the base of a mountain like a gathering avalanche.

There is nothing better than seeing nature's home movies up close and personal.

Such experiences often earn the distinction of being a "runner's high," which, loosely translated, suggests being completely caught-up in the moment, totally captivated as if in a spiritual trance. Although my running days, as I said, had long given way to a slower-paced form of exercise, walking still served the purpose of getting my heart rate up and experiencing all the tender touches of nature. As I happily continued this walk, effectively oblivious to both time and space, it suddenly dawned on me that I had traveled far beyond my designated route.

Such experiences often earn the distinction of being a "runner's high," which, loosely translated, suggests being completely caught-up in the moment, totally captivated as if in a spiritual trance.

Pausing momentarily to glance at my watch, I suddenly realized that I was fully six miles from the hotel and more than an hour beyond the appointed time of my breakfast with Dianne. Ordinarily, this is when that desperate state of panic would set in.

This time, however, I sensed something entirely different. I wasn't gripped by the throes of panic, which would ordinarily be the case. I was peculiarly and completely at peace, and I actually did a slow and deliberate about-face while continuing to soak in the awesome beauty of this gloriously magnificent day.

As I calmly reversed direction, back toward the hotel in the hope of replicating nature's wondrous presentation all over again, I realized this was a uniquely special moment. It was then and there that a decision took shape – solidly and firmly and deep within.

I suppose that it may well have been my personal encounter with my own version of the biblical "burning bush."

For the very briefest of moments, I stopped dead in my tracks, pausing to wrap my arms around what I was feeling and experiencing. It was no mere epiphany, but rather a reckoning with a lifelong, but long-buried, dream of walking across the United States of America. Somehow and in some way, I was being told by Mother Nature and the heavens above that it was long past time for me to fulfill a promise that I had long ago made to myself – to fulfill a dormant dream that was simply destined to be.

It was if a sign had descended upon me from the heavens. That beautiful morning was the gift outright that pointed me in the direction of that dream.

Call it a magical epiphany or a reckoning, or an awakening or a moment of truth, it was time to fulfill a life's mission, no matter the consequences. Like Scarlett O'Hara in Gone with the Wind, I too, there and then, made my solemn vow to embrace my fate, damn the realities, challenges and prospective obstacles, and walk across the United States. The thought of walking across America had never appeared daunting to me, not for a second. I and the seemingly insurmountable liked each other. Whether it was being the first in my family to earn a college degree or becoming an All-American athlete or winning a Super Bowl trophy, notions of negativity were neither in my vocabulary nor in my mind.

Immediately resigning myself to the fact that I was going to follow a peculiar road, and one far less traveled, it became clear that the obvious

It was a happy August morning in Ohio when I decided to walk across America, and I was still smiling 18 months later as the spring rains beat down in Arkansas.

It might sound a little trite to say the road was calling me, but there certainly was a sign out there in Tennessee with my name on it.

task of determining the specific purpose and logistics of such a mission might well be far more daunting.

But I was in a "Damn the torpedoes, full speed ahead" mindset!

It was as if all was already affirmed, and a wide-eyed smile became a permanent fixture on my face. I was going to walk across America as I long ago promised myself, and serve some greater good in doing so. Up to that point, I had spent my entire adult life busily serving charities and causes that I passionately believed to be worthy of attention, and there were a multitude of worthy choices that warranted consideration. Walking across America could be an extraordinary accomplishment in its own right, but it would certainly not be a mere stand-alone event.

Call it a magical epiphany or a reckoning, or an awakening or a moment of truth, it was time to fulfill a life's mission, no matter the consequences.

I was still walking underneath an early August Akron sun and thinking that a deserving charity would, as a beneficiary, have to be attached to this coming journey across the continent. Struck by lightning as it were, there I was scheming and thinking and fashioning a design for my madness before I even got back to the hotel – as if the dream would be lost should I fail to give it meaning at the very moment of its inception.

During my long walk back, my mind was teeming with the elation of fulfilling a dream – and already dealing with the consequences and practicalities of actually achieving the same. As I pondered prospective causes, several well-deserving charities that had been part of my life quickly came to mind.

For several years, I had served as honorary chairman of the highly accomplished Tomorrow's Children's Fund. Its rise to national prominence was largely made possible through the help of an often controversial disc jockey, Don Imus, formerly of WFAN radio. Imus had championed this initiative and raised tens of millions of dollars for children stricken with cancer. He eventually built both a hospital wing and a huge children's ranch retreat in New Mexico.

Then there was the Colleen Giblin Foundation, a wonderful children's charity founded by Paul and Vickie Giblin. I had served in a similar capacity as chairman for that organization as well. The Giblins and Martins were a close-knit, extended family, even though they are of Irish descent and we are African-American. Paul served as godfather to our four children, and I in turn am godfather to their son, Todd. Paul was also, at one time, my NFL agent and to this day he serves as my personal attorney. Vicky and Paul had lost their beautiful daughter, Colleen, to a brain tumor when she was but an infant, at which time they founded a wonderful foundation to channel the undying love they had for their little princess into other good works.

There also had to be serious consideration given to Minority Athletes Networking, Etc. Inc., or "MAN," a 501(c)(3) organization founded by former New York Football Giants Harry Carson, Ron Johnson and myself some 20 years ago. MAN, a permanent fixture in the tri-state region, had garnered great support over the years. Its mission is to target and serve inner city youth by providing scholarships, mentoring and exposure to job opportunities beyond the confines of the urban backdrop. Its proud motto is simply "Making a Difference," and I can assure you that many former New York Football Giant players diligently did so over the years.

These and a host of other organizations would have been great choices to benefit from this endeavor. However, when I had time to canvass the inner recesses of my brain, it suddenly dawned upon me that the obvious was staring me right in the face. I would later, with the help of others, stop dead in my tracks, realizing what the perfect mission was. For several years, I, like so many New Yorkers, had become completely frustrated over the ongoing treatment of the 9/11 first responders and rescue and recovery workers. The refusal of our political leaders to deal with their concerns and needs and health maladies was both unbelievable and deplorable.

*****

As fate had dictated, on the evening of September 10, 2001, I was returning from an out-of-town business trip to Kansas City, Missouri. I was then vice president of AXA Equitable's Sports Marketing Division and I was flying into Newark International Airport shortly before midnight. Again, being the country boy with longing in his eyes, I always insisted upon a window seat to take in the wonders of the planet.

They had heroically served us and they were suffering and they were ours.

There was a female passenger who was seeing the New York region for the very first time and she politely asked what sights she should take in during her visit. It was a brief exchange as we were on final approach for landing, but I was delighted to share my thoughts with her.

Flying southward and parallel to the Hudson River, a magnificent view of the New York skyline illuminated itself against the blackness of the Atlantic Ocean. I took the liberty of pointing out several marquee landmarks that she might consider. "Central Park is a must," I suggested, "and, of course, no visit would be complete without a visit atop the world-famous Empire State building. If you're interested," I added, "you also might want to take in the David Letterman Show at the Ed Sullivan Theater on 51st, and no trip would be complete without a visit to the Statue of Liberty."

What made the conversation so memorable is that my second to last suggestion before the Lady in the Harbor was the Twin Towers of the World Trade Center. As we were arriving around midnight, she indicated that she was going to sleep in the next morning and get a start later in the day. Little did either of us realize that this would be the last day anyone would see those magnificent structures intact. I had always been captivated by the visual majesty that the Twin Towers provided. I suppose that was neither novel nor unique, but, from the sky, their breathtaking splendor differentiated these towers from all surrounding competitors. Especially at night!

I have often wondered if that young lady followed her own advice and chose to sleep in as she intended. I sincerely pray that she did.

As for me, as I had gotten home late the night before, on the fateful morning of September 11th I was persuaded to follow the suggestion of my fellow passenger and to sleep in and ignore my customary 5:00 a.m. wake-up call. The following morning, Dianne had already awakened and was downstairs preparing her coffee. She has sworn by her morning cup of Joe ever since high school.

Rising from my abbreviated night's slumber, I turned on the television and quickly searched for my morning dose of Lori Stokes, long-time anchor of Channel 7 Eyewitness News. The volume was reduced to a whisper, as Dianne would occasionally watch TV while battling her insomnia, dialing down the sound so not to disturb me. As I glanced toward the set, I was struck by an eerie case of déjà vu as clouds of black smoke were pouring from the top of one of the Twin Towers.

Just at that moment, Dianne thoughtfully entered the room to bring me a cup of coffee as well. Believing this to be a rebroadcast of the 1993 WTC bombing, I asked Dianne, "Why are they showing this old clip of the WTC bombing"? But as she began to respond, it hit me that the original attack occurred in the underground parking garage and that the smoke would have been nowhere near that high.

Something was terribly, terribly wrong. Little did I know in that moment just how wrong!

Little did I know that we were about to cry and mourn. Little did I know that we were about to be shocked and horrified and forever changed.

But on that wonderful morning in Akron, I mulled over every possible beneficiary save for the one I would ultimately settle on, before I got back to the hotel. Although she did not then know why, I was too happy and too elated for Dianne to remain angry with my tardiness. We went on to enjoy a celebration with my friend, Harry, one that was truly worthy of the day's beginning.

I would return to New Jersey with a firm hold on this dream, and before the week was out, Dianne, my children and my company would all be on board.

I was clearly on my way across the United States of America – but only just.

6 – FIRST STEPS

Loud and boisterous and proud

I took my first physical step on the *Journey*, onto the center span of the George Washington Bridge ("GWB"), at 7:00 a.m., September 16, 2007, six years and five days after 9/11. In that step there was an explosion of joy inside me. Oh, I was all cool on the outside, but the bells were peeling powerfully within.

It was a day that dreams are made of, and we got very lucky that this particular September 16th, a Sunday, dawned bright and beautiful, just like September 11, 2001.

The level of activity the night before and the morning of September 16th was mind-blowing. Boxes of shirts, flags and banners, and the human beings carrying them, kept scurrying back and forth as a media frenzy of TV crews set up their cameras and readied their satellite trucks and newspaper photographers snapped countless images in their sharp-looking *a Journey for 9/11* tees. Brigades of staff and supporters moved out in teams with the precision of a military force. The only difference was that my troops were all smiling, rather than fearful or tearful about what was to come.

On this special, once-in-a-lifetime day, we had the right lane on the upper level of the GWB to ourselves to launch the *Journey*. I could feel the rhythm of the traffic on the huge suspension bridge as passing drivers waved and honked their horns in support. Stepping to the microphones, I made a promise to the crowd that I would not fail.

Finally, and elatedly, I put my right foot forward on the 3,500-foot center span of the Bridge, and the *Journey* had begun.

We had set it in motion and we were going to travel the country, giving voice to the plight of the first responders, rescue and recovery workers, and celebrating them as the best of America.

At mid-span, suspended more than 200 feet above the Hudson River by steel cables hanging from the GWB's majestic 604-foot towers, I paused for a few seconds, just for me. First I looked north toward the Tappan Zee Bridge, with its distinctive profile hugging the broadest section of the river. In the woods and hills beyond the Tappan Zee Bridge was Bear Mountain State Park, about 13 miles north of my home in New Jersey and a frequent walking destination as I religiously trained for the *Journey.*

Then I turned south to take in the island of Manhattan and it struck me, before I took my next step toward an eventual total of 5,206,082, how much was missing since the Twin Towers fell.

As I crossed, I was very, very proud that for the first time since September 11, 2001, for these first steps of *a Journey for 9/11,* that a part of the George Washington Bridge was to be closed for any event. The work done to get the approval alone was staggering. We were to begin on the New York City side of the bridge, so we had to coordinate that morning with the New York Police Department, Port Authority of New York and New Jersey Police, the New Jersey State Police and the New York Fire Department.

We had to coordinate with the press – with the local New York media, with ESPN and NFL Films – and since we were beginning in what was the most densely populated corridor in the United States of America on what were heavily traveled roads, safety and security concerns were paramount.

Our own security and emergency medical personnel had to coordinate with the police departments and emergency services units in every municipality we would cross that first day – Fort Lee, Leonia, Englewood, Teaneck, Hackensack, Hasbrouck Heights, Wood-Ridge,

Carlstadt, Rutherford and East Rutherford – since critical intersections along the way had to be staffed and prepared for closure.

And that was just to get to Giants Stadium!

Not one but three primary *Journey* events were being staged during the day: the launch at the bridge itself, a presentation at Hackensack University Medical Center in Hackensack, and the halftime show at the New York Football Giants and Green Bay Packers game at Giants Stadium in East Rutherford, New Jersey (what was the Giant's 2007 home opener).

Sunday, September 16, 2007, the day *a Journey for 9/11* officially began, was going to be one impossibly extraordinary day.

Timing was everything. We had to launch from New York at precisely 7:00 a.m. to get to the 10:00 a.m. event at the hospital, to get to Giants Stadium by 1:00 p.m., in time for the halftime show that just happened to be featuring the *Journey.*

There, where I had played football on so many other Sundays, I was surrounded by many of my former Giants teammates, everyone from Phil Simms to Lawrence Taylor to Stacy Robinson to Joe Morris to Brad Van Pelt to Perry Williams, and so many others.

Giants Stadium was deafening. I had played 14 years in that stadium and this topped it all. To say the crowd went wild is an understatement. I was walking across the field carrying the American flag and you could see tears in their eyes in the stands. You could see America – the young, the old, the rich, the poor. I tried to make eye contact and wave to everyone that I could.

At this wholly loud, classic American celebration, we collected $11,030 in tin cups – $11,030 to add to $911,000 from Joseph and Carol Reich, and to the NFL's $50,000 and to the Giants $25,000, and to the $10,000 from Coach Parcells that put us over $1,000,000 for the 9/11 responders.

Presentations were made as a marching band cheered us on our way. My friend, Timmy Shinn, gave me a brand new Chevrolet Trailblazer outfitted with my image and the *Journey* logo. A field-sized American flag was unfurled for us. Out of that Old Glory, we were sent off by those fans who never forgot.

Loud and boisterous and proud they sent us off – out of hordes of photographers and so many quick interviews and TV sound bites and Giants Stadium panorama and spectacle.

Only when we left Giants Stadium would the pandemonium and craziness begin to subside. Only then would we normalize – or rather, sustain – the normal level of crazy that was to prove to be part and parcel of the entire *Journey,* every day, day in and day out.

Crazy would accompany us like the fully loaded and *Journey*-decorated, 52-foot-long RV that General Motors had loaned us through the intercession of David Jurist, which would provide some needed shelter and opportunities for a catnap as far as Roswell, New Mexico, when *Journey's* complimentary loan of the vehicle was up as the walk went longer than anyone had imagined.

After the fanfare died down and the crowds thinned out, it was just Dianne and I; Lee Reeves; George Diaz, the 24-year-old EMT from Fuchs E.M.S. and Medical Transportation Services of Fair Lawn, New Jersey; and Sergeant Bill Markowski, the security officer from the New York private investigation and security firm Beau Dietl & Associates – and the sound of the crickets in the Meadowlands.

But reverberating in my memory of that day will always be how Harry Carson, at the launch site at the Bridge, before the beautiful spectacle of the Palisades across the Hudson in New Jersey, pulled me aside and said, "George, I want you to know that should anything happen to keep you from finishing, I will, I promise, finish it for you." As always, my brother on the field and my brother in life.

Harry, of course, was in a way responsible for those first steps on the bridge – and the 5 million plus that followed. But between my inspiration at his Hall of Fame induction in Ohio and his words at the start of *Journey*, there was much work to be done. First we had to build the team.

*****

After a pleasant but exhausting weekend celebrating Harry Carson's induction into the Hall of Fame in Canton, I returned home determined to walk across America on behalf of the 9/11 first responders and subsequent rescue and recovery workers. But before I could take my first step, I knew that I would need to put a first-rate support team in place. I had won a Super Bowl, but only because I was led by one of the greatest coaches in the game and part of a great team, one of 11 men on the field who would go through hell for each other and take risks for each other. We had each other's backs and we had been prepared for every contingency by a meticulous and exacting leader who demanded everyone's best.

It would take no less an effort, no less a team, to implement a purposeful and potent sojourn across these United States of America, and it would fall to me to emulate Bill Parcells. And while there is only one Bill Parcells, I had spent seven successful seasons with him and I had learned from him. Largely because of him, I knew what it took to lead.

Naturally, I was apprehensive about building my team, but I also was enthusiastic and confident that I could assemble the allies needed to make it happen.

I had the honor and privilege of playing 13 seasons with one of the greatest middle linebackers who ever played the game. A brother forever, there he was on that inviting and brilliant September 16 in 2007, standing by my side at the George Washington Bridge. "George, I want you to know," he quietly but firmly said, "that should anything happen to keep you from finishing this, I will finish it for you."

My initial plan was simple. I would first approach the friends who I most respected and whose trust meant the most to me, and do my very best to coax them into buying into my dream – or, depending upon your perspective, my insanity.

Embarking on such an unorthodox undertaking was indeed a new thing for me and I fully expected some of my friends to balk or to try to talk me out of it, but no one did. Not a single person I approached did. All of my enthusiasm and confidence notwithstanding, even I wasn't prepared for the overwhelming show of support that I received.

I had never been a subscriber to the celestial notion of having the "stars aligned" in one's favor, but they certainly did so for me. Of my initial laundry list of "go-to" friends, people who were important to me, people who I felt I needed on board, every single one rather remarkably embraced my own enthusiasm.

They were people who were close to me and whom I needed to hold close, people whose opinions and smarts I knew well. There was one who had an exhaustive knowledge of business, another with not-for-profit experience, and still another who knew the New York business community intimately. Coincidentally, the last was the good and gentle man who just happened to give me my very first post-football career opportunity when my Giants' playing days ended.

David Jurist was the celebrated co-owner of a very successful commercial printing company, Tanagraphics Inc., one of the largest sheet-fed commercial printing operations in New York City. He also was president of the celebrated Tomorrows Children's Fund ("TCF") at Hackensack University Medical Center, a great organization focused on building one of the most successful pediatric cancer treatment centers in the country. Dave and I had worked closely together over the years for TCF after his middle daughter, Eileen, a cancer survivor, had been stricken at an early age.

I was the lucky beneficiary of his friendship, for it was he who initially hired me as his vice president of Human Resources, Security, and Industrial Waste Management when football was to be no more; and believe me, I learned a hell of a lot from this iconic New Yorker. Having Dave Jurist in my corner would give both me and my dream instant credibility in business, for he was, as they say, "the man."

I had left his employ a few years earlier, under very good conditions, to pursue other opportunities, but Dave and I had remained close friends throughout. So I quickly arranged to have lunch with him once our schedules allowed.

Dave was kind enough to come uptown near my new office and we met for lunch at Ted's Montana Grill on 51st at 6th Ave. We both ordered the signature Bison Burger and I nervously began sharing my vision and explaining the plan that I had in mind. Dave knew me as well as anyone in my circle of friends, since I had worked for him for nearly 10 years. He also understood just how determined I could be and how willing I was to go off the deep end.

This was a pivotal juncture in the early stages of *Journey*, because I had tremendous respect for Dave, my mentor, and had he given it a resounding thumbs down, I'm not certain that *a Journey for 9/11* would ever have come to fruition. I should also note that Dave had never been a proponent of vigorous exercise over the years that I had known him, though he might wildly dispute such a claim. So the concept of walking across America on foot could have been incomprehensible to him, but I attempted to explain.

As I completed my passionate pitch, Dave paused momentarily, though it seemed like an eternity. I think that I actually began expecting the worst, and as one who was rarely prone to letting pessimism in, I well remember the moment. But after Dave went through a litany of patented, non-committal gestures, he sympathetically reached out his hands and embraced mine as if to console me – or so it seemed. He took a deep breath and then another pause before he finally leaned over, gingerly kissed me on the forehead and said, "This, my friend, is an absolutely brilliant idea."

We had actually begun and I was at peace. In that first step, there was an explosion of joy inside me. Oh, I was all cool on the outside, but inside, the bells were peeling loudly.

"Saints be praised," I thought to myself, because with that single statement, there was a veritable avalanche of validation, unleashed by someone whose opinion was especially important to me. The dominos, I thought, might now begin to fall into place, and I had David Jurist to thank for that.

I felt overjoyed, and ideas and suggestions just started to pour out of me. I was throwing them out like a Louisiana auctioneer at a hog-selling contest. But after a moment of this insanity, Dave looked at me, snickered aloud, and then very calmly said, "George, first things first." With that, we began to sort out the pieces of one very important puzzle.

In one, very intelligent follow-up question, Dave asked if I had decided on a name for the venture. I began babbling out suggestions, which a desire to avoid embarrassment will keep me from repeating here.

He interrupted my rant and said, "You're walking across America – right?" Yes, I replied. "And this is going to be an effort on behalf of the first responders and rescue workers of 9/11, correct?" Yes, I again replied. "Then, why not simply call it '*a Journey for 9/11?*'"

Sometimes silence can be deafening.

It was a moment that reminded me of an old and familiar adage of my father's. "Sometimes it's better to remain silent and be thought a fool, than to speak out and remove all doubt." So I silently nodded in agreement.

a Journey for 9/11, it would be, and why not?

*****

Upon leaving that luncheon, I was on an emotional high, one that would eventually come to carry me clear across the United States of America.

Dave and I had quickly compiled quite a to-do list. We agreed that strategically a formal launch should coincide with the start of the 2007 National Football League season, giving us nearly a year to put it altogether. Partnering with the Giants and the NFL as we anticipated would help give us star power – and there was no doubt that we would need all of the star power that we could muster – along with a team of professional experts who were outstanding in their respective fields.

The initial list of necessities, as well as the accompanying human capital, would grow exponentially. Prior to taking a single step, we had to legally establish a not-for-profit, tax- exempt 501(c)(3) entity, which would ideally require some pro bono legal work. If corporations and the general public were expected to contribute to this adventure, it was imperative that we have a clean and legitimate tax-exempt status. Public relations also loomed as a vital component in the scheme of things, in that it was impossible to elicit support without getting the word out. Here, Dave had just the right person in mind, which we will explore in much greater detail a bit later. Security, which Dave absolutely insisted upon, was another essential component.

As I gazed intently at the list that Dave and I had formulated on napkins, it immediately became clear that this would be anything but a "mom-and-pop" operation. Walking across America would require a small army of staffers and many, many volunteers. There were logistics, sponsorship, marketing, collateral materials, printing, apparel, branding, fundraising, website development, information technology, medical assistance, field coordination, route development and a list that went on and on – to long to think about. By the time I finished reviewing *Journey's* needs, I was dizzy and overwhelmed, and more than a bit discouraged.

But just when I started to think that the task at hand was becoming insurmountable, inspiration abounded in the image of Bill Parcells.

As a professional athlete, I had marveled at the detailed planning and operational precision that my greatest NFL head coach, Bill Parcells, always brought to the fore. How could someone be so gifted and accomplished as to have considered beforehand each and every detail and circumstance and possibility that a football season could manufacture? I was always fascinated by his absolute attention to detail and I was determined to incorporate his approach into our *Journey*.

Having the ability within myself to physically, mentally and spiritually embark upon something of this magnitude was one thing, but being able to get the time off from AXA Equitable, my then employer, was a horse of a different color. This was the first of the absolute necessities that had to be addressed before my dream could see the light of day. Without AXA Equitable's buy-in, I was going nowhere.

At the time, AXA's Senior Vice President of Human Resources was a very nice gentleman by the name of Steve Schulman. Steve had been extremely supportive of many of my out-of-office charitable endeavors in the past, and I was fairly confident that this would yield similar results. But I was well aware that this was something that he would undoubtedly have to run up the corporate chain of command.

When I first approached Steve with the idea, I was once again met with the same kind of overwhelming enthusiasm that Dave had shared.

But, naturally, Steve noted that his personal embrace was not to be confused with the corporate imprimatur that he would pursue. Needless to say, I had already done my homework on the matter, and knew that, like most large corporations, AXA had a corporate Executive Loan Program in place.

This is a unique and creative method through which corporations can have a profound impact on charities and outside organizations within communities. By loaning human intellectual capital to a chosen event, activity or organization, corporations can amplify and accentuate their corporate social responsibility efforts. As I was a high-profile employee and 9/11 efforts were generally well received, I hoped my request would prove to be a no-brainer. It was, to be sure, high stakes, since I needed to maintain my salary during my proposed humanitarian sabbatical. But soon, Steve happily informed me that my leave of absence had been approved. There was, however, one major strategic miscalculation, born of my zestful euphoria that would come to muddy these waters: I was very comfortable with the notion that I could actually accomplish this massive undertaking in only four months.

Yes, I said four months. In my early training regimens, I was racking up better than 30 miles per day. My initial intent was to aggressively ratchet that up to 50 miles per day and maintain that for the duration of the *Journey*. Needless to say, I received more than a few raised eyebrows. There were so many factors that I had failed to consider at the outset. Eventually I realized that press, educational, political and community-related components of the *Journey* were to eat up a great deal of time, so we had to dramatically revise our estimates and more reasonably project how long it all would take. Thankfully, AXA agreed to an extension as well.

My elation at AXA's response was short-lived, as I quickly realized that my to-do list just kept expanding rather than contracting. Getting the green light from AXA was indeed a major milestone, but there was little time to celebrate. I needed to give rise to both a strategic game plan as well as a formidable and functional board of directors.

Eventually, I realized that press, educational, political and community-related components of the Journey were to eat up a great deal of time, so we had to dramatically revise estimations and more reasonably project how long it would all take.

As I paused momentarily to catch my breath, it suddenly dawned on me that I was truly wading into the deep end of the pool. I needed a major band of qualified supporters and a great deal of good fortune. It came next in what was, to me, the most unlikely of places, the person of one Lee Reeves. Like Lee, I was among the former MONY employees who were acquired by AXA, where I headed up the sports marketing division.

Lee was my polar opposite. The term "macho" was a foreign concept to Lee, who was every bit a nerd dipped in milk chocolate. But polar opposites or not, Lee and I had collaborated on many projects in our corporate lives and I knew him to be a very dedicated and focused individual.

As I paused momentarily to catch my breath, it suddenly dawned upon me that I was truly wading into the deep end of the pool.

A few months earlier, Lee had requested a buyout from the company and was now the independent master of his own fledgling firm called Intelligent Design. At the time, he and I were friendly acquaintances, as were our respective significant others, Dianne and Flora.

Lee hadn't quite gotten his business off the ground at the time I approached him about *Journey* to see if he would be interested in creating a website for us. Up until that point, I had always viewed the actual *Journey* walk as a solo endeavor, not wanting to impose on or endanger anyone else with my self-proclaimed missionary vision.

Lee was originally from Tennessee and he took pride in being a country gentleman of the first order. Yeah, right! To me, Lee's impression of a hard day at the office was not having air conditioning in his car for the commute. I, by the way, took great delight in teasing Lee at every possible juncture, and he loved it, not that there was much that he could do about it anyway.

As Lee's girlfriend, Flora, was still working for AXA after his departure, Lee would often come into the city to have lunch with her (whenever she could afford it, that is).

On one occasion, I audaciously invited myself to one of their luncheons and began to loosely lay out the initial plans for the *Journey*. Lee, who knew me well, could immediately discern that details were anything but my strong suit, so he, just like Dave, began to throw a barrage of pertinent questions at me. As I stuttered and stammered through his surgical inquiries, Lee could easily see that I was heading down a one-way street in the wrong direction.

There we were lost, somewhere in what had to be the bowels of Oklahoma. Lee had checked with Jennifer Skor, our "Wizard Behind the Curtain" back in New York, when we last had cell phone contact. She assured us that we were going the right way, but what had been a road had disappeared and what then became a trail also had disappeared. There were no trees, no markings, no bearings, just a lot of empty, wide open space. "Lee, I roared, you have got to be (expletive deleted) kidding me," to which he calmly responded, "George, if I'm not mistaken, these have got to be mountain lion tracks."

"Who's going with you – what routes are you planning on taking – what's you're starting point – where will you end – what support will you have out on the road – where will you stop – how will this be funded – do you have any sponsors – do you have a launch date – or a projected end date?" By the time lunch was done, I was dizzy once again, and confounded. However, as much I hate to give him credit, the truth was that Lee's penetrating probes had been spot on.

I left that meeting so angry at him that I wanted to cry.

Here I was approaching the seminal moment of my life and he was pissing all over it, or so I thought. After I got back to the office and cooled down a bit, I realized that Lee was asking all of the right questions that had to be addressed, and that his keen insight was both cathartic and revealing. I, along with the *Journey*, needed someone who was not only going to ask the tough questions, but find the right answers as well.

Like a boxer whose eyes are getting swollen, I needed an experienced cutman in my corner; Lee would become a true wingman as well, a co-pilot whom I could trust and depend upon throughout.

I needed someone whose ego would remain in check and whose motives would not become muddied. *Journey* and George Martin needed a manager who could identify all of our needs and figure out how to meet them. We needed someone who would arduously sweat through the details, since I was obviously too close to the blood, sweat and tears of it all to maintain perspective. As strange as it seemed to me at first, I had just discovered the perfect candidate:

Of all people, my polar opposite, Lee.

Shortly after that first meeting with him, I quickly went about devising a strategy to cleverly elicit Lee Reeves' services. I figured that I could sweeten the pot by asking him to officially come aboard and join *Journey* as our IT specialist and assistant manager. Thinking that Lee might see through my not-so-subtle game, I asked if he would be willing to meet with me again to bring me up to speed on the website. Then when the moment was right, I would casually spring the greater trap on my unsuspecting buddy. So the meeting was set, but before I could get into my agenda, Lee asked if I would indulge him because he had an important matter that he first wanted to discuss. Not wanting to upset the apple cart, I was perfectly willing to accommodate him.

"George," he said, "This has the making of being something really special. It could be the signature moment for you and your legacy. You are a beloved and respected athlete in the New York region, and the 9/11 cause is homegrown and close to the heart of every New Yorker. There's no margin for error here, and this should be a reflection of the best that New York has to offer. To be perfectly candid, I see this as a seminal moment for you nationally. So, George, I'd like to come aboard, not only as your IT guru, but also as your road manager. You need one and I'd also like to join you on the walk, if you think that it would be a good idea and not too much of an imposition?"

Without missing a beat, I paused for a moment, pensively looked up at the ceiling and then down at the floor, before saying, "Let me sleep on it for a while and I'll let you know."

"George, there's no margin for error here and this should be a reflection of the best that New York has to offer. To be perfectly candid, I see this as a seminal moment for you nationally."

Lee Reeves

You see, Mama didn't raise no fool. I played him like a two-dollar fiddle and he's none the wiser to this day – or at least I have allowed myself to believe. He was, of course, the answer to my fervent prayer. But I did my level best to keep Lee in the dark. I didn't want him to know just how absolutely delighted I was to hear him make that timely overture to me, since his overture would otherwise have been my plea to him.

*****

Lee was just what the doctor ordered. He would come on as a full-fledged member of our board of directors as well, and no one, beyond me, would give more of himself to the *Journey* than Lee Reeves. He became my certified partner in crime, but there was an ebb and flow and paradox that often came with working with Lee. Like a good firefighter, he never failed to show up, but he never quite brought enough water to completely douse the flames. In a word, important things lingered. There will be more on this later.

After pointedly, but it appeared to him, begrudgingly, giving my blessing to Lee and welcoming him to join my then-traveling asylum of two, I wanted him to think that he ought to be beholden to me, his compassionate and benevolent companion. Yes, I have a bit of an evil streak in me, because the truth is that I was actually desperate for him.

Figuratively joined at the hip, like Sidney Poitier and Tony Curtis in *The Defiant Ones,* Lee and I went on to walk into America and into time together. But I still needed to bring more hands on board.

There was David Jurist's business credibility and the all-important macro perspective, and there was Lee Reeves' building blocks of business and his equally all-important micro perspective. With those two believers by my side and in my corner, I went off in pursuit of the third vital member of my *Journey* team.

Like Sidney Poitier and Tony Curtis in the movie, 'The Defiant Ones,' Lee and I went on to walk into America and into time together.

By all accounts, Brie Ingrid O'Neal was heaven sent.

At the time Brie was a freelance humanitarian who championed certain causes that suited her fancy. Whenever I think about the collective talents that eventually surfaced to fashion the success of *a Journey for 9/11,* I concluded that I was truly the beneficiary of "divine intervention." It was so indeed with Brie O'Neal as well.

I had met her a few months earlier when she was helping my football brother, Harry Carson, out with one of his many charitable endeavors. Highly efficient, workmanlike, meticulous and smart, she was an executive director for hire, a top gun who could bring projects to fruition.

When I first met her, I had no particular need for her unique services, but we struck up a casual friendship and we'd talk from time to time, largely about political issues. She thought provocatively, and in the pre-Obama era she forecast that such a presidency was actually possible, and then she proceeded to explain, in insightful detail, just how such a historical event might come to pass. At the time it appeared to me to be just wishful thinking. But to her it was simply a matter of impeccable timing and strategic planning.

As a friend and conversationalist she dazzled, and she had been a veritable champion for all sorts of social issues and causes.

Knowing that Brie had loftier aspirations and that she was in the process of relocating to the D.C. area., I didn't feel that helping to launch *Journey* would particularly excite her, but as my friend Lee advised, "If you don't ask, the answer is always no!" My apprehension in approaching her was multifold. First, I truly felt that she might just be too big for us, and secondly, there was so much about what we were planning that was still in the wind. In our infancy, we were high on the big picture but extremely short on detail and certainty.

But I had already jumped out of the plane and I definitely needed to pull the cord on the parachute – and we needed someone like Brie. So I nervously called and asked if she would be willing to meet me for lunch.

Realizing that lightning never strikes twice in the same place, I decided that she was unlikely to fall for the Lee Reeves approach. Who, after all, but Lee would? I'd have to rely upon my charm and devastating good looks alone. I didn't have a chance.

So it was time to put on my best suit and throw myself on the mercy of the court. We agreed to meet at a small diner in Jersey City of all places, which was not too far from her apartment. I wanted to make it easy for her, because I was the one coming on bended knee with hat in hand. But even though 14 years in the NFL had taught me that punctuality is always a must, I got turned around and lost.

After retracing my steps and frantically finding a parking spot a few blocks from the diner, I rushed into it and spotted Brie sitting alone at the table with the body language of a serial mugger. In a not-too-subtle attempt to defuse the situation, I politely flashed my signature smile at her and extended a greeting accompanied by my lengthy "hate to be late" apology. But she wore this unmistakable look of annoyance on her face and I was a bit taken aback by it. Before I was able to even sit down, she looked me squarely in the eye and said, "I'm upset with you, George Martin!" Damn, I thought to myself, I may as well ask for the check now and avoid the coming painful humiliation of public rejection.

Thinking that my tardiness had pushed her over the edge, I again sheepishly expounded upon my apology, but she cut me off in mid-sentence. "I'm not upset with you for your being late, that's understandable. I'm upset with you because I've heard that you are developing a 9/11 walk across America and you haven't invited me to participate in it. Why not?"

Man, sometimes it just pays to be living right, I thought to myself.

If I had been wearing false teeth at the time I would have dropped them right there on the floor, as I stood there with my mouth wide open. I could not believe what I had just heard.

"George Martin breathes but not for himself. He breathes to help others. That is the kind of player he was and that is the kind of man he is."

Bill Parcells

With a warm smile, she then turned towards me and apologized for stating her case so emphatically. "I'm sorry George," she quickly added. "What did you want to meet with me about?"

If she only knew, I thought. She was all about unique and challenging experiences, and we just happened to be right up her alley – an unvarnished, start-up charity with potentially national implications. Before my inexplicable good fortune even began to settle in, Brie and I began discussing my vision and, more importantly, the vital role that she might play in it.

No doubt about it, Brie was a doer, a drum major and band leader.

She sketched out a launch outline that was so precise and intelligent that even I could understand it. In her head already there were timelines and chronological to-do lists. It was abundantly clear that Brie had already given *Journey* considerable thought. From an experiential standpoint, it also was obviously clear that she had been there and done that.

As a prospective senior manager, she proposed to direct the launch for us. A born leader, she wanted no interference or debate as to her authority. She wanted no outside interference from any well-meaning or well-intended ally, a decision that would inevitably ruffle more than a few egotistical feathers, but one that was absolutely necessary. She wanted it understood and agreed upon, from the very outset, that our mission was to be the only thing that was sacrosanct. That included everyone and everything else – even yours truly!

I understandably agreed that even I was not to interfere with her authority.

Now that Brie's situation was settled, we concurred that the tax-exempt 501(c)(3) status was simply a must. Not a problem noted Brie. "I have a contact in the legal world who might be able to do this on our behalf and better yet – pro bono," which are two of my favorite words in the English language. Brie was paying huge and immediate dividends before we even left the diner.

Courtesy of Brie, the law firm of Proskauer Rose LLP, in the persons of Rob Palmese and Ron Projansky, stepped in, the legal stalwarts who were to be our knights in shining armor. And if you'll be so kind as to excuse the vulgar vernacular, these two gentlemen worked their collective asses off for *Journey*.

Committed from the word "go," Rob and Ron were not only the undisputed legal dynamic duo that would secure our 501(c)(3) non-profit status, but also the authors of the by-laws and the legal construct of *a Journey for 9/11* itself. Despite many challenges that were placed in their way, they got these done in no time at all – except for the 501(c)(3), which took the Washington muscle and mojo of former U.S. Rep. Vito Fossella and his staff to get past the bureaucrats. Rob and Ron stood by our side as *Journey* progressed to assure that we were in compliance with regulations in every state that we passed through.

Shortly after Brie had secured the legal services of Rob and Ron, we then set our sights on aligning *Journey* both spiritually and practically with New York City law enforcement. This was at the heart of our mission, as they, along with the New York City Fire Department, were the primary sources for most of the rescue and recovery workers that sad day. I knew that there was a cadre of governmental departments and agencies that all selflessly descended upon the site of the Twin Towers during our time of need, but it was New York City's Bravest and Finest who were the heart and soul of it all.

Whenever I think of New York's Finest, I conjure up the "bad-ass" image of an intimidating, fire-breathing, Sergeant York type, replete with a vocabulary that would shame most sailors and NFL coaches alike. But imagination aside, I can tell you with a degree of certitude that New York is one of the toughest places on the face of the planet and it is not for the faint of heart, and that's no joke.

Yet there was something very gentle about Ed Mullins, the president of the New York Sergeants Benevolent Association ("SBA"), whom I had the pleasure of meeting. All of my preconceived notions and thoughts evaporated when I met Ed, who has never raised his voice above a whisper or used profanity in all of the years that I have known him. With the prototypical good looks of a choirboy, he is a throwback to that bygone era when police officers were called to get cats out of a tree and when they always tipped their hats to the ladies. With a killer smile and personality to boot, he was and is a professional's professional.

Whenever I think of New York's finest, I conjure up the "bad-ass" image of an intimidating, fire-breathing, Sergeant York type, replete with a vocabulary that would shame most sailors and NFL coaches alike.

Ed and I hit it off instantly, largely because we have very similar moral values.

To both *Journey* and to me, he became a most trusted advisor and friend. Despite an always ingratiating outward appearance and gentlemanly disposition, he was never afraid to tell you exactly what was on his mind, and he would stand toe-to-toe with anyone. You've got to admire a man like that.

Ed and I have had many long and painful discussions about the immediate aftermath of 9/11. From his perspective, when you've lost close friends and colleagues whom you've respected and formed lifelong bonds with, it was no easy task to attend funerals, make bedside visits at the hospital, or offer consolation to grieving widows. But that's what life and 9/11 demanded, and both he and his organization clearly wore their passions on their sleeve as they went about the business of emotionally doing all of this and more.

When Ed decided to come aboard and support *a Journey for 9/11*, it was indeed a happy day. However, when he decided to come aboard as a member of the board of directors, it was a validation that genuinely touched my heart, because they just don't come any better than Ed.

There is an appropriate footnote, and I would truly be remiss if I did not mention the role of Ed's beautiful and wonderful executive assistant, Theresa Ashton, his indisputable gatekeeper. She was his first and last line of defense; no one would ever get to Ed without the blessing and approval of Theresa. For some unknown reason, she took a liking to me and I must say with absolute joy that the feeling was mutual. Ed may very well have been the ultimate decision-maker, but it was Theresa who was the unchallenged queen of implementation at the SBA.

At this stage of *Journey's* development, the vital pieces of its foundation were miraculously falling into place. In a very short time I had secured a much-needed road manager, a director of the New York launch and some outstanding members of the board of directors, and we had strategically allied with a number of the rescue and recovery organizations as well. But there still remained a few more key slots to fill before I could be completely comfortable with my overall team.

It is a rule of thumb that you always save your best for last, and in this case the adage rang absolutely true, because next in my sights was another dear friend, Kenneth T. Vehrkens, the Dean of Fairleigh Dickinson University's ("FDU") Petrocelli College and a Vice President of the University. Ken and I went back well into my NFL playing days and he and I have collaborated on countless educational and charitable initiatives over the years. He has been an intricate and influential part of my adult life, as well as that of the entire Martin household.

I first met Ken when I was seeking to complete my college degree in 1985 while playing for the Giants. Ken was already involved with the New York Football Giants as part of FDU's negotiating team, which was responsible for administering the practice camp that the Giants then conducted at FDU's Florham Park campus. At that time, fully 75 percent of all NFL players did not have a college degree, and the average career span was a paltry four years. I was not only one of the 75 percenters, but I was also on borrowed time, playing in my 10th NFL season. The proverbial clock was ticking away on my career, so I decided to seek out Ken Vehrkens to see if there might be a way for me to complete my degree at FDU during the later stages of my Giants playing days.

When it comes to promoting continuing education, Ken Vehrkens is as passionate as I had once been about getting to the quarterback. He has spent his entire career in higher education, and countless individuals such as myself owe a great deal to this modern-day Johnny Appleseed, who chooses always to sow countless seeds of educational opportunity. It became my pleasure to join him in forging many of his educational initiatives.

The pinnacle of our tag-team efforts occurred when the NFL decided to replicate the New York Football Giants *Degree Completion Program* that was established by Ken and myself in the mid- '80s. So successful was the initial program with the Giants that the NFL saw fit to establish it with all 32 team franchises. Ours was the prototype that started it all and we both took justifiable pride in that milestone achievement.

Ken and his lovely wife, Karen, own a small farm upstate in the Albany, New York-area, close to where the Giants once conducted their training camp. A kind of gentleman farmer, he raises an impressive variety of vegetables during the abbreviated summer months. On Sunday evenings on his way back down to Fairleigh Dickinson, he would kindly and invariably drop off a large selection of fresh vegetables for my family and me at our Ringwood home. This afforded us the opportunity to chat regularly and conspire to do so many great things together.

On one occasion I took the liberty of talking to him about my plans for *Journey*, and true to form, Ken was immediately on board. In retrospect, I realize that the term being "on board" was a definitive understatement in Ken's case. He signed on as one of the original members of the board and an officer as well.

Ken was instrumental in persuading FDU to develop the entire walking route for *Journey*. Coast to coast, this presented an enormous challenge as we were prohibited by law from walking on any major U.S. highways. Together with his colleague, Joseph Thomas, they forged a class project – with credits going to the participating FDU students –

utilizing the most sophisticated technology available at the time to plot the route, which also had to head south to avoid the worst winter weather. We also initially planned to turn back to the north and end the *Journey* in San Francisco, but I called an audible along the way and we finished in San Diego instead.

"George and I had joined forces for many causes over the years, so immersing myself and our university in Journey was only natural. Our students actually plotted the course and got academic credit for doing so. We also were involved in marketing, fundraising and public relations. And why not, because George is a reaffirmation of the fact that there is still goodness in this world."

Kenneth Vehrkens

Ken also was the only board member who regularly came out on the road to tangibly show his support and get "up close and personal" with the *Journey* entourage. In fact, Ken set the record for the longest distance covered by a board member, logging more than 23 miles with me in New Mexico in a single day. Several other board members joined me on the road at least once, but Ken was the only one with multiple visitations. He conducted several FDU fundraisers, garnering $15,000 on one occasion, and he regularly marshaled FDU resources throughout. If *Journey* had named an MVP, Ken would have definitely been one of the front runners.

At this point, it should be fairly obvious that there was an almost unbelievable groundswell of support from every conceivable corner for *Journey.*

In rapid-fire fashion, Beau Dietl, a highly decorated former New York City police detective who had formed his own security firm, came on board; as did Kevin Fuchs of Fuchs E.M.S; as did Andrew Giangola of NASCAR, as did Jennifer Skor; Lee's "Wizard Behind the Curtain;" as did Jay Winuk, who would spearhead our public relations operation. Beau committed to providing the security personnel who would be with us throughout, and Kevin to providing the emergency medical technicians who would also be there with us. Andrew engineered a couple of NASCAR events for *Journey* along the way, and Lee as overall manager would not have survived had there been no Jennifer to shed some light; and as we criss-crossed the country, often in the most obscure of places, Jay somehow always got news of our impending arrival to them.

And just for the record, when I say these good people provided, I mean almost all of them did it completely, or certainly as much as they possibly could, *pro bono* – FOR FREE.

I was grateful that board members, distinguished and highly accomplished men and women, would continue to sign on, but with the above team in place I was confident we were ready.

Rather remarkably, everyone I personally approached had said yes. I was, to say the least, blessed with great friends and colleagues, without whom we would never have gotten under way.

Without this battalion of friends, my *Journey for 9/11* would, no doubt, have remained just a dream.

7 –THE REALITY AFTER THE LAUNCH

On the Path of George Washington

Then, it was, oh so suddenly, just my beautiful Dianne, Lee Reeves, George Diaz, Sergeant Bill Markowski and myself.

"You'll Never Walk Alone," or so the song goes. That was the rule for *Journey* – part of the plan to make sure we did what we set out to do. On a couple of days many people would walk a short distance with me at an event planned around the walk; many members of my board walked for part of a day here and there; but most times and for most of the distance, it was just me and members of my team.

I was never allowed to walk by myself, though sometimes I wanted that solitude. Lee would walk with me in the morning, and my security officer in the afternoon. I would talk with Lee about the things friends talk about; with the security people, who changed many times during the walk, I'd talk about their work as rescue and recovery workers.

You see, most of the security guys who came out were connected with 9/11, and none of them had been ordered to go to Ground Zero. These brave people went and worked there of their own volition.

Journey had begun on the western portal to the greatest city in the world, over the banks of the majestic Hudson River where an explorer by the name of Henry Hudson sailed in 1609.

There atop the George Washington Bridge, directly across from the incredible New Jersey Palisades, we took the path that General

Washington and his ragged Continentals did upon being driven from New York City by the British. Our very first steps on *Journey*, in fact, were toward and into the terrain of Bergen County, New Jersey, where Washington found hope and solace when all seemed lost, and where Thomas Paine wrote in his immortal The Crisis: "These are the times that try men's souls".

Yes, we began there, just two miles from Yankee Stadium, where Babe Ruth and Lou Gehrig and Joltin' Joe DiMaggio and so many others wrote the history of America's Pastime – there but a mile and half from the beautiful Cloisters and five miles from Old Broadway and Lincoln Center and the museums that memorialize our culture, there in northern dogleg of Manhattan with the New York City Fire and Police Departments and the Port Authority Police Department by our side, those who had given their brothers to us forever on 9/11, there out of the sometimes mean streets of the Bronx, there where Washington returned to first serve the new nation as president, there into that land where he found hope and strength and victory.

*****

Lee Reeves struggled mightily to keep pace that first day, on what was to be the first of 187 days of walking, and, as I never tire of reminding him, he kept refusing to be rescued again and again by auto as he should have been.

I think that Lee was shocked by how demanding keeping the pace that we needed to set was, but to his credit, he strove to improve each and every day. There was a "wow" moment later in Virginia when I realized that he was finally in game shape. We memorialized that milestone with one mighty and memorable fist pump.

As I wrote earlier, Lee and I were polar opposites, physically and otherwise, but what a team we made. On his plate were scheduling, routing, and the no-so-simple matters of where we slept and where we ate every day. It was Lee who dealt with the schools and the churches and the municipal and other civic leaders we visited with along the way. He was also our on-site intercessor, whose role was clearly to intercept and deflect any and all unexpected intrusions away from my attention, no matter how well meaning they may have appeared at the time. It was Lee who constantly bore the initial point of impact and assessed whether or not my mission and focus was to be interrupted and altered, and he did it with impeccable, successful fortitude, day in and day out.

Lee was my confidante, my brother, my antagonist, my touchstone and my Energizer Bunny. Looking back, Lee was, in truth, the Godsend who delivered us. As I write again and again, without him, I don't think we ever could have gotten this done.

His children were grown, but what a remarkable fiancé, Flora DeJesus, he had, and whom he would marry in San Diego on the day after *a Journey for 9/11* concluded – a journey that I originally targeted for four months, but one that would end up taking nine. Just imagine planning a wedding under those circumstances.

Lee had his own emotional memories of September 11, 2001. "My fiancé and I were both at work in New York City on 9/11 and we got to experience the chaos and fear first hand. As we desperately made every effort to evacuate the city, we noticed all those heroes rushing toward the disaster. In the days after 9/11, we would often go back into the city from south Jersey, and as we cleared the Holland Tunnel, we would see what appeared to be armies of pedestrians lining the median of the West Side Highway cheering on those entering Ground Zero."

So Lee took that memory and that image and our friendship, and translated it into nine and a half months by my side and millions upon millions of steps – even if he was in such less-than-optimal physical shape at the beginning that I had to insist that he ride in the trailer car for a spell.

Of course, I wasn't exactly at my peak, either. But once an athlete, always an athlete, or so Harry Carson and I believed. I began my professional football career one year before Harry, but we decided to retire together after 14 and 13 years, respectively, of playing an intense warriors' game. While our bodies had been worn and damaged by the rigors of professional football, one of the pledges that we made to each other when leaving the field together was that we would remain in top physical condition. There were, we promised, to be no bloated beer bellies between us.

We had, for as long as we could remember, been conditioned to train and conditioned to treat our bodies with respect, on the field if not off it. So we went out promising each other that we would continue to respect our bodies, because we had a whole lot of living yet to do.

'It was a day that dreams are made of.'

But at the age of 53, while I was still in excellent physical condition, that didn't mean I was ready for what this would demand. Excellent shape or not, I was no spring chicken and this would require serious training – maybe not as demanding or as brutal as those annual camps with my revered friend Coach Parcells, but training nonetheless!

There is a bit of a Parcell-ism: Preparation is always important.

So I prepared to build my way into a 20- to 30-mile-per-day regimen at Bear Mountain State Park, knowing I had to add some hills to my routine. I was in pretty good shape, but I was suffering under the delusion that I could accomplish this *Journey* in three to four months, which is exactly what I first told my superiors at AXA, John Kirksey, Andrew McMahon and Steve Schulman.

The initial projection was based upon a goal of 50 miles per day and six days a week. It was a pace that only an athlete in great condition could sustain.

I was training to be that athlete, but I had forgotten that I also was going to be the public spokesman for a cause, who would have inordinate demands placed upon his time. As it was, I was going to be asked to regularly engage the New York, national and local press, as well as school children and town and state officials. I was expected to attend fairs and barbecues and church meetings and assorted events. I was to make presentations and pay our respects at national monuments.

But most of all, I was to take time out for the tens of thousands who would go out of their way to welcome me and greet me on the road. These were tens of thousands of conversations that we, initially, simply did not think about. Tens of thousands of conversations that fed my soul and made what was to be a walk of wonder!

Ours was a political, educational, fundraising, and media event. It would take time, and targeting even 20 miles per day under the circumstances was to be moving at a breakneck pace.

Once, too, we envisioned visiting 15 states, but in the end, we touched 13: New York, New Jersey, Pennsylvania, Delaware, Maryland, Virginia, Tennessee, Arkansas, Oklahoma, Texas, New Mexico, Arizona and California, plus Washington, D.C.

The Natural Beauty of Our Land

Oh, this land of ours, with its common denominator of sunrises and sunsets, with what God has given and man has wrought, and with what has been built up and torn down! State by state, so much of it moved and stunned me, and there were the occasional wonders that left me breathless.

Remember, I was an art major who appreciates collages of colors, "the amber waves of grain", "the purple mountains majesty," and all that makes "America the Beautiful."

As to any discussion of the natural beauty of our land, it is important to consider that we began by crossing the majestic Hudson River, with the burnt, rusted glow of the New York skyline behind us and the mighty Palisades staring us in the face. It is an awesome panorama and it is, to me, where America begins. It was the first of ten thousand or so sights that would move me and stop me in my tracks as *Journey* progressed. God's television set, you see, never shuts off and, for me, a simple country boy from Greenville, South Carolina, what I was to see of our land, up close and personal, quite literally and daily, blew me away.

*****

On the second day, September 17, 2007, we began to do what we continued to do clear across the United States of America, and that was to visit firehouses and the occasional police station. Truth be told, there was hardly a city, town, village or borough whose firehouses we passed that we failed to visit, and there were many that we went out of our way to get to.

There, we met thousands upon thousands of brother and sister first responders, who, through us and our mission, were able to join us in honoring both the 2001 fallen and those still in need of care and assistance, who we were all determined to serve.

In the first week alone, there were the Franklin Park Volunteer and the Metuchen Volunteer, and the Edison, Menlo Park and Lawrence Township Fire Departments. At each, there were babies and young teenagers and spouses and elderly parents and the folks from the neighborhood. We were pleased that our outreach to local media was getting results and that people were aware of and looking to embrace us as we passed through.

Early on, we realized that we were never going to be alone, as Jay Winuk's press releases were everywhere preceding us and paving the way.

*****

Washington and his bruised and blue Continentals would crisscross the length and breadth of New Jersey – which we would traverse but once – no less than three times. Like him, we walked just east of Morristown and directly into Princeton and Trenton, where both he and we crossed the Delaware River. Notably, two of his early and key victories were in those towns.

The Battle of Trenton was especially important, as Washington moved his army over the Delaware in the wee hours of the morning after Christmas Day into the teeth of a blizzard. They force-marched nearly nine miles south into Trenton. Washington utterly surprised the English and some 1,400 Hessian mercenaries, of whom 22 died, 83 were seriously injured, and fully 896 captured. Remarkably in this stunning surprise attack, Washington lost only two men. He had written "Victory or Death" on a note two days before, and it is also written that his men left a trail of blood in the snow as they marched on feet that were bound by rags, because they had no shoes, to Trenton. There, they sustained the birth of the very nation that was attacked on 9/11.

As we walked in honor of those who sacrificed their all on 9/11, we walked alongside the very path that these 2,400 soldiers, the whole of the Continental Army at the time, rendered sacred on the morning of

December 26, 1776. And we dwelled upon the tremendous sacrifice of those men more than 230 years before in whose footsteps we trod that day. Out of the heart of men who trudged through snow in the heart of a blizzard and into a battle, we walked. Out of that kind of sacrifice, we walked.

Compared to George Washington, we moved through our home state of New Jersey in a veritable flash, as the only other major people gathering was at the New Jersey office of the generous firm that gave me the leave of absence to do this. There must be nearly a hundred of us AXA Equitable types in the picture taken in front of our General Motors-loaned *a Journey for 9/11* RV.

One other memorable Jersey moment was when I was joined by my friend Ken Vehrkens, who rushed from a nearby meeting on September 20 to catch up with me close to Princeton. With both tie and dress shoes on, totally unprepared and looking every bit the same, he hung in with me for 10 miles or so, for what was, to me, taking friendship to a whole new level.

My New Jersey offered the most picturesque and well landscaped of suburban communities. Despite the northern I-95 corridor of the New Jersey Turnpike, it is, as advertised, the "Garden State" replete with beautiful individual homes that make you pause and take notice. It has its renowned lakes and a heralded shore line, and I walked through towns that by their very appearance invite you to stop and take up residence. But quickly we were moving toward Pennsylvania, even as we replayed the history of the American Revolution in our minds.

From the place where we would cross the Delaware we could see the Trenton Barracks, and we also walked within a couple of miles of Jockey Hollow in Morristown, where the Continental Army was twice encamped in 1779 and 1780, under conditions that were even more unbearable than those at Valley Forge. Valley Forge just gets better marketing.

The watchword upon which we couldn't help but dwell, again and again, was sacrifice. Out of the sacrifice that gave rise to our nation a spirit of sacrifice resounded in a people who would answer the call again without reservation, in World War I and World War II, and on the infamous morning of 9/11, when into the burning buildings, Americans went.

We walked alongside the very path that these 2,400 soldiers, the whole of the Continental Army at the time, rendered sacred on the morning of December 26, 1776. Out of the heart of men who trudged through snow in the heart of a blizzard and into a battle, we walked. Out of that kind of sacrifice, we walked.

As we proceeded to cross over a bridge on the Delaware River into Pennsylvania, we looked up at a road sign that interestingly read "New Jersey – Pennsylvania – New York – San Francisco," the last being what was then our designated end point. The three immediate states and San Francisco, and just about the oddest for-real road sign ever come across. With only 50 miles or so to cover in Pennsylvania, south through the streets of historic Philadelphia, and fewer miles still in Delaware, the *Journey* rapidly moved through New Jersey and its neighbors and poured cheap champagne at the passing of each.

And just for the record, there's nothing particularly exciting about drinking cheap champagne in front of places like the Morrisville Filtration Plant. We had made the decision not to reach for the good stuff until we earned it. Maryland, too, was to be short, and then in Virginia it would finally begin to get serious. The real problem was that the quick transit of these first three states forever spoiled us, and contributed to our moments of despair in what seemed the endlessness of realms, like the great state of Tennessee, which stretches 440 miles east to west, the longest of any state.

Once in Pennsylvania, our steps took us into the very heart of downtown Philadelphia, within blocks of what was once Carpenters Hall, home to the First Continental Congress, and Independence Hall, where 56 men from 13 colonies pledged "their lives, their fortunes, and their sacred honor." There John Adams, Benjamin Franklin, Richard Henry Lee, Thomas Jefferson and so many others came together to give us the magnificent statement of human values that is the Declaration of

Independence. "We hold these truths to be self-evident, that all men are created equal, that they are endowed by their Creator with certain unalienable Rights, that among these are Life, Liberty, and the pursuit of Happiness." You cannot help but ponder the magnitude of monumental events like these when you brush by the neighborhood in which it all occurred.

As an African-American, it also is important to note that in order to win the vote for independence, the delegates to the Continental Congress had to shelve the question of slavery, and removed Jefferson's stirring "He hath waged cruel war against human nature itself" clause. Declaring independence required a unanimous vote of the 13 colonies and the colonies of the Deep South insisted upon their "peculiar institution." Leaving the question of slavery on the table in Philadelphia destined the new nation to seemingly endless conflict, to 600,000 dead in a Civil War, to a century of Jim Crow and overt racism and persecution, and to a then 50-year, later-20th-century struggle to assure equality and civil liberties.

How's that for but one simple thought to consider on a late September afternoon – a thought about the dawning of our nation during the dawning of my own *Journey* across its heartland.

In the early states we crossed, there were smiles and handshakes and the occasional request for autographs, but the pace was rapid, the ground covered extensive, and the out-of-the-box was not truly encountered until we met a character's character in Maryland.

There, walking somewhere east of Interstate 95 on some nondescript road, we encountered a magician, replete with black tux, tails and top hat traveling in a gleaming black convertible. He made repeated stops to perform for us right by the side of the road. His magic practice, he informed us, wasn't going all that well and his cash was limited, so he said that the only contribution he could make was to perform for us and bring a smile to our faces, which he certainly accomplished.

He generated the occasional "ooh and ahh" from us and he certainly made us laugh – the image of him alone couldn't help but make you laugh – on no less than three occasions, as he tracked our progress on the web and dropped in for an impromptu show. And so we learned that sometimes the spiritual contribution that a vagabond magician makes on the side of a road is as great as if it were worth a fortune. As it happened, I don't think we ever got his name. We just called him "Magic," and "Magic" made his mark.

*****

Having grown up in the most rural of towns on a small sharecropper's farm in Greenville, South Carolina, where I played with dogs and pigs and rocks and dirt, I had dreamed of seeing America up close and personal from my earliest of days. I sat by the window in the back seat of an overloaded station wagon as we moved west to California before my teen years, and there, entranced by the map and the odd names of places and the occasional historic site, I had dreamed of seeing America all the more.

Then for years as a member of the New York Football Giants, I crisscrossed this land from the glorious skies above and continued to dream of seeing it truly up close and personal one day.

In Akron, Ohio, that memorable Hall of Fame weekend, the dream oh so suddenly just happened to get up close and personal with me and it was as if some alarm long dormant inside me went off.

Along with an entreating and yet foreboding internal warning: if not now, never!

Some might refer to it as a "wow" moment. For me, it was a moment that clarified, a moment that demanded and dictated that this finally be done.

Yes, I had responsibilities to my family and to my employer and there were a thousand practical considerations that weighed heavily against doing something so very, very impractical – so altogether unlikely and impractical.

But by the time I showered and left the hotel in Akron, it was as if I was walking on air because I was determined to make it happen. Then and there, no question in my mind, I decided to make it happen! I also knew that I had to attach this lifelong yearning of mine to a cause that would make it worth the price to my family, my employer and others.

And hopefully to a cause that would make it winning, formidable and invaluable to many who were then unknown to me.

Some might refer to it as a "wow" moment. For me, it was a moment that clarified, a moment that demanded and dictated that this finally be done.

It was a matter of attaching the dream to a cause, a simple matter of assuring that it would be about "paying it forward."

While I was personally invested in so many charities, I knew that such an undertaking would have to be attached to a cause with which all of America could identify. To the extent possible, I also knew that I would have to trade on whatever celebrity value there was in having been captain of the New York Football Giants and a Super Bowl champion.

After looking out my office window in New York toward Ground Zero and having the inspiration that I might help the increasing numbers of 9/11 rescue and recovery workers suffering from and succumbing to many different respiratory and other diseases, and the many of them who were without medical coverage, I determined to research the issue and to see if this might not be the cause worth attaching my yearning to.

I quickly learned just how compelling the Ground Zero workers' plight was, and before I had even spoken to my Dianne or my superiors at AXA Equitable, I knew exactly what I hoped to attach my *Journey* to and who I hoped to do it for.

Ground Zero workers had 12 times the normal rate of asthma, and one in eight of the 30,000 were already suffering from post-traumatic stress disorder (PTSD). Many had already developed or were in the process of developing tumors related to the toxins unleashed on that site. What they had worked in and breathed in the months surrounding the attack was contributing to the onslaught of heart disease, emphysema other bitter respiratory ailments, and cancer.

There was absolutely no doubt about it.

These heroic people were the latest victims of September 11's vile and horrific act! And I could help them.

*****

It was one of those rare days when Lee was not walking with me, again in the bowels of Oklahoma in a place so remote that it was unclaimed by any municipality. It was a completely desolate no-man's land, yet there on the side of the road was an old bicycle and a boy of no more than 8 or 9 with shaggy brown hair and with a brown paper bag that contained his savings of $3.78, all of which was being donated to the 9/11 rescue and recovery workers. I should have gotten Lee to take his picture, because he should have been the poster boy for *Journey*. And hell, I should have gotten his name. I rather got bits of his heart and soul. Remarkably, this young soul was willing to give his fortune away to those he believed had served him. He understood, he wanted to be held accountable. What was in him should have been bottled and force-fed to all Americans.

*****

9/11 was a day unlike any other for the United States of America. There was the wholly surprising, sudden and vicious nature of the attack. There were the unforgettable and appalling images of the planes coming over the Hudson and of the crumbling buildings and of the falling bodies and of a suddenly dark downtown New York City. There was a profound shock and deep sorrow that enveloped the lives of all Americans.

Yet, as so many ran away from the fire and smoke and plummeting steel and concrete to save their lives, there was this almost unimaginable and heroic rushing into as well – firefighters and police and paramedics and a host of others who poured in to help as thousands strove to get out.

For me, there were a number of close friends who lost someone that day, and one young neighbor of ours from Ringwood and a son of a friend. There was the wrenching, agonizing heartache of acknowledging the names and putting a number upon the dead. There were wakes and memorials to attend, somber ceremonies that tried to make sense out of the madness and extract some kernel of meaning and purpose for the loved and the lost.

I have since come to look upon Christian DeSimone, Tyler Ugolyn and others killed that day as angels who were called to serve some higher purpose. In the end, their deaths made it personal, as did the simple fact that the attack, which occurred just blocks from my office, was aimed at all that I hold dear, at my family and friends, at a way of life that I treasure, at values that mean everything to me, and at the country that I love.

Yes, the focus had to be upon the rescue and recovery workers who were being left behind and forgotten about. U.S. Reps. Carolyn Maloney and Jerry Nadler of New York had sponsored a bill in Congress that would make their care the responsibility of the people of the United States, but it had gained no traction and there was no immediate hope of its passage. So my thought was why not raise some immediate revenue for these heroes, while calling attention to their plight and to this bill and winning support for it nationally.

I looked at the possibility of what we could accomplish as life-affirming, and deep inside those mystic chords of memory that we all share, I kept hearing my father's voice reminding me, "Make sure that you leave the world a little bit better than you found it." A lifelong dream and a great cause were to come together as one to make a difference. From the great movie Shawshank Redemption, the cry of "Get busy living or get busy dying" kept playing in my head. I was determined to get busy living and to pay the bounty and the success and the goodness in my own life forward.

This is what I thought about and talked about to my wife of then 33 years, to my children and to the mentors in my life, and to my closest personal friends and then finally to the folks at AXA Equitable, for whom I just happened to be the Vice President of Sports Marketing.

"Make sure that you leave the world a little bit better than you found it."

George Martin Sr.

*****

Dianne saw me for the crazy man I was, the always crazy man in her life, in whom she had great faith and trust.

"Once I realized that it was coming from his depths," she said, "once I realized this notion was being driven by his soul and spirit, I knew there was only one place for me to be and that was beside him."

As to my children, they looked upon it as "just Dad being Dad," or as my son Aaron proposed, it was "just another one of his mid-life crises." As to mentors and friends, they were universally supportive.

Being right with Dianne was first and foremost.

Her complete support was absolutely critical to me. If she didn't sign on, there never would have been a first step. As high school sweethearts, we had lived it all together and been through it all together. Having watched me try to conquer the world, she knew me better than anyone, and everything about it had to be right with her. We did not yet have grandchildren, so in that sense the window of opportunity was perfect, a window that would likely begin to close in the not too distant future.

Fortunately, not only was she supportive, she bought in hook, line, and sinker. Almost overprotective of me at first, Dianne stayed on the road with the *Journey* and often walked by my side during the first three months. At one point she even drove the big RV! It took her quite some time before agreeing to leave me to my own devices and return home, where naturally she had to preoccupy herself with something easy like redecorating the entire house.

Getting to do so without me looking over her shoulder seemed the perfect opportunity to tackle such a project.

Somewhere just north of Christiansburg, Virginia, Dianne spotted it as we rounded a curve in the road. There on a rolling green hillside sat the perfect red farmhouse barn with a huge silo. Freshly painted, it radiated light and it was surrounded by a colorful field full of autumnal mums. Dianne said, "Now that takes my breath away, that is just incredibly beautiful." She claimed it as her takeaway picture. While the beauty was everywhere, if I were forced to choose, I'd take the incredible, ethereal sunsets over the sweeping mountains of Western Tennessee. It had me wondering what made old Davy Crockett ever set out for Texas.

As to everyone I approached after Dianne, everyone who mattered most in the immediate Martin world, their response was an almost universal "How can I help?"

And help they did, every single one!

Before approaching my superiors at AXA, of course, I thought it wise to build support and the semblance of a hopefully burgeoning organization. I wanted to make sure that I could get the people who had the right skill set so I could concentrate on the task at hand.

"Once I realized this notion was being driven by his soul and spirit, I knew there was only one place for me to be and that was beside him."

Dianne Martin

First, I called upon those who had played and bled in the trenches with me, many of my former Giants teammates, who immediately came on board, either tangibly or spiritually. The initial group most notably included great ballplayers like Harry Carson, Phil Simms, Perry Williams, Stacy Robinson, as well as one of the greatest coaches ever in the game, Bill Parcells.

Then there were my mentors.

David Jurist, the first kind soul to ask me to work for him at Tanagraphics when my playing days were over, was also the first to agree to be a board member of our *a Journey for 9/11* organization. He helped me to get John Ferguson, then president of Hackensack University Medical Center, to commit to matching every single dollar we raised in providing free services for ailing Ground Zero workers.

This snowballed into getting both Mount Sinai Hospital and North Shore LIJ Medical Center.

Ken Vehrkens, my great friend and the Dean of Petrocelli College at Fairleigh Dickinson University, channeled his energies into marketing, direct fundraising, and organizing a team to physically plot out the course that I would walk.

Two X-factors stared us in the face from the very beginning. First, we could not walk along the interstates, so there would be no getting on

Route 80 and heading west. Secondly, unpredictable winter weather in the north warranted our blazing a trail to the south.

We were destined to walk off the beaten path, on the by-ways, not the highways. We were advised to keep our distance from important governmental facilities, missile sites, etc. and it certainly wasn't going to hurt to avoid mountain climbing in the high Rockies and the potential blizzards there. Ken was charged with configuring our best path.

And then, there was Bill Parcells, who stayed in touch with me throughout the *Journey*! While his personal contribution of $10,000 would push us over the million-dollar mark, his greatest contribution was in teaching me the importance and value of an organizational construct. His coaching influence inspired me and I could hear his voice throughout: "Be prepared, plan, organize, control – establish your rules of engagement, adhere to them, never be late, be unyielding, be perfect, be honorable."

This resulted in our 6:00 a.m. daily meetings, our 7:00 a.m. starts, and our allowing no distractions or headphones or iPods on the road, in the interest of safety and security.

We had a prescribed route that we went over every night. We had a minimum objective every day of 20 miles. I would not let the day end without accomplishing our objective, though that at times took some creative improvisation.

To make it, we had to set targets and goals and deliver on them and in all we did, therefore, we did our best to emulate one of the game's greatest coaches.

"Be prepared, plan, organize, control – establish your rules of engagement, adhere to them, never be late, be unyielding, be perfect, be honorable."

Bill Parcells

I played for the man for a long time and no one in my life ever pushed me harder or demanded more from me. And because he did, he got my best. His tactics worked, leaving me one of his biggest fans.

How often along the *Journey* he'd call and say, "Martin, where the hell are you? You better get the heck out of there and get moving. For God's sake, Martin, get moving now! You won't make it by standing still and pontificating!"

My team, like the Giants in the 1987 Super Bowl, couldn't be beat. Board members included Phil Simms and Harry Carson, David Jurist and Ken Vehrkens, Andrew Giangola of NASCAR, John Kirksey, the Senior Vice President and Diversity Officer of AXA Equitable, Ed Mullins, president of the Sergeants Benevolent Association, philanthropist Joseph Reich, and others.

Among the sponsors were the three world-class medical centers – Hackensack, Mount Sinai and LIJ – Fairleigh Dickinson University, NASCAR, AXA Equitable, Bear Stearns, UPS, Nike, KeySpan Energy, Hunter Douglas, the National Football League, the New York Football Giants, WWE (World Wrestling Entertainment), General Motors, Sprint, Big Blue Travel, Beau Dietl & Associates, Fuchs E. M. S. & Medical Transportation Services, and later, Best Western Hotels.

Each would play a role and contribute in a variety of ways – some, of course, far more than others. I remain grateful to them all, even if their role was just lending a great name to our efforts.

Most importantly, there was the question of building the road team. But it got done, despite my occasional skepticism. How was it, after all, that one close friend of mine, an IT nerd of the first order who was moving on from AXA to do his own thing, agreed to put his own life on hold – even his romance and marriage, for that matter?

As crazy as I am, or as he was, there were to be two of us. Since Lee was to be responsible for handling all of the in-the-field activities and business, he also was the liaison to the support team back in New York.

"Martin, where the hell are you? You better get the heck out of there and get moving. For God's sake, Martin, get moving now. You won't make it by standing still and pontificating!"

Bill Parcells

Then there was our great and generous friend Beau Dietl, the president of Beau Dietl & Associates, the author of *One Tough Cop*, and one of the most respected private investigators and security consultants in New York City, who so kindly agreed to provide ongoing field security. Revolving in and out, someone from Dietl's team would always be with me.

Kevin Fuchs of Fuchs E.M.S. & Medical Transportation Services, another great friend, likewise agreed to provide emergency medical technicians from start to finish. Ed Mullins, president of the NYC Sergeants Benevolent Association, one of our initial board members, also pledged to work with Beau. It should not get lost in the details that what Beau and Kevin together contributed was worth well in excess of $200,000.

Jay Winuk of Winuk Communications, who lost his brother and 9/11 rescuer, Glenn, when the South Tower collapsed, signed on as our national public relations lead. To honor his brother's memory, Jay had co-founded the non-profit organization MyGoodDeed, which successfully worked to establish 9/11 as a National Day of Service and Remembrance. Some 11.5 million people participated nationwide in that day of service in 2012, including the President and First Lady of the United States, Barack and Michelle Obama. The numbers only spiraled upward in 2013, and the anniversary is now the largest annual day of charitable engagement in the nation's history. Jay was to do an outstanding job for the *Journey* with the New York and national media, but he also remarkably maintained ongoing contact with and secured coverage from local press all along our route. If there was a two-page weekly in Podunk, Wherever, he and his team didn't miss it. Winuk's agency got to every editor, reporter and producer from New York City to San Diego, and he was nothing less than a warrior on our behalf.

Then there was the remarkable launch team led by Brie O'Neal, with the assistance of Andrea Juett and my beautiful daughter-in-law, Michelle. Brie organized an array of volunteers from AXA Equitable and our great friend Nancy Pellegrine and her team at Valley National Bank, some of whom were there for the official launch at the bridge and others who were stationed to help with the kick-off event at Hackensack

University Medical Center, and still others who were there to help with the halftime event at the Giants home opener at Giants Stadium.

Tasked with high-profile press events on the same day on three stages – the George Washington Bridge, HUMC, and Giants Stadium – Brie was not unlike a five-star general commanding her troops during a complex invasion.

Jennifer Skor, who Lee aptly dubbed his "Wizard Behind the Curtain," also warrants a grateful mention. She worked daily with Lee revising and updating the schedule, the route, the events, the contacts. If we were to meet anything untoward or challenging on the road ahead, she gave us the heads up. I leaned on Lee constantly, and Lee, in turn, leaned on Jennifer. While far, far away from us physically as she was home-based in Connecticut, it was as if Jennifer, too, were right there with us always.

Dozens of others will be appropriately recognized in an appendix. It includes every single member of the Martin family, I can assure you.

"You are as good as the people who surround you. George taught me to be aware of that," said Perry Williams as Journey began on September 16, 2007. "And then he taught me that if you aren't making a difference for them, you're failing. That commitment to making a difference fostered **a Journey for 9/11.** ***It was behind every single step he took."***

*****

The team acquired some unique adjuncts along the way. When we had difficulty expediting our not-for-profit 501(c)(3) papers, allowing us to fund-raise, U.S. Rep. Charles Rangel first stepped in to help facilitate, and later Rep. Vito Fossella pushed us over the line.

Recently censured by his colleagues, the sadness in Charlie Rangel today seems palpable and tangible, but he vows to stay the course and hold onto the seat that he has held for decades and continue to serve his constituents. As for me, I see only the public servant who kindly served us and we wish him all the best.

While Nike was a sponsor, contributing walking shoes and sneakers and some athletic apparel for which we are grateful, Massai Barefoot Technology, the manufacturer of 'MBTs,' truly stepped in to save us, as they outfitted everyone in-the-field with their extraordinary walking sneakers.

Before trying MBT, every shoe I used left me with some measure of discomfort. But the Masai footwear was like bedroom slippers on! The best shoe, the longest-lasting shoe – on average about 192,000 steps per pair during *Journey* – the most comfortable shoe, we went to San Diego on MBTs. We can't thank Massai Barefoot Technology enough for kindly outfitting us and saving our feet.

Now I venture into the thanks-is-just-too-small-a-word category.

No matter how I phrase it and no matter how many times I say it, it is not enough. It can never be enough.

Joseph and Carol Reich are good souls who happen to have succeeded in life and who live in Manhattan and love their city. All it took for them to do the absolutely extraordinary was to read a small article in The New York Times about my intention to walk across America for the benefit of 9/11 rescue and recovery workers – nothing more. Long concerned themselves about the plight of the 9/11 workers and convinced that both the city and the United States of America were collectively failing them, this remarkable couple after reading the article agreed on a most remarkable course of action and contacted me personally.

They wanted to thank me for what I proposed to do and to personally share their intentions with me, which were greater than I could have imagined. In effect, they were metaphorically plotting to fire me out of a cannon at the George Washington Bridge launch.

They committed an astounding $911,000 to *a Journey for 9/11.*

In telling me, they left me numb. Years removed from the moment, it still leaves me numb. Joseph and Carol Reich read about our plan to raise revenue for and awareness about the plight of the Ground Zero responders, who were the first to stand up for America in the immediate wake of a profound tragedy. The Reichs believed that every single American owed them a debt of gratitude.

What I proposed to do, after all, was nothing when juxtaposed to and laid upon the altar of their sacrifice. But the Reichs saw *a Journey for 9/11* as an opportunity to repay a bit of that debt. No one could possibly have blessed what we were embarking upon more.

Prior to their involvement with me, the Reichs had opened their own charter school in Brooklyn, Beginning with Children, a creative, successful and energized example of what primary education should be all about. At the Reich's invitation, I had the opportunity to visit and speak to their bright and engaging student body prior to the launch. The students kindly presented me with a gift to light my way, a jug full of 911 pennies.

911 pennies and $911,000 to light my way!

The official press event formally announcing *a Journey for 9/11* followed soon after. Joseph and Carol Reich joined me for it, as did my Dianne and members of our family. With the help of the Reichs, we also were joined by then-New York City Chancellor of Education Joel Klein and Port Authority Police Officer Joseph Szczepanski, a first responder, who was facing many physical challenges as a result of his selfless acts on our behalf.

"I had read about it in The New York Times ... read about what a wonderful man intended to do, and my wife and I, who had happened to make some money, wanted to become a part of it. New Yorkers and Giants fans, we embraced George."

Joseph Reich

At the press conference, I remember speaking about the influence that 9/11 had upon us all, and of how it brought us together as one people – united and wholly committed to one another. Flags flew everywhere in America and a nation of people all joined hands as one. But 9/11 had later morphed into a wound that we were reluctant to open up again. Interest in it and even in what it meant to us had waned. I argued that this should not be, and that we Americans truly belong as we found ourselves in the days after the attacks – a people united and willing to dare and risk and sacrifice for one another.

I argued that this is where we needed to be again, back in that place where we longed to be of service to each other, rather than that awful place where we just selfishly worry about ourselves.

Years removed from that day, years removed from the *Journey* itself, I still think that I feel exactly the same way, which is why, I suppose, I have determined to write about it. 9/11 was an abominable, almost incomprehensible tragedy, but it had made – tragically and sadly and even mysteriously made – you and me and our families and our neighbors better people, better Americans. It reminded us that we all – the sea of strangers that we all too often and sadly become – belong to each other and owe a duty to each other.

*****

As we approached September 16, interest in what we were about to do continued to grow. Through the help of Andrew Giangola, we had already planned two NASCAR events along the way, one at the Charlotte Motor Speedway in North Carolina and one in Phoenix, Arizona, and now on September 13, just three days before the launch, WWE embraced *a Journey for 9/11.* Among other things, WWE pledged to keep their 20 million fans advised of our progress. Not to be petulant or unfair, but I have often thought, if only each fan donated a buck.

I'll admit that I was totally unaware of the rabid fanaticism surrounding auto racing, a sport that isn't usually popular with the "Brothers," a.k.a. African-Americans. At the Charlotte Motor Speedway I was one of two honorary guests, along with former NBA basketball sensation Rick Barry. To witness nearly a quarter of a million fans gathered in one location all adorned in their favorite NASCAR attire was awesome, as was being led down "pit row" to see all of the drivers and their mysterious speed demons revving up like hungry tigers.

NASCAR racing facilities are enormous, especially when compared to NFL stadiums. The raceways are large enough to accommodate hundreds of thousands of fans, along with their RVs, SUVs, 5th-wheelers, countless 18-wheelers, and all manner of home-away-from-home accoutrements such as barbecue pits, assorted children's toys and camping equipment. It almost resembles a mobile village during the weeks leading up to the big races.

The ultimate real thrill was having the honor of being strapped into racing legend Richard Petty's No. 43, and zooming around the track in excess of 150 miles per hour. Boy, am I glad that they didn't have an underwear check after that experience. It was exhilarating and nothing short of awesome. And when you factor in the reality that their cars are not made for 6'5," 270 lb. behemoths such as myself, it adds significantly to the notion that if things went wrong there'd be a bit of difficulty getting me out of the vehicle, considering how hard it was just to get me into the required racing jumpsuit, let alone into the car itself.

*****

Little at first had I realized the magnitude of what we were getting into or all of the demands that would be placed upon us. Why, the significance of simply taking the first step on the first day overwhelmed.

Yet, the sea of faces from that incredible September 16th swims back across my mind even now.

Always there is Brie O'Neal at the helm, that toughest of task masters, bellowing out commands, but right there with her are Andrea and Lee and our Michelle and Dianne and all of our children and board members and sponsors. I see Beau Dietl and Ed Mullins and Harry Carson and Kevin Fuchs and Ken Vehrkens, and teams of uniformed police and firefighter brigades and honor guards to see us off, and what appeared to be an army of volunteers in those sharp-looking *Journey* tee shirts.

Later at Giants Stadium, Joseph and Carol Reich were there as well. It took some persuading, as they are not fans of the limelight, but they agreed to make a ceremonial presentation of the $911,000 check there as my Giants embraced *a Journey for 9/11* at a dazzling halftime show.

A lifelong dream, a child's yearning, an idea, and a truly humbling purpose had come together to make September 16th happen, to make this improbable *a Journey for 9/11* happen, an entity and undertaking that was far greater than anything I had ever imagined. It was still going to require placing one foot in front of the other and taking one lonely step at a time, but we had somehow, on the fly, built an organization with a board of directors and a website (thanks to Lee) and a resource team. In what seemed the blink of an eye, Dianne said "yes" and my superiors at AXA Equitable said "yes" (and "we'll continue to pay your salary while you explore our country") and somehow suddenly, there was all of this.

All of these people and all of this stuff, from *Journey* tees to MBTs, to a sharply decorated recreation vehicle in Giants' blue no less, had come together to make my dream a reality. Not only had it come true, but it had transformed into a reckoning, into a cause, into something that was uniquely and purposefully American.

As we entered Arlington National Cemetery, our national sanctuary, you could feel the presence of all of the fallen heroes whose markers bear witness to their great courage and sacrifice. Although we had all seen the beautifully landscaped vistas and the precision-placed white vertical crosses on television, there, up close and personal, we realized that each marker represents an American Hero, whose life was, more often than not, cut short in battle. It takes on a far deeper feeling when seen in person. In parting, I couldn't help but think about how so many were lost in the prime of their lives. Who knew what further contributions they could have made.

8 – 'I WANT A HUG!'

Washington, D.C. and The Commonwealth of Virginia

The Red Knights of the Perryville Fire Department and a group of Maryland State Troopers joined us early on for a welcome and well-appreciated reception, and soon we passed through Baltimore, the home of Fort McHenry, where the valiant defense of our country during the War of 1812 inspired Francis Scott Key's "The rockets' red glare, the bombs bursting in air," on my way to the city where all of our history comes home and where all of it is memorialized, Washington, D.C.

A marching band, cheerleaders and a color guard greeted us at the Friendship Public Charter School when we crossed into "the District," as residents call it, pulling out all the stops to make us feel welcome. As I entered the auditorium, I was blown away to find nearly 400 students dressed in *Journey* t-shirts. Behind the podium arranged for me loomed a moving and dramatically large mural capturing the heroic efforts of our first responders on 9/11.

It had been designed and painted by these young students, and what a fantastic job it was.

In art and song and dress and words, and through youthful and spirited fundraising, these young children were prepared to embrace us in a manner that few ever could.

By the end of that afternoon, my arms were tired from hugging and I was so moved by having looked into the heart of the youth of America and been touched by their apparent devotion to service itself. Child after child, inspired by the 9/11 rescue and recovery workers, spoke to me of wanting to help others in the work that they did. We could well use more Friendship Public Charter Schools, and the great young kids who the school was clearly in the business of molding into young and caring citizens.

The *Journey* had a good deal of business in Washington D.C., including a press conference on the steps of the Lincoln Memorial no less, and another press conference on Reps. Maloney's and Nadler's proposed legislation for 9/11 rescue and recovery workers, legislation that our *Journey* would garner support for and both spiritually and practically advance.

There is no spot in this D.C. that does not stir emotion. We paused to visit the spectacular and solemn Korean and Vietnam War Memorials. Vietnam for me is, of course, personal, as my generation was greatly touched by it – and how emotional it is to take in those 55,000 names.

The new Martin Luther King Jr. Memorial was then under construction, and nearby, of course is the singular Lincoln Memorial!

Upon entry there, standing before the imposing figure of President Lincoln, you are confronted by the words, "In this temple, as in the hearts of all the people for whom he saved the Union, the memory of Abraham Lincoln is enshrined forever." The immortal Gettysburg Address is etched in the marble there, but the document that most moves me, Lincoln's Second Inaugural Address, delivered on March 4, 1865, also is enshrined in the Memorial. And it just doesn't get any better than his stirring conclusion:

"With malice toward none, with charity for all, with firmness in the right, as God gives us to see the right, let us strive on to finish the work we are in, to bind up the nation's wounds, to care for him who shall have borne the battle, and for his widow, and his orphan, to do all which may achieve and cherish a just and lasting peace among ourselves and with all nations."

With the incredible trial of the Civil War finally coming to a close, Lincoln neither celebrated nor hailed victory, nor pointed the finger at nor laid blame upon the vanquished and defeated. So magnanimous and humble, he always saw the bigger picture and never looked upon the rebels as anything but Americans.

Oh Lincoln! I look up upon him there and it's as if he speaks to me about how much better the journey for African-Americans might have been – could have been – had he been around to forge a more viable Reconstruction. The wonder of Abraham Lincoln to me lies not merely in his extraordinary accomplishments, but in how much more he was likely to have accomplished in that second term had he lived. Would less bitterness, less demagoguery, less vitriol, and less hatred have led to less racism, less bigotry, and a far less viable Ku Klux Klan?

I thought largely about the legislation to help the rescue and recovery workers that we were fighting for at the time, our own personal contribution to living history. But the drumbeat of historic sacrifice enveloped me – for how Lincoln sacrificed and King sacrificed and our 9/11 rescue and recovery workers sacrificed.

Sacrifice is at the core of our history.

There is such a pathos and truth in all of this, for our country is, above all else, both the beneficiary and the repository of this always churning legacy of sacrifice.

Would less bitterness, less demagoguery, less vitriol, and less hatred have led to less racism, less bigotry, and a far less viable Ku Klux Klan?

Had we been there just one year later, I would have been dwelling quite a bit upon the fact that Barack Obama, the first African-American president, would soon be residing in the White House. He was elected just five short months after our walk across America concluded.

The next day, October 4, was a journey among a succession of ceremonies. I gathered first with a group of former NFL players, who on behalf of the National Football League Players Association presented *a Journey for 9/11* with a check for $10,000. Among them were Stacy Robinson, Andre Collins and George Starke, a former nemesis I was matched against many times when he was "Head Hog" of the Washington Redskins' once-famous offensive line. The setting was incredible, the company was great, and the contribution, like all contributions, was deeply valued and appreciated. My NFL colleagues also presented me with an Alumni Award of Courage, which I still cherish to this day.

We then moved a few blocks to a promenade outside the Cannon House Office Building, where we had worked with concerned members of Congress from New York to organize a press conference in support of the James Zadroga 9/11 Health and Compensation Act of 2007, or HR 3543, Rep. Carolyn Maloney's bill, co-sponsored by U.S. Rep. Jerry Nadler, U.S. Sen. Bob Menendez and many others, aimed at providing care for all 9/11 rescue and recovery workers negatively affected by their service. Mr. Zadroga was an NYPD officer who died of a respiratory illness attributed to his work at Ground Zero. The symmetry between it and *a Journey for 9/11* was almost perfect, as both the bill and the *Journey* were after the same thing, and we could mutually support each other's efforts.

The difference was that we were reaching out to the heart of American citizenry and to the generosity of a people, while the bill maintained that it was the actual responsibility of that same American citizenry through specific legislation!

By the end of that afternoon, my arms were tired from hugging and I was so moved, in having looked into the heart of the youth of America and been touched by their apparent devotion to service itself. Child after child, moved by the 9/11 rescue and recovery workers, spoke to me of wanting to help others in the work that they did. We could well use more Friendship Public Charter Schools and the great young kids who they were clearly in the business of molding into young and caring citizens.

U.S. Rep. Peter King spoke and then U.S. Reps. Bill Pascrell and then Vito Fossella and then Jerold Nadler and finally U.S. Rep.Carolyn Maloney – Republicans and Democrats. All from New York City or the immediate impacted region, they all pumped the bill, arguing that 9/11 was a national event with national impact and that the consequences of it were a national responsibility.

Concluding the star-studded presentation that day were two distinguished rescue and recovery workers who had been with us from the very start of *Journey's* launch and planning. Their stirring accounts of the actual bitter aftermath of 9/11 were in my opinion gut-wrenching, and had the most profound impact among the crucial gathering and its goals. One, who prior to 9/11 was your typical everyday union worker, recounted that in the wake of his 9/11 efforts, he now must take more than 65 different medications on a daily basis.

Truly, what the 9/11 rescue and recovery workers incurred was selflessly done so on behalf of all of us in the United States, and our entire nation was honor-bound to come to their assistance. I was kindly described as a "hero," an "inspiration," and as "one driven by compassion and dedication."

"George is a true inspiration to those of us in Congress who are working hard to establish a comprehensive federal health monitoring and treatment program to help those exposed to and sickened by 9/11 toxins," Congresswoman Maloney kindly said.

But this gathering was about the bill, and the *Journey* and its purpose, and not about George Martin. People like to paint portraits of heroes and they generally apply the term all too liberally. On the *Journey*, it was all too often applied to me.

I guess this is done because people need heroes so very much.

Just as my walking across America was not heroic, and neither is playing football a heroic act. If you have the skills, all you need do is to apply what is but a gift from God. Neither, too, are trying to make a difference in this world of ours, nor being kind, heroic. It should fall to all of us – each and every one of us – to do the same. Thousands of times along the *Journey*, I spoke of this and added, "If you want to look for heroes, look to folks like the first responders. Heroism is in their DNA. Look to those who are willing to lay down their lives."

Winning support for the James Zadroga bill, which was signed into law by President Obama in 2010, was one of the greatest contributions of the *Journey*, and perhaps its most heroic result.

Later on that ceremonial day, I walked with Dianne along the Mall, between the United States Capitol and the Lincoln Memorial. There was the architecture and majesty of Washington D.C., and the structures and all they symbolize. However sad the news may be from Washington, and no matter the ugly partisan divides nor the sordid unwillingness to compromise, that ground and those hallowed buildings do something to you. Just being there makes you feel that our country is still somehow bigger than our aspirations, even though our leaders all too often come up short.

The National World War II Memorial was a stunning tribute to America's military heroes. With its circular configuration of precisely sculptured individual states saluting the men and women whom they honor, it should make any visitor beam with patriotic pride and reverence. The concentric fountain that adorns the center of the monument was simply stunning to see. The Korean War Veterans Memorial, its eerie life-like statues of soldiers outfitted in their flowing rain ponchos while combing a distant and foreign field of battle, is especially gripping and imposing. In the distance across the Reflecting Pool, the black granite of the Vietnam War Memorial supports the earth with the names of the fallen. Across the Potomac, the U.S. Marine Corps War Memorial in Arlington depicts a stirring moment of national pride. All of them conspire to pierce the heart. The sacrifices of America's heroes come home to you in stunning clarity.

Playing football is not a heroic act. If you have the skills, all you need do is to apply what is but a gift from God. Neither is trying to make a difference in this world of ours nor being kind heroic. It should fall to all of us – each and every one of us – to be willing to sacrifice for others.

Members of the NFL Players Association turned out in D.C. to make a $10,000 donation to *a Journey for 9/11*. To my left are my longtime nemesis from the Washington Redskins, former Offensive Tackle George Starks and his teammate Andre Collins. Presenting the check is my former Giants teammate Stacy Robinson.

After a scary ride at the Charlotte Motor Speedway, I was happy to be back on my feet and named an Honorary Race Official by NASCAR.

Lee Reeves and I take a brief energy break while discussing course corrections and alternatives, which took place on a daily basis.

An impromptu autograph session for Mrs. Marty Beets and her husband, Richard, at their famous and very friendly Pig & Chick, the "Home of Swine Dining," in Rogersville, Tennessee.

Senior Security officer Bill Markowski and I cross a lonely overpass, past a crumbling train trestle, in De Valls Bluff, Arkansas.

The sign and the expressions on the young faces in the crowd say it all. I, too, was amazed at this point. A third of the *Journey* completed, and celebrated in Sawyers Mill, Tennessee.

Paying tribute at the Oklahoma City National Memorial to the 168 victims of an earlier act of terrorism. After respectfully dipping your hands in the reflecting pool, placing them on the memorial wall will forever retain your handprints.

I was brought to tears as I realized that each chair represented a death at the Alfred P. Murrah Federal Building. The smaller chairs are for the 19 children lost that day.

The children were an inspiration throughout the *Journey*. Here I met several kids in a school parking lot in Binger, Oklahoma, home of Major League Baseball star and Hall of Famer Johnny Bench.

Communing with Mother Nature and some magnificent Clydesdales as I passed a horse farm in Tennessee.

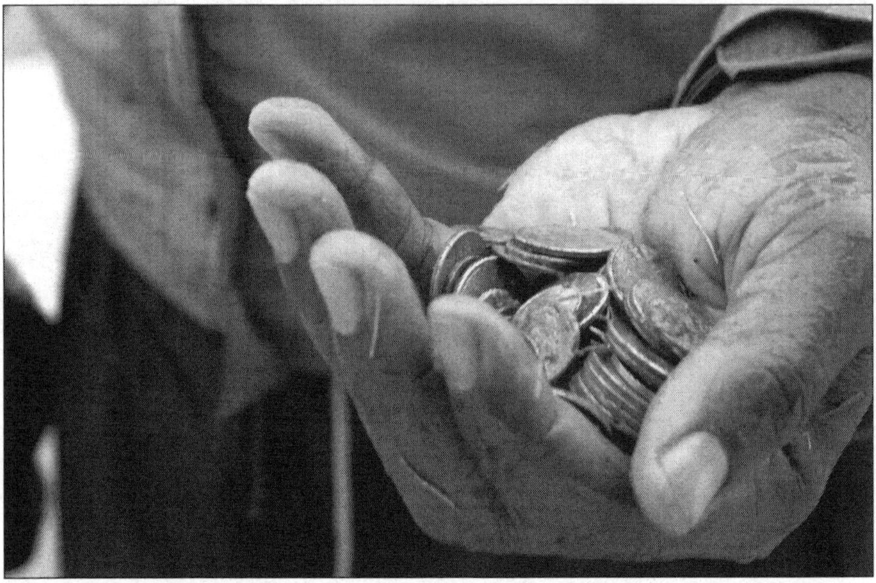

It's not just when you're driving that you should keep your eyes on the road. While walking 3,003 miles, I picked up $196.36 along the way.

Journey brought an unusual Thanksgiving Day for Dianne and me. Rather than hosting football players for dinner in New Jersey, we spent part of the day planning the next stretch of the walk in Tennessee.

*****

Journey crossed the Potomac into Virginia, walking first through Arlington National Cemetery, where an eternal flame burns above the grave of President John Fitzgerald Kennedy, and nearby lies his brother, Robert Francis Kennedy. But it is the endless sea of thousands upon thousands of immaculate white headstones that washes over you and carries you away – a sea of soldiers who served this country, and many of whom sacrificed all for this country, lie there. At Arlington, a sacred place, the spirit of sacrifice overwhelms, leaving you humbled and weak.

It takes your breath away, as truly looking upon the face of sacrifice always does.

You wonder who they were and where they lived and what they left behind and what they may yet have done, these silent dead who lie beneath those immaculate white headstones.

It seems as if every town in the great state of Virginia, truly God's Country, is linked to living history. The path we cut through Virginia took us away from the coast where Washington, at Yorktown, resolved the struggle for freedom we relived walking through New Jersey and brought a victorious end to the American Revolution. No, we rather walked the ground where General Robert E. Lee's Army of Northern Virginia and General George Meade's Army of the Potomac fought a different battle 85 years later. Our path brought us past and through towns and cities or regions with names like Winchester and Richmond and Shenandoah and Fredericksburg and Charlottesville, by places like Yellow Tavern and Cold Harbor and the Wilderness. We walked, quite literally, through a valley of tears with the ghosts of so many other "sons of sacrifice" who gave their all in what Winston Churchill once suggested was the "least avoidable conflict"' in the history of the human race, the American Civil War.

You wonder who they were and where they lived and what they left behind and what they may yet have done, the silent dead who lie beneath those immaculate white headstones.

"God's will," said so many leaders in blue and gray, as it became for Lincoln a sacred reaffirmation of the principles upon which the nation was founded, a rebirth for that magnificent phrase, "all men are created equal." And as redundant as it sounds, the word that comes to mind as we walked with the ghosts through the incredulity and heart of that conflict, again and again, was sacrifice. For no matter what army or side they fought for, Lincoln so powerfully suggested that all ultimately sacrificed themselves for the same cause. They were, whether victims of inherited bigotries or believers in the "divine spark" that lies within all children of God, after all, all Americans.

As we walked, day after day, in the name of and on behalf of the 9/11 rescue and recovery workers, we thought long and hard about where "the all of the American people" were. We were working so hard to effect each and every donation that we allowed ourselves to believe that contributions should just be flowing in.

We also were puzzled because we received such a stunning and moving reaction from people personally as we moved forward, in every state and every region and town, but it was a reaction and reception that just didn't resonate nationally as we had hoped.

*****

We left D.C. and wound up right back in the arms of the firefighters who would be with us all along the *Journey*. For our first few days in Virginia, we rarely moved without an escort from one of them.

I always told the firefighters I am here to give honor to you and your brothers. They would reciprocate by giving me one of their arm patches, which I was always honored to receive. I have proudly kept them all in three large picture frames prominently displayed in my office across from my desk. They continue to represent such an inspiration to me each and every day.

Virginia was a most welcoming state, and I was besieged by roadside visitors in what was the heart and the beauty of autumn. I also was introduced to what became the never-ending roadside mini press conferences and photo ops (and be assured that the picture of me napping atop a picnic table in a rest stop, which Lee likes to show off, was an anomaly).

There was the "take my breath away" countryside of the Commonwealth with its red barns and white silos and pumpkin fields and prodigious oak climbing trees. Virginia has long laid claim to the slogan, "Virginia is God's Country," and its rolling and sweeping lush green hills, cascading brooks, picturesque waterfalls and Rockwellian feel undeniably lend truth to this claim.

It was in Virginia where I first took note that yesterday's homes and barns and farms can be so noble and proud and even beautiful in their dying. Shattered and broken vestiges of what they once were, vines and ivy and bushes and tree branches would so richly embrace them and render them among the reborn. It has always struck me when I go by old dwellings that the structure tells me a story about people's lives: Long-abandoned porches that once held the laughter of countless family gatherings, holiday events, weddings, rocking cradles for new babies, and even waking the beloved departed; farm yards that saw the cheerful play of children growing to adulthood. I'm curious about who their inhabitants were and the lives they lived.

In these homes and farms, we witnessed endless cycle of years now revealing the frailties of wood, brick and mortar, as well as our very own lives. They represent the inevitable decline and demise of us all, the ravages incurred with the passage of time. These irrefutable truths became abundantly evident as we carefully observed the ever-changing world in which we all live. I had requested that the trail car and members of the riding staff capture photos of these road signs, , mile markers and yes, old dwellings as well, and I now in retrospect fondly gaze and relive the poignant message that each silently conveys. At one point we had amassed an inventory of more than 18,000 pictures during our nearly nine-month *Journey* excursion.

Our Virginia "character's character," who really sparked my curiosity, was a middle-aged woman whom we knew only as Sylvia. For the better part of a week, in the Richmond region and below, as we moved south in the direction of Lexington and Roanoke and into the heart of that beautiful state, she kept reappearing. For at least 100 miles, she joined us for just a few minutes at a time, to pamper us with cool bottles of water, fresh fruit and granola bars. We'd say, "Enough is enough. You're making Exxon rich," and she'd respond that, "This is the least that I can do to thank you for what you're doing for all of us in the brief time that I have."

Wherever it was that Sylvia lived, there was no question that she had gone a hell of a long way out of her way for us.

Sylvia almost came to serve as a symbolic enigma, for while we met her early on the *Journey*, she and the kind of interest and goodness she represented stayed with us throughout. The point is that whenever things began to get ragged or dark, the memory of Sylvia – in reality, of the many Sylvias that we met along the way – was a tonic that continually helped pick up our spirits. As I write this, the *Journey* just celebrated the seventh anniversary of its completion and Sylvia is still fresh in my mind, still up close and personal. Her genuine spirit shall not be forgotten.

Alan Ross, an author who walked with me for a while at a time when we were silhouetted by the great Blue Ridge mountains of Virginia and the bluest of skies in the universe, interviewed me at length about both the *Journey* and my previous charitable work. We all enjoyed his company, his ready friendship and enthusiastic response to what we were about. As it happened, he wound up featuring me, as one of three athletes who went above and beyond to serve, in a book that he published entitled *Away from the Ball.* His extensive focus on *a Journey for 9/11* there certainly helped to spread the word, and we owe him a great debt of gratitude. So many Virginians, encountered day after day, seemed to wear their appreciation for its history on their sleeves. Virginians are a proud people and a people who are aware of their unique heritage.

Now I don't know how Jay and Lee and Jennifer Skor, our "Wizard Behind the Curtain," pulled it all off, but we celebrated our 500th mile in a town that was notably called Christiansburg, leaving me to dwell upon the cry of Ralph Waldo Emerson in *Self-Reliance*, "But in Christendom, where is the Christian"?

He, of course, suggested that true Christians are generally hard to find, but in Christiansburg they appeared to be everywhere.

We celebrated the 500th milestone right on the roadside at a green, rolling Virginia field. It lied in a veritable sea of lush, green, rolling Virginia fields.

This one was appropriately framed by a stately red barn in the distance and a prodigious climbing tree, the kind with the sea of branches that your childhood longed for. And yet atop that field, surrounded by virtually nothing but open space, we were joined by an army of school children, who were excused from their ordinary day and bused to meet us. They were accompanied by the now ubiquitous firefighters and legions of Virginia State Troopers, and local officials and moms and dads and grandparents, and even some disabled in wheelchairs. It was just an extraordinary turnout of what was an ad hoc army of kind and giving people who shook my arm that beautiful day until it was ready to fall off.

That crowd of smiling and good people forever remained the face of Virginia to us.

Lee's daily contributions were nothing short of phenomenal. Masterfully, he would have to estimate dates and times of arrival in order to coordinate the events far in advance; manage the participants, the dignitaries, the location and the crush of media. He was constantly on the phone, arranging and rearranging everything from caterings to carpools, interviews to timely exits, from making certain that everyone got on the bus to occasionally throwing me under it. Lee may not know the difference between sports and bad case of hemorrhoids, but he does indeed have professional skills.

I'll now let Lee share the story of his Virginia highlight himself. It features the two of us.

"What was it like? Well there is another Lee story of Virginia to be told. There was Robert E., of course, and me.

On the surface, ours was a nine-and-a-half month odyssey with what most people would consider two people who were polar opposites – the jock and the geek.

George ran the sports marketing division and I ran the marketing technology division for a Fortune 500 company; however, we both had strong Southern roots and shared common values.

The fact that an athlete and a geek had undertaken this adventure became painfully evident on Day One when I barely made it to Giants Stadium and George had to terminate the walk early because I simply couldn't keep up.

It took nearly three months, before I was able to actually keep stride with George, and climbing a mountain in Virginia and having George acknowledge my accomplishment in the form of a fist bump was one of the proudest moments of the trip for me.

And, there we were, two African-American males who were about to walk into the eye-teeth and heart of Klan country."

*****

"Not thrones and crowns, but men," Ebenezer Elliott declared. And women, of course. "Oh God, save the people."

And what people they were!

Each and every one of those met along the way!

Journey was and remains, first and foremost, a story about people – about friendship and relationships and the tens of thousands of people met – some of whom loom very large in the membranes of my memory, but all of whom matter.

It is a story about the friends and compatriots and co-conspirators and teammates and colleagues and associates who backed me and stood with me throughout; and it also is about the inherent goodness of the American people who carried me, while I walked, from the beginning, September 16, 2007 until the end, June 21, 2008.

Earlier, I wrote about the sea of strangers that we Americans all too often and sadly become, as opposed to the one people who serve and stand up for each other that we ought to be – the one people who are inextricably and spiritually and morally bound – the one people who together have the capacity to truly retool and to breathe new life and new light into our fragile and vital American dream.

Today I know who they are, because day in and day out, for the 9½ months and 171 days that I walked across America, I met them, the courageous Americans who are capable of reaffirming and resurrecting the American dream. In schools and churches and town halls and parks and on the road – always on the road – I met them.

During all hours of the day, I met them. In all shapes and sizes, I met them.

Working in every occupation known to human kind, I met them.

By the Atlantic and by the Pacific and in 13 states and Washington, D.C., and on each bank of the Mississippi River and the Rio Grande, I met them.

Good and strong and decent, I met them. Bright and articulate and committed, I met them. Enthused and dedicated, I met them. Gay and straight and black and white and Hispanic and believers of all faiths, I met them. Old and frayed and broken, young and strong, dismayed and determined, I met them.

Those on whom the sun was setting and those for whom it was just rising, I met them.

The salt and soul of America, I met them.

Now, having done so, I know that we are better than that which is daily projected on the evening news, better than we allow ourselves to believe, and oh so much better than that damned reality TV of ours, which purports to be a window through which to touch base with our national soul. Oh, what an outrage that is, an outrage of truly monumental proportions.

*****

In stark contrast to the artificiality of reality TV resides the truth of American greatness within the hearts of ordinary, everyday people. Stereotypes in general represent an idiotic presupposition cloaked in myth, a notable lesson and one that we would experience time and time again out on the unvarnished and unabridged American countryside.

Shortly after entering the wonderful back country of Virginia, Lee and I, being of African-American descent, were acutely aware of the reputation of this particular area of the country being the birthplace of the infamous Ku Klux Klan. Therefore, our historically based suspicions were already on high alert. Were that not enough, earlier in the day we had been pulled aside by a supposedly well-meaning local police officer, who questioned us regarding our presence out on the road. It was more curiosity than a formal interrogation, as he informed us that our presence (meaning Lee and myself) would normally invoke a bevy of "concerned" phone calls from the residents to the sheriff's office, alerting officials that the anticipated invasion was perhaps underway.

Thus far he said, his office had not been contacted to report that "we" were in the vicinity, and he thought that was strangely odd. By the way, he said, "Have a nice day, and be certain to be off the streets before night fall for your own safety."

Well, you certainly don't get greetings like that every day. Call it the locals' version of the Paul Revere-like civic duty of sounding the alarm that something different was coming, and in our case it certainly wasn't the British!

Sure enough, later that day, as luck would have it, an older-model, camouflage-painted, off-road pickup truck, complete with the ubiquitous gun-rack and Confederate flag prominently displayed in the rear window abruptly pulled up behind us, which immediately had us on alert. Now, I consider my-self a rather sizable individual at 6'5" and 265 lbs., however out stepped what looked like the reincarnation of professional wrestler Man Mountain Mike – tag team partner of Haystacks Calhoun, for trivia buffs – complete with a "Duck Dynasty" beard and XXXL bib overalls. Our "Mike" looked to measure a whopping 6'6" tall and only a biscuit away from 350 pounds. In the back of my mind I could quietly hear the *Deliverance* theme jangling its familiar refrain.

I then decided to confront the situation head-on by offering a warm handshake and greeting of friendship. But as I cautiously approach this human version of King Kong Bundy I could see that he was offering no means of reciprocation in return. Gentle beads of sweat were forming on my forehead and it wasn't from the pace of the day's activity. Just was I was in striking distance of Man Mountain Mike, he slaps my hand away and utters the words that momentarily stopped my already nervous heart:

"I DON'T WANT NO HANDSHAKE!" He then continued in a loud and jolly voice, "I WANT A HUG," and gave me a great big bear-hug, literally and effortlessly lifting me off the ground with a Santa-like laugh. I have never been so happy – or relieved – in my life.

"Hello," he said, "They call me Big Dave (Gee, I can't imagine why). I saw you guys on TV last night and I wanted to come out to meet y'all and invite y'all to my barbecue joint." Dared we say NO? After such an unusual and wonderful encounter, one that would repeat itself many times throughout our *Journey*, we had a wonderful day eating, drinking and sharing one another's experiences for the balance of that afternoon.

What a fantastic day that was. Here we were, a group of individuals who could not have had less in common socially, economically and racially, but were together bound by a common event, 9/11, and as a result, any barriers of difference had been bridged forever. We were just a group of Americans, boys out on the town for the day celebrating our commonalities rather than focusing on our perceived differences. Wow, what a concept!

Please stay tuned as there are certainly others.

Good and strong and decent, I met them. Bright and articulate and committed, I met them. Enthused and dedicated, I met them. Gay and straight and black and white and Hispanic and believers of all faiths, I met them. Old and frayed and broken, young and strong, dismayed and determined, I met them.

*****

We are still the same people who rose up as one in the aftermath of 9/11, the same people who took each others' hands and dedicated ourselves to something greater still, the same people who watched in awe as first responders fearlessly went into that horror on behalf of all who fell that day, and their families, and for all Americans.

But who we are, in fact, was determined long before 9/11.

We are still the same people who manned the rugged embankments on Bunker Hill and at Lexington and Concord, the same people who took increased and renewed devotion from Lincoln's *Gettysburg Address*, the same people who stormed the beaches at Normandy and refused to quit at Bastogne, the same people who rose up, after the Depression and the 2008 financial collapse, and refused to be beaten.

We are and we remain a people of hope and a people of enduring faith.

9/11 and its consequences, both good and bad, belong to each and every one of us. But as we deal with the bad and the ongoing threat of terrorism, it is the good that prevails and that drives and that altogether sustains us.

That good is in America's DNA.

In the earliest of Colonial days, the ministers who preached and the documents that gave rise to government and to civil authority were preoccupied with the word, "good." The very propagation of the good was our self-mandate, and our obsession with "good" bore into the soul and sinew of the American experience. It was goodness that was found in the words, "That all men are created equal, that they are endowed by their Creator with certain inalienable Rights." There was great goodness in a *Gettysburg Address* that celebrated a government "of, by, and for the people;" and in Martin Luther King's "Free at last, free at last, thank God almighty, we are free at last."

It is this inherent goodness that trumpeted the Allied advance in Africa and in Europe, and liberated Dachau and Buchenwald in World War II.

Goodness is at the very core of the American experience itself and in our ongoing and sustaining effort to perfect the concept of freedom, an effort that is always challenged and yet one that ever endures.

And it was that very goodness that I met, again and again and again, as I walked across America on behalf of the 9/11 rescue and recovery workers in 2007 and 2008.

We save each other in this life, and with God by our side we also redeem each other. I am forever moved by the story of the firefighters who struggled to take one disabled woman down the steps of the second tower after the first had fallen: the "Miracle of Ladder Company 6." Aware of their grave danger, they refused to abandon her and in the end found themselves in that reinforced structural cavity on the 4th floor, which stayed intact during the collapse. Ironically, it was she who saved her would-be saviors. Yes indeed, we save each other, and with grace, we redeem each other.

I have often been taken by this thought that this is ultimately a book about redemption.

Early on in my NFL career, I also learned a most important lesson. In my daily communications, including fan letters, appearance requests, and the like, there was a note from a boy who introduced himself as a Tomorrows Children's Fund ("TCF") kid, a sick child being treated at Hackensack University Medical Center, who so hoped that I could visit him at his home sometime. I marked and noted it and with all good intentions, placed it aside. As it happened, he lived right next door in a neighboring town to Ringwood in Oakland, New Jersey, so about three weeks later on one of our rare off days, I headed there. But I didn't meet him. I rather spoke to his young and grieving mother who had buried him just the week before.

For whatever reason, this beautiful 10-year old boy looked up to me – me who unintentionally disappointed him – me who failed him – me who took it all so casually – me who would never again assume that a sick child has time – me who would forever after remember the *precious urgency of now.*

We are still the same people who manned the rugged embankments on Bunker Hill and at Lexington and Concord, the same people who took increased and renewed devotion from Lincoln's Gettysburg Address, the same people who stormed the beaches at Normandy and refused to quit at Bastogne, the same people who rose up, after the Depression and the 2008 financial collapse, and refused to be beaten.

That was the world that I walked in with David Jurist, the friend who gave me a brand new automobile and a 25 percent raise before I even showed up at the office for the first time. In many ways, David was a surrogate father and a mentor, who saw what I didn't even realize was in me, and he nurtured it and cultivated it. I spent nine years in Utopia with him as vice president of human resources at Tanagraphics, before flexing my wings and flying on my own to new and greater challenges. Leaving was heart-wrenching for me personally, but as he wanted only the best for me, he made it all so easy.

While focusing on great givers like David, I also think of Joseph and Carol Reich and I have a confession to make, because I actually hung up on him when he first called to contribute to the 9/11 charity. Come on, who wouldn't have thought that $911,000 was a prank? It just doesn't happen every day and my apology to him was, of course, one for the ages.

What great character Joseph and Carol both have. Unfailingly kind and genuine and introspective, they played their life's hand by building their own innovative charter school in Brooklyn and by such things as marching with Dr. Martin Luther King Jr. many years earlier and by remarkably supporting crazy vagabonds like me. There are very few, true and genuine guardians of humanity as I have witnessed, however there's no doubt that Joe and Carol are unquestionably the "real deal."

I played with No. 10, Brad Van Pelt, a former All-Pro outside linebacker during my early years with the Giants. He and I anchored the left side of the Giants' dominating defense back in the day. Understand that playing with is to go to war with and all that noble band-of-brothers stuff applies. You rely upon one another, you give your all for the other, and you either rise up or fall together.

To have played with Brad is an honor that I never took lightly.

Brad Van Pelt had it all. He had great talent and he was blond, blue-eyed and ruggedly handsome. In him was absolutely everything Hollywood looks for – but having it all can be a curse for those who are not grounded or rooted to their own.

Brad, in youthful selfishness, got lost in the party scene and squandered that which mattered most in his life. Later on, he caught hold of himself, but it can be a difficult thing to pick up the pieces and to make amends. I respect him for trying hard to do so and for the courage that he displayed in talking to me about it all.

I mention Brad because the very first day of the *Journey* was the last time I saw him. The illness that would take him not long after was already ravaging him alive, but his Van Pelt smile still won out and carried that day for him.

When Brad first heard about my *Journey*, he told some of our old teammates that it was the kind of thing that they'd expect old George to do, and that it was a classical George maneuver. And when he saw me that day, he actually said, "I wish that I would have known earlier, George. It would have been fun to walk with you."

So, I said, "Join me, Brad. You are most welcome."

But regretfully he responded, "I wish I was up to it, George, but I'll just have to follow you on the website for now and, maybe, catch up with you later on."

And that's how I remember and see him, as ever hopeful and alive and undefeated. Sure, the illness took him physically and broke and destroyed his body, but it never got his spirit, one that will yet, I believe, catch up with me later on.

The vagaries and unpredictability of life impact us all, in that we know that life is unfair and in that it comes for some too young. Unlike Brad, my former teammate Stacy Robinson was able to generously contribute his time and his person to the *Journey*, both walking with me and joining us for celebrated events like the assembly at the Hall of Flame Fire Museum in Phoenix.

Yet Stacy, too, succumbed to cancer just three years ago.

Both Brad and Stacy, in their dying young, loudly remind us all to do all we can for others in the time that we have, which is now. They too, like that cherished 10-year-old boy, remind me of that *precious urgency of now.*

The precious urgency of now should compel us every single day of our lives.

*****

Every day on the *Journey*, we embraced that urgency, as there were miles to cross and people to embrace and hearts to win and service to satisfy. Now, in the living present which – alone – is what we are guaranteed, we – you and I – must continue to do all that we can possibly do.

It was that spirit that launched us on September 16 as we felt the goodwill and good wishes of so many thousands of people at the George Washington Bridge, in Hackensack and at Giants Stadium.

Perry Williams, one of the cornerbacks on our '86 Super Bowl team and a great friend, who has stood with me for multiple causes since, was there at the stadium, and I took his great smile with me on the road. I took also the reassurances of Phil Simms, our Super Bowl MVP and one of our *Journey* board members, a pat on the back from running back Joe Morris, and the overarching concern for my well-being bestowed by our Hall of Fame middle linebacker and my closest friend on the Giants – and yet another *Journey* board member – Harry Carson. They were among the many veteran Giants being celebrated on that opening day against Green Bay and the four who reside most prominently in my memory.

All of that left with me on the *Journey*, as did the ovation of the more than 77,000 fans who welcomed me at halftime and the good wishes of all who joined us at the G.W. Bridge and at Hackensack University Medical Center. I also took another pat on the back from the medical center's president, John Ferguson; and the presentation of the check from the Reichs at halftime and the handshakes from the grounds crew who were waiting with me in the tunnel. I took all of it as I made those first steps out of Giants Stadium on my way across the United States of America.

Every day on the Journey, we embraced that urgency as there were miles to cross and people to embrace and hearts to win and service to satisfy. Now, in the living present which – alone - is what we are guaranteed, we – you and I - must continue to do all that we can possibly do.

Out of all the noise and activity and swirling pandemonium, there were two final and extraordinary people encounters on that beautiful, promising, and oh so gorgeous and sunny day that particularly stood out.

The first, unsurprisingly, was with Harry, who, as you already know, pulled me aside to tell me that if anything happened to prevent me from finishing the *Journey* that he would finish it for me. "That's a promise," he said. "If anything stops you, I will finish this for you, George." He meant it and he wanted, and almost needed, me to know it then.

In every game we ever played, you see, we had a defensive game plan, but should A or B happen to make plans go awry, we also had contingencies.

Leave it to Harry whom I affectionately call "Old Warrior," and he refers to me as "Old Reliable", my fellow comrade in arms, as what I was embarking upon was about to be one of the biggest games of my life, to know that I needed the peace that comes with having a back-up.

And just as I was about to leave the noise and excitement of the stadium behind for the quiet of Sunday afternoon's roads, just as I was exiting the tunnel of my own Giants Stadium, out of all the emotional electricity inside, came the quiet poignancy of the goodness of Timmy Shinn, who likes to do his good deeds in secret, as the New Testament lovingly suggests. A huge Giants fan and owner of a very successful construction company called United Crane who practices selfless philanthropy, Timmy handed me the keys to a brand new, fully loaded Chevy SUV that had been adorned on the outside with images of me and *a Journey for 9/11.*

A great and good man, Timmy Shinn is, but please keep it as quiet as he'd like us to.

The goodness and generosity of people comes in many different forms and guises, and sometimes it just comes from out of nowhere and it stuns you. Timmy Shinn stunned me that September 16th. There I was about to take my first steps out on Paterson Plank Road and over the Meadowlands into the residential neighborhoods of East Rutherford, N.J., where I played for the New York Football Giants, and his overwhelming goodness propelled me like a bullet-pass out of there and into America. Thanks, Mr. Shinn.

9 – THE HEART, OR THE SALT AND SOUL, OF IT ALL

The Long State of Tennessee

Ever onward, from southwestern Virginia on November 6, 2007, we entered the Volunteer State of Tennessee. We would do well to get used to it, for we were going to be there until what seemed to be the very end of time.

No matter where in Tennessee, dusk always seemed to find me walking toward a glorious, low-lying mountain that provided the vista for the most spectacular, heart-thumping and soul-wrenching of sunsets. Each had to be the very handiwork of God, who wanted to remind us, in the most stunning of ways, just how glorious is his creation. There, like Davy Crockett, who was "born on a mountaintop in Tennessee – greenest State in the land of the free," I immersed myself in the sights and sounds and textures of nature, in the rays of sunlight shimmering through white cloud cover or pouring over a black creek or magnifying a spectacle of orange and red autumn leaves. Whether it was the sweeping yellow foliage, a lone red maple by the side of a barn, or the broad sweep of retreating clouds as a storm relented and gave way to the breaking light from the west, I was, in Tennessee, relentlessly introduced to slices of heaven.

One could not help but encounter God there.

I also took away images of log cabins and barren trees in the coming of winter's wind, and of the wonder of a mist that encapsulated mountains, and of the incongruity of a small home with its white peeling paint and its two Confederate flags and its Christmas wreath and a sign above the door with a torn screen that read, "Silent Night, Holy Night."

And at the far end of the state, oh, the wonder of Memphis! I was so moved by this city. It boasted of out-of-the-past plantation-like structures, the mighty Mississippi River, an array of fantastic bridges and engineering marvels, and a long avenue that was everywhere "the Blues'" and everywhere Elvis at the same time. And make no mistake about it, Elvis still lives in Memphis.

But we felt that we were destined to be in Tennessee forever, so long was our stay in the great Volunteer State. We were to spend more time there than in any other state – and it should be noted that more than any other state besides Virginia, Tennessee witnessed the horrific carnage of the Civil War.

We walked directly into those memories in cities like Knoxville and Nashville, and when we passed places so rich in lore and legend like Chattanooga and Chickamauga and Shiloh and Lookout Mountain and Forts Henry and Donelson. In fact, it was at Forts Henry and Donelson where an obscure commander by the name of Ulysses S. Grant and his Army of The Tennessee won the first Union victories, and he earned the nickname of "Unconditional Surrender" Grant – indeed a moniker that would write its own history. Then too, it was at Shiloh – "Bloody Shiloh" – where both sides were stunned by the price paid in the loss of human life, and stunned by the realization of just how unimaginably costly the business that they had unleashed was going to be.

Yes, Tennessee and the Civil War were one and Tennessee cried just as Virginia cried, and you cannot spend time in either state, if your eyes are open, and not get up close and personal with a history so defined by human tragedy. It is a history that still haunts, just as the ghosts we passed by still haunt.

We walked, quite literally, through a valley of tears with the ghosts of so many other "sons of sacrifice" who gave their all in what Winston Churchill once suggested was the "least avoidable conflict" in the history of the human race, the great American Civil War.

A century and a half removed from that war, its history still palpably reverberates. We were, of course, just walking through, but the reminders and signposts stared us squarely in the face. We long walked along Andrew Johnson Highway – Andrew Johnson who was, of course, Lincoln's Vice President, the Tennessee Senator who remained loyal to the Union. Personal limitations, an impeachment trial and a taste for alcohol aside, he struggled to advance Lincoln's reconstruction policies. The legacy of the war is in everything from the names of the roads, to the names of the schools, to the names of public parks and buildings and avenues, and so much more.

Yet, Tennessee's story was ever so much richer still.

In northern Tennessee, well north of Knoxville, we passed a sign directing us to the birthplace of Davy Crockett, who Walt Disney had made known to me as a child. Who among my generation had not been touched by his tragic death – and yes, dare I say it, sacrifice – at the Alamo or by his wholesome goodness and lifelong pursuit of justice?

Next, we walked by a sign that said we were literally standing upon the very site of the Last Stagecoach Hold Up in Tennessee history on October 15, 1882, when Bug Hunt and the Edwards Boys robbed a stage driven by John Rayburn. I did no research on the particulars here but it struck me that child in this country ought to be struck and fascinated by things like stagecoaches and the Pony Express and the Wild West. And lest you think that I have mastered the history of the Civil War, please keep in mind that the entire countryside of the South is strung with historical markers denoting pivotal events that took place at these very locations. Just walking through the hallowed ground that these markers commemorate gives one an eerie sense of the rage, glory, sacrifice and uncommon valor that was the War Between the States.

Then on November 19, 2007, in the middle of nowhere in Tennessee, there on the side of Andrew Johnson Highway was this well-preserved memorial with its own eternal flame. It read simply and only this – "To all who have died so that we may live" – simply this and nothing more. It bowled us over and left me numb. There was no claim of ownership, no belonging, just the poignant power of the words, "To all who have died so that we may live." Thank you, Tennessee.

It was also during this time that I discovered that my senior security guard, Bill Markowski, had a deep and abiding interest in the Civil War. Bill was constantly collecting Civil War souvenirs and memorabilia to take home to his two children after his two-week rotations ended. I found out about Bill's obsession because he was always stopping, photographing and reading intently the numerous markers that lined the side roads near the key historic locations we would pass. So one day I asked Bill why the interest, and he, somewhat cautiously, said he was obsessed with accounts of our history, and that he and his family would visit many such sights while on vacation. I sensed that Bill's initial reluctance was because he felt that I would assume that he was a closet Confederate sympathizer or something, so I assured him that the Civil War had mercifully ended and that I, for one, was pleased and overjoyed with the outcome.

We spent some time at both Long George Creek and Coon Creek in Tennessee. Can you imagine that, a Coon Creek? It is hopefully the vestige of a bygone age. (Then too, in Arkansas, we came across Long George Creek. I had no idea how celebrated I was.)

In Tennessee, our southwesterly pitch would level off and we would begin to move due west. All you need to do is look at a map to realize just how much of our due west was in that one state.

We would visit dozens of schools in Tennessee, just as we did on the entire *Journey*. Schools, especially charter schools, were among the top stops where I gave what were eventually more than 500 public presentations.

The theme of my primary speech was a constant. Again and again, I said that it was not about me, and that we cannot allow the event to supersede the cause, and that neither I, nor Lee, were the real heroes. To walk, to serve, to care, and to put oneself out for others is laudable, but it is not the stuff of heroism. Those who raced into the flaming towers and marched into the smoldering debris after the buildings fell, those rescue and recovery workers, whose health was now at risk, were the heroes for whom we walked. Our mission was to bring their plight to everyone.

For the record, I never took any visit with children lightly, as I did my best to teach them that a life well lived had to be a life of service, and I took strength from their smiles and enthusiasm. I told them that the people you want to respect and emulate are the people that you can call in the most difficult times in your life. And those that we make into our artificial heroes – the noted celebrities and professional athletes of our world – are not among them.

November 8, 2007, was an exceedingly busy day as we walked through a region in northeastern Tennessee that is home to many members of a noted clog dancing team. We also received the key to the city at a local elementary school and visited a local high school town there. To say that we met many unforgettable people would be an understatement.

Our journey southwest on U.S. 11W toward Knoxville brought a most memorable encounter at Volunteer High School in Hawkins County, home of the national champion clog dancing team, the Tennessee Hoedowners. Unscheduled, I wound up scaling a mini-mountainside upon being prompted by a handful of students on a promontory above. I did so because one was in a wheelchair. They were a great bunch of kids, who had been informed by a teacher about *a Journey for 9/11* and a handful had been on the lookout for me.

Again unscheduled and unwieldy, it wound up being one of my longer school visits, as the crowd kept growing and I kept talking football and politics and, most importantly, the importance of heroes like their own teachers, with them.

Receiving the key to the city was a great honor, but we did so humbly, aware that we were not the heroes whom our *Journey* celebrated.

As I left that elementary school where the mayor presented us with the key to the city and began thinking about what it was that made Southern school children different from their counterparts in the North, I was quickly struck by two images, the first of a man sitting on his porch with a rifle nestled between his legs – putting me in mind, I'm afraid, of Lee's occasional references to Klan country.

The second was of an elderly woman in homespun clothes that betrayed her likely impoverished life. The first, thank God, just sternly watched me pass by, and the second, despite her considerable years, appeared likely and ready to tackle me if I did not stop.

As it happened, that elderly white woman, named Tammy Horton, with scraggly and unkempt gray hair and a broad, bright smile that conveyed little or no concern about the great loss of teeth, was not alone. Three young boys and a little girl, looking somewhere between the ages of 7 and 14, stood patiently behind her. From Surgoinsville, she warmly introduced them as her grandchildren and she said that she just had to meet us so that they could see, up close, just what sacrifice and dedication and devotion is.

Tammy's praise for us was so effusive that it was almost embarrassing.

She pointed at us and loudly said, "Look, boys, this is sacrifice, this is what it means to be an American, this is what it means to dedicate yourself to others. And that's how you must live."

Turning to me, she added, "Mr. Martin, I wanted my grandchildren to witness and be a small part of this history."

There was no virtue that this magnanimously kind woman did not attribute to us and beg her grandchildren to ascribe to and to internalize. No effort on our part to dial down what she attributed to us impeded her and, in truth, any effort on our part to do so only added fuel to her fire.

Any "well" we uttered only swelled the wellspring of Tammy's sweet chorus.

For she was truly and sweetly on fire for us and she was almost begging her grandchildren to emulate what she insisted we represented. Her humble and unbridled sincerity both stunned and humbled us, as did her transparent desire to transform these gentle young souls in her care into instruments of good.

My hand was nestled in hers when her appeal finally subsided and her body language invited the bear hug from me that followed. Tammy Horton had tears in her eyes as we thanked her and did what we could to return the praise, which she would not have. As we moved to part, she hurriedly reached into her little black pocketbook, grabbed a $10 bill, and handed it directly to me. I literally said, "No, that's not necessary," as it seemed wrong to take from her obvious poverty, but she assertively cut me right off again. Lee, my ever-present companion, witnessed what was transpiring and quietly whispered in my ear that to refuse her gesture would be inappropriate. That she was teaching her grandchildren a very valuable lesson, one that was far more valuable than the $10 she was sacrificing. Her grandchildren weren't the only ones who learned a very valuable lesson that day.

This extraordinary woman who wanted so to win her grandchildren for kindness and charity, and who would give from her poverty in order to do her small part to light a candle and lift the darkness. Her profound act of kindness, generosity and civic responsibility had as much of an impact upon me as did the tremendous generosity of Joe and Carol Reich. This encounter remains to me as one of the most powerful and moving interaction of the entire *Journey*. It serves as my personal anthem of a *Journey for 9/11.*

Ever onward, on November 6, 2007, we entered the Volunteer State of Tennessee. We would do well to get used to it, for we were going to be there until what seemed to be the very end of time.

Time after time I have dwelled upon the fact that poverty knows generosity and that those least able to extend themselves are far more likely to do so. Of course, there are those with plenty who do so as well, but there is a gaping disparity, as the impoverished are ever so much more likely to give what they do not have and the rich are less likely to give what they do have.

Sure, there are so many exceptions to the rule, like our Reichs, but a rule it seems will remain. This grandmother, whose poverty certainly knew generosity, was one of the more larger-than-life characters encountered on the *Journey* and certainly one who stayed in our hearts throughout.

Later on that same memorable November day, already memorialized by the grandmother and the Volunteers, we met Richard and Marty Betts, the owners of the Pig & Chick Restaurant in rural Rogersville. They invited our party of five to a great dinner that night, where our money was not welcome. We went back for breakfast again the next morning and they again picked up the check. Our EMT, George Diaz, then had a dental emergency and it was they who got the dentist for him, they who paid all the bills, and they who easily lured us back for dinner again.

In fact, we frequented "The Home of Swine Dining," the Pig & Chick, for a record five straight days, running up through November 12, 2007, and the Betts repeatedly caught up with us on the road as well. They, as much as anyone met on the *Journey*, literally laid out a red carpet for us and showered us with small town or heartland of America love. Topping it all off with a cash donation, in the end, that was over the top!

Their relentless insistence upon serving us pumped me up and inspired me so that I left them feeling as if I could have walked forever.

On November 15th, we enjoyed the company of Captain Tom and a crew from the Morgan County Sheriff's Department at Captain Tom's Hickory Smoked Barbecue; on the 21st, we visited with the Smyrna Rescue Squad; and on the 22nd, we had a memorable walk with locals from Carthage, Melissa and Darin Taylor, all a prelude to a special Thanksgiving Day celebration.

On Thanksgiving eve, the simple sight of a worn old white clapboard house with chipping and peeling paint struck me, as it was decorated with a bright new red, white and blue American flag, so staking its place in history. The contrast between the house and the flag was poignant, suggesting to me that out of all that is broken and coming apart, there is still the brightness of our flag, and so too of our future. To the extent that we cloak ourselves in that flag, there is hope. For both the tattered homes it dresses and for you and me.

As I stated earlier, Thanksgiving had always been a special day for Dianne and me, who began a tradition of taking in the lonely hearts as far back as my first season with the Giants in 1975, when we invited all my teammates who were without family and alone for the holiday to join us. Over the years this tradition took on a life of its own, often with upwards of 15 players and their significant others joining the Martin family to celebrate this most American of holidays. After the Giants years, our Thanksgivings continued to be about more than just the Martins, and we found other needy people with whom to share our bounty. My long-standing charity, Minority Athletes Networking Etc. Inc. ("MAN"), would offer turkey, stuffing and all the fixings to as many as 500 seniors in Paterson, New Jersey, a tradition that was started by none other than Mr. Harry Carson himself.

Thanksgiving, therefore, had always taken on special meaning for us. We were just a Thanksgiving people, a Thanksgiving family.

So on this 2007 Thanksgiving, in the heart of central and endless Tennessee, we hooked up with Girl Scout Troop 1540 in Carthage, near Nashville. They, with the support of their families, planned on preparing and delivering Thanksgiving dinners to the elderly shut-ins and indigent in the area. It seemed like a great way for us to warm up for our own meal later in the afternoon, and oh what an early afternoon and memorable Thanksgiving it proved to be.

It all reminded us that there is much more to this sacred holiday than football, pictures of Pilgrims and Indians, Snoopy, the Cat in the Hat, and of course, the Macy's Thanksgiving Day Parade!

Lee, better than I, recalls the details of a situation early that afternoon that seemed destined to get out of hand prior to my arrival. He remembers the small white house with the chain link fence and the broken shutters and the hysterical family inside who were frantic because the police had just shot their dog. Lee told me that folks in the neighborhood were all screaming and yelling at each other and the aggrieved family was crying, and feelings, both pro and con about the killing of this dog were freely flying. Lee maintains to this day that my arrival and the simple word that the captain of a Super Bowl champion was there immediately helped to calm the waters and restore a modicum of peace to a situation that the police were previously unable to control. Why that is, I'll never entirely understand, but I do remember visiting the family who lost the dog and sympathetically talking to them about their loss, for there are few among us who haven't lost a dog. They were poor enough to be on our delivery list, so it was good to offer them Thanksgiving dinner, but they felt poorer still for the loss of a dog they loved, a dog who sadly had committed the apparent sin of terrorizing certain neighbors.

The most memorable visit for me that afternoon was, however, with a gentleman who had to be well into his 80s, who lived alone, and who appeared extremely frail and broken. We arrived there all caught up in our good-deed doing mode, wrapped up in our own goodness and generosity.

But as we walked into his humble little house to set up his meal, we noticed an array of faded black and white photos of him and his deceased wife on a mantle, along with pictures of a young and vibrant Marine who had served his country, our country, in World War II. In one, he was pictured crisply saluting an officer. Our attitudes immediately took a course correction as we talked to him and learned that he lived through the horror of Iwo Jima, where he had watched many brother Marines fall.

We arrived there thinking, "Good God, we never want to be in this guy's position. We never want to be poor, old, and sadly, so very alone like him." But then you spot that handful of photos and the humanity comes rushing through and you are stunned, because you realize that this feeble, old, poor, lonely guy sacrificed himself for you. The wheels turn as you dwell upon the fact that he is to be honored rather than pitied. You are transformed by his quiet dignity, by what he paid forward for you in another lifetime, and by the "Once a Marine always a Marine" spirit lurking in the sinew of his proud soul. We were, therefore, moved and humbled to realize that our own Thanksgiving should become a celebration of him, of this old man from Carthage, Tennessee, who was being momentarily embraced by our goodness, but inevitably left to his solitary loneliness.

Deo Gratias and thank you for your service, I thought.

Leaving him to his turkey and to the stillness of his now-lonely life was difficult and bittersweet, for he had stood up for something and delivered for us and there he was almost forgotten by the nation and people he so proudly served. He was also one of the people we were walking for, a first responder from another time and another war. This old soldier was the single most memorable person I met on the *Journey.*

In Nashville, of course, we walked past the history of country music in the Country Music Capitol of the World. Our steps took us past the Grand Ole Opry and the Nashville Sound, and Dixieland Heights and the Rock Country Bar & Grille, and the Cadillac Ranch and red-and-white trolleys and one mighty big component of the soul of America. Lest we forget, this good old country boy's teenage roots may have been solidly grounded in the heart and soul of Berry Gordy's Motown, but the origination of my music appreciation was unquestionably anchored in country.

Yes, I said country. Jimmy Dean's "Big Bad John," Walter Brennan's "Old Rivers," and of course the original African-American country crooner Mr. Charlie Pride's "Is Anybody Going to San Antone," among many others, have a prominent and cherished place firmly affixed among my 5,000 song iPod collection.

Do we have a problem?

*****

Then there was Casey Jones Country Village and a tribute to railroading history; and I was fascinated by the downtown street we walked along in Waverly that housed the Humphreys County Court House with its own Liberty Bell and a mountain-sized, fresh Christmas wreath, an old "Main Streets" Americana theatre that happened to be playing *Fred Claus*, along with a pharmacy that was right out of *It's a Wonderful Life.* It was late 2007 and there we were, journeying for 9/11, through a downtown that was right out of a 1930's postcard. We were in the midst of living and breathing history.

At this point I feel a strong compulsion to remind the reader that although these wonderful and yet tangible memories stream seamlessly in retrospect, each and every one was acquired one arduous, solitary step at a time. They're an accumulation of events that are the result of repeated blisters, sore and constantly aching muscles, and an endless ocean of sweat and bitter determination on a daily basis. These memorial snapshots were not attained in the casual confines of automobile travel nor the expedient luxury of any modern mode of transportation, but rather were the result of the most basic and rudimentary form of human travel – walking!

The next couple of weeks, leading up to Christmas, generated a familiar whirlwind of what became established as the usual – a great visit with the guys at both the Dickson and Jackson Firehouses and with the locals at Carl's Perfect Pig Barbecue & Grille in White Bluff, and with the patrons of an auction that we held at the Pig Pen Lounge. Then there was a time with the young children at "Our Peaceful School," or the Parkview Montessori Magnet School – and with the middle school gang in Dickson – and with the older students at J.D. Leftwich High School in Magazine, Tennessee.

The above speaks to two truths. First, we visited with students of all ages always, and second, that pig and pork and barbecue form the single-most identifiable food staple in the Deep South. You can't travel a mile without coming across one kind of barbecue joint or another.

The "Holy Trinity" down South was barbecue, pork – and the Lord Jesus.

And there is, sadly, nary a salad to be found.

But then, you spot that handful of photos and the humanity comes rushing through and you are stunned, because you realize that this feeble, old, poor, lonely guy sacrificed himself for you. The wheels turn as you dwell upon the fact that he is to be rather honored than pitied.

The wheels turn as you are transformed by his quiet dignity, by what he paid forward for you in another lifetime, and by the once a Marine always a Marine lurking in the sinew of his proud soul.

The daily grind of averaging more than 20 miles from sun up to sundown can extract a monumental physical and emotional toll on even the very best of us. Couple that with the endless public interactions both scheduled and impromptu and it can weigh heavily upon one's fortitude over time. Which is exactly why we incorporated a "one day in seven" restful recovery plan. A rather divinely inspired equation, which we wholeheartedly adopted.

We had several unforgettable gatherings with people in mid-December. Certainly, our incredible Sunday morning with the wonderful and welcoming parishioners of Lee's uncle's church was among them. His 84-year-old uncle, we noted, wore the struggle of the civil rights movement on his face, and oh, what a gentle soul he was. December 13 was an especially good day. Local guest walkers included Robin Parker, Pam Autry and Austin Cowan, who joined me for about 10 miles prior to a reception conducted by the Carroll County Chamber of Commerce, which preceded the Hollow Rock Police Escort to our 1000th mile celebration with the enthusiastic students of Hollow Rock-Bruceton Central High School, serving Hollow Rock, Bruceton and Brownsville, Tennessee. With Christmas in the air, it proved to be quite the celebration.

Then on December 17, we enjoyed a great visit with the patrons of the Olde Country General Store at Casey Jones Village in Jackson, where they conducted a local radiothon for us that heralded their own native son, Lee Reeves. The wizard behind this effort and one of our *a Journey for 9/11* heroes was the energetic and ingenious Deborah Shaw Laman, the marketing director of the store, who engineered a slew of productive programs and activities. She was assisted by Mayor Jerry Gish, who gathered in a circle with us and local firemen and led us in prayer, and by Wendy Isom of the *Jackson Sun,* who described our walk as "a labor of love."

Together, they raised more than $26,000 which was, by far, our largest single daily total out on the road.

While we passed much that was falling down or breaking down, I did, on December 18, make particular note of the touching site of a thoroughly rusted tractor that was complemented by a barn that half fallen-in and an old shed that was literally covered in brush. I wondered who last rode that tractor? When was the last time that fresh hay was carried into that barn? What happened to life here? Ours were questions in search of history and understanding, and we asked them of ourselves and of each other, again and again, as we strode forward. Each empty farmhouse or dilapidated barn or rusted gas station begged the same questions. Each had untold stories to tell. Each was wrapped in mystery.

To the extent that we cloak ourselves in that flag, there is hope. For both the tattered homes and for you and me.

Then on December 19, in Covington in Tipton County, we encountered another recent piece of history, the birthplace of '70s R&B singer Isaac Hayes, who was born amidst the cotton fields in the tin shack of his sharecropper family, something that I can so directly relate to, as my Dad, too, was a sharecropper.

Somewhere between Jackson and Memphis, I got that now near-infamous call from my dear coach and mentor, Bill Parcells, right in the midst of a freezing rain storm. He, among many other talents, is a master at timing things perfectly. Phrasing things pretty well, too, and always preferring to call me by my surname. This is the essence of what he said: "Martin, are you still in Tennessee, Martin? You got to get the hell out of there, Martin. You've got to get moving. You don't want to get caught in the snow and ice there." Sage advice from my coach – though, as they say, a day late and a dollar short! The ice was all around us. But Bill's approach was always sheer genius as it was part motivational, part harassment, and always calculated. Bill can sometimes be just like that old-school magical medical elixir, castor oil. You know that it's good for you and that it almost always works, but it's always pure hell to swallow.

You have got to love my coach. I sure do.

Then the stately southern mansions out of *Gone With The Wind* were upon us, as were the incredible, beautiful bridges that connect the Memphis of Tennessee and the ghost of Elvis to the West Memphis of Arkansas and the spirit of B.B. King. History, I was increasingly discovering, is not merely to be found in the names and events gone by, but in the buildings and structures that surround us and in the music of our lives, and in the songs that we sing and in the movies and shows that we watch.

Memphis is history on parade – the structures, the architecture, the homes, the cafes and bars, the music. I was first taken by King's Blues Club and that old 1950s-era Pepsi Cola sign that dominates the background. The blues and B.B. King are everywhere, and the names so many Memphis institutions are all in harmony. There's Mr. Handy's Blues Hall and Superior Bar and The Blues City Café, and The Pig on Beale and B.B. King's Company Store, and the Blues City General Store. Everywhere, there's the blues and B.B. King and large pictures of Elvis and cafes that never close, as the music never dies.

There also was the incongruity of my being interviewed by a local TV station at Jefferson Davis Park, of all places. I, an African-American son of a sharecropper, who was born in the still-Jim Crow South, was the subject of a press event in the president of the Confederacy's park, in what had been the heart of his slave-holding Southern aristocracy. I thought then, as I do now, that we just can't make stuff like this up – and it just doesn't get any better than this.

There I was, in Memphis, being escorted by a phalanx of friendly police officers, right in the heart of Klan Country, where they used to hang uppity "niggers" from the limbs of trees for sport.

I can't leave Tennessee, where we spent the bulk of November and December, without giving a shout-out to the wonderful men and women of the Memphis Police Department, who met us on the morning of December 21, on what was a sun-scorched yet high-cloudy day, to escort us over the mighty Mississippi River. With us, in great numbers, from morning through night, they were just fantastic.

Crossing the Mississippi as we were finally exiting Tennessee represented a huge milestone for *Journey*. NFL Films would occasionally send out a crew to record our achievements and report on our progress to our faithful followers. Raul, who was part of the NFL film crew, was fast becoming familiar with our team, and he and Lee were always giving one another strategic updates. That particular morning the *Journey* team was very excited as we had conquered the crossing of the widest state in the union, and to cap it off we were all anticipating our celebratory crossing of one of the greatest natural landmarks in America.

Because the bridge that we would be using was a major thoroughfare, Lee had made his usual meticulous arrangements with the local highway patrol to escort us safely across into Arkansas. Coordinating two different state law enforcement agencies and an NFL film crew, and all the while making certain that my pace and progress were unabated so there were no unexpected delays, was something that Lee masterfully perfected, though it slightly goes against my nature for normal greetings and cheerful salutations to be cut short or abandoned altogether for the sake of expediency.

Starting out the day with the intense stress of absolutely precise timing places incredible pressure on you, and can be a needless and worrisome burden if you are not aware of the consequences.

A word to the wise: Never allow a motorized escort to take the point, because despite your very best intentions, you cannot maintain pace with a moving mechanical object. Always be the lead sled dog in that case. After briskly meandering through the prescribed Memphis route at an elevated pace, we reached the entrance to the bridge and the celebration began. We were more than a bit exhausted, but Bill, Lee and I all high-fived one another and the police sirens and truckers' boisterous horns all rang out with acknowledgement of our hard-earned achievement.

That was an extremely special day. But after the excitement and festivities subsided, reality set in as it had upon leaving Giants Stadium in the New Jersey Meadowlands, and the ever-looming "miles to go" once again prescribed our marching orders.

*****

Memphis is history on parade – the structures, the architecture, the homes, the cafes and bars, the music.

There's a sidebar that I want to share now that is important and telling, for as Lee said so often as we prepared for the *Journey*, "Two black men are about to take a long walk into the heart of Klan country."

At the beginning, to be honest, our perceptions were skewed and outdated, and all of our rudimentary fears and pre-conceptions proved to be unfounded. We met with nothing but the inherent goodness that is rooted in the American people. We met with appreciation and gratitude for our mission generally, and with kindness and gentility for us personally. Every day, we met and encountered this. In overwhelming numbers, in the hotels, the restaurants, the schools, the town halls, and on the road, we met this goodness.

There was quite a difference between the way the Memphis police treated us and the way in which they treated Martin Luther King in another harsh day and time.

Day by day, in the moment, there could be hundreds of quick introductions or hellos, explaining why I did a poor job processing names. In the moment, there was no thought of a book, so I spent my time extending gratitude and goodness in return and not on record-keeping. I processed the events, the settings, the emotions, and all of the global and macro stuff, but only rarely the names. I wish that this were different now, but what matters is that I internalized their goodness – their overwhelming goodness – to share with you, because that is what was captured in abundance.

I'm not suggesting that skinheads or neo-Nazis are non-existent, but I am suggesting that they are not at all representative of who we are. And I am further suggesting that goodness and decency prevails.

There are, we know, people who still, with blind bigotry and hatred and in sublime ignorance, hold onto Klan sentiments, but there is no longer a Klan Country. It, like the great, pre-Civil War plantation economy and slavery itself, is long "gone with the wind."

We had thought that the farther we got away from New York City, the less people would care about our *Journey* and our cause, but we discovered exactly the opposite. We were delightfully wrong and as we went through the process of finding out just how wrong we were, it lifted and raised us up. It took us higher and made the work that we had to do easier. It made our steps lighter.

We met with nothing but the inherent goodness that is rooted in the American people.

A quick anecdote to cement my point. Shortly after our arrival in Arkansas we had just passed a sleepy little rural town whose name escapes me at the moment. What matters most is that as we were exiting the town and proceeding along a fairly deserted highway, an SUV filled with young white adolescents came screeching by us at an alarming speed, then they abruptly began screaming and yelling at us and came to an abrupt halt.

I was a little alarmed, to say the least. Their shouts were barely decipherable as at least six young adults got out of the car and started running headlong toward us. Again, please understand that in the historical context I am accustomed to this could have signaled only one palpable conclusion. I was about to soil myself from the sudden rush of fear as I slowly began to understand what they were saying. "It's him, it's him, let's go, come on guys, let's go, it's really him."

Thinking I was about to be the guest of honor at an old fashioned PICNIC, for which the original derivation meant the very worst for blacks, I was petrified, only to find out that what they had in their hands were not guns and knives, but rather pencils and pens. What this overly enthusiastic young crowd wanted for themselves was simply a rare celebrity autograph.

Unbeknownst to the young men, because I hid it so well, I was shamelessly embarrassed, so I did what I usually did in situations such as that and blamed the entire overreaction on Lee. What are friends for, after all?

In truth, I was so pleased and pleasantly shocked that these kids had no concept of color or bias, but only wanted pictures and autographs of a person that they were simply admiring. How's that for progress?

Afterwards, Lee and I privately had a hearty laugh about the entire situation, along with a much needed shower as well!

*****

By Faith Alone Though a Nation Under God

Let's face it. I don't think that I ever could have made it without God being there to give me that gentle push or prod whenever the need dictated. There were times when the wind blew so mightily that it almost lifted my defensive end frame off the ground, and all that separated me from the four and six and 18 wheelers brushing by me was twelve inches of shoulder and a little stripe of fading white paint. The cars would blow by me at breakneck speeds while the ice pellets pummeled in the Smoky Mountains or the sun blinded me in Devil's Canyon.

In those moments where Lee left my side to quietly attend to business in our ever-present *Journey Mobile* or trailer car, the loneliness of the road would take me. When it was just me and the machines blowing by, or just me and the vastness and, more often than not, the beautiful spaces surrounding me, prayer was how I breathed. God was there to provide 53-year-old me with the health and strength with which to finish, and the peace of mind that would enable me to unlock the joy and the purpose within the venture in the first place.

There were times when the wind blew so mightily that it almost lifted my defensive end frame off the ground and all that separated me from the four and six and 18 wheelers brushing by me was twelve inches of shoulder and a little strip of fading white paint.

Everything about the *Journey* couldn't help but put me in touch with that something inside that was just bigger than me. The purpose was bigger, the people served were bigger, the people met along the way were, the country was, the capacity to serve was. It all was. It all was of God to me. In Him and through Him!

As to engaging the natural beauty and God words just fail, for that is where He is made manifest. What I witnessed daily and over and over and over again were sights that literally made me want to drop to my knees. In the magnificence and bounty and spectacular beauty of this sacred land, there is God. In every sunset, there is God.

In Virginia, somewhere below Skyline Drive and in the Shenandoah Valley, there is a well-landscaped, lush green farm on a series of rolling hills. It had a wrap-a-round porch with huge swings and no less than a dozen rockers. There in the center of the property was the most spectacular climbing tree that I had ever seen. Branches, enormous branches, magnificently twisted and turned and intertwined while reaching upwards, ever higher and higher, for the heavens. As proud a tree as I have ever seen, it was to me more than the mightiest of cathedrals or quaintest of churches, a testament to the wonders of a God who gave us all of these unbelievable gifts, of a God who never boasts or brags, but yet daily props the stuff of wonder and inspiration in our laps.

In those huge, uniquely interwoven yet seemingly disjointed branches, I saw our human family, for though seemingly disjointed, so too are we uniquely intertwined and made one.

Prayer was how I breathed.

We met the cross, the universal symbol for suffering and sacrifice, and for extending oneself, even unto death, on behalf of another, everywhere we went.

It is my belief that all of us in life, no matter our faith, are our brothers and our sister's keepers. It is my belief that we all, each of us, belong to one another.

I believe that life requires each of us to pick up our own crosses and to sacrifice, so as to become the redeemers we are destined to be.

This belief has everything to do with the life that I have tried to live and with the example that I have tried to set. It is behind every charitable endeavor in which I have engaged, behind every organization that I have founded, and behind every single step that we took and every mile we walked on *Journey*.

Often, we would pass by a synagogue as well, where the Star of David would be depicted, that ancient and beautiful symbol of Judaism, the inverted triangles or hexagrams that were the protective amulets of a people who had known much suffering. Occasionally, we also would pass by a mosque, the house of worship for the faithful people of Islam. Both were reflections of the rich religious as well as ethnic diversity of our people. As the demographics changed, however, and we left eastern megalopolis and ventured into the heart of the Bible Belt, those steeples with the crosses clearly predominated.

I believe that life requires each of us to pick up our own crosses and to sacrifice. This belief has everything to do with the life that I have tried to live and with the example that I have tried to set.

On November 1, the 46th day of the *Journey*, a sweet autumn day and now well below the Skyline Drive in Virginia, we passed by a horse farm on an off-the-beaten-track country road. While the colors of the leaves hadn't yet fully turned, the promise was in the air. Speaking of air, amid the picturesque scenes that were so often prevalent in this region of the country are naturally teeming with a variety of livestock. Very often we would encounter a cattle truck, and if you have never had the pleasure of a fully-loaded cattle carrier passing you out on the open road, please do yourself a favor and pass on the opportunity. There is nothing, and I mean nothing, more foul and aromatically disgusting than a fully loaded beef wagon dispensing its signature odor along the roadside. It just so happened that I had a ringside seat on many such occasions. Yuck! So much for being a country boy.

Everywhere we looked, the scene, so pleasant and easy, smacked as if it were the inspiration for Norman Rockwell's America, complete with the barns and the silos and the white fences and the horses and the cows and the family dog. Coming on up over a rise in the road, there was a quaint, inviting church up ahead, with its white clapboard and stained glass. As we rounded the bend and came closer to the church, I could read the bold lettering on the message board out front. It read. "Our friends, trust in the Lord with all thine heart."

Reflecting upon what we were doing on the *Journey*, I remember thinking to myself, "You know, I think we are." Never been one to take church message boards lightly, I think that they are posted just for me.

We'd walk through towns of what appeared to be no more than a few hundred souls to save that had main drags that consisted of a tiny café, the smallest of general stores and three different Baptist churches.

Only in the Bible Belt and only in America!

We'd also be taken aback by the subtle ironies of sorts that are commonplace in the Deep South, where generally friendly and engaging people happen to revere two commodities, their Bibles and their guns. So, it wasn't uncommon to see on Highway 66 South a sign like "Welcome to a Guntown community and a Church of Christ community," hallmarked by the Guntown Community Church of Christ at Rogersville, Tennessee. Similarly, I ran into a young teenager not far from there who wore a t-shirt that proclaimed, "We'll shoot 'em all dead," with an image of many poor creatures of the forest, while wearing a cap that exclaimed, "All for Thee, Jesus."

Again, ironic to those in the Northeast, but not at all to those in the South!

On December 10, I gladly detoured back to New York City to accept the Heisman Humanitarian Award – presented annually to "exemplary selfless individuals who give of themselves to serve those less fortunate." Sure I was proud – only the second recipient of that great honor. And it included a $15,000 contribution to *Journey*. Accompanied by my PR director Jay Winuk, we participated in a press conference prior to the awards dinner to address the media, and then attended the Heisman ceremony at which Tim Tebow was announced as the first-ever sophomore to win the legendary Heisman Trophy.

Toward mid-December, in the heart of a Tennessee that seemed to have no end, cold rains and sleet often fell and biting winds cautioned us of winter's prospective bark. But we were warmed by the Christmas lights on pine trees and homes, and on Main Street storefronts and old movie theaters, and on warm neighborhood restaurants and rustic town halls. Let's hear it for the pine wreaths with bright red ribbons that color the world. Let's hear it for the lights that proclaim the "Light of the world" and the pines that signal eternal life.

On the morning of December 12, Lee and I had the honor of meeting with the faithful parishioners of Blair's Chapel CME Church, where Lee's Uncle George is a member. Upon arrival, it was easy to tell that the church was thriving. It was pleasant, well appointed, and made you feel, as churches often do, both at home and in the company of God. The parishioners, predominantly African-American, treated us wonderfully and we were blessed to be able to talk to them about the

Journey in the bright light and spirit of Christmas and the holiday season.

Interestingly, Lee's Uncle at age 96 just happens to have a remarkable and telltale face.

In which lay the haunting memories of untold suffering and denial and of the rugged and roughhewn and bitter struggle for freedom. In it were the cries of anguish and the rivers of tears, but also the strength of a Rosa Parks and of a Jackie Robinson and the pride and dignity of a Martin Luther King and of a Malcolm X. Right there, in his beautiful face, there was this window bearing witness to a magnificent journey of faith.

Let's hear it for the pine wreaths with bright red ribbons that color the world. Let's hear it for the lights that proclaim the 'Light of the world' and the pines that signal eternal life.

Faith is to hold dear and to abundantly value that which you cannot see or touch, but yet believe – with your whole heart and whole soul.

Journey daily affirmed my own faith. The reason was obvious. In everyone who I met, on the road or in schools or in local restaurants or at town halls, God was making Himself known to me.

We are all, I deeply believe, of one body and of one loving God.

We walked through the heart of the southern Bible Belt, where people may be poor and wanting or hard and loud or tired and worn, but where faith is part and parcel of breathing. As we got well into the trip, I started to pay more attention to the church sign boards that we passed, like the one that we read in Virginia, and to make an occasional note referencing the prayer that they hoped would give we passers-by some guidance.

On December 17, the signboards on both the Union Missionary Baptist Church and the Zion Hill Baptist Church outside Jackson, Tennessee, both said, simply, Romans 10-9. So typical of the South, you might have had difficulty spitting between these two churches, but that's what you so often find there – communities where it seems as if there must be more churches than people.

'One God, so many trees'

Not exactly on the tip of my tongue, Romans 10:9 reads, "If you declare Jesus is Lord and believe in your heart that God raised Him from the dead, you will be saved." Yes, but for the record, I stand with the good Rabbi in Mitch Albon's wonderful book, *Have a Little Faith.* When asked why he is friends with the priests and so fascinated with eastern religions, he points out that God didn't create just one tree. He created the oak and the poplar and the willow and the maple and the redwoods, all beautiful and all of which raise their branches towards the heavens, as if to God. "One God, so many trees," he said. One God, he suggested, with so many portals or pathways or roads that might be traveled in order to reach Him.

In short, I also have faith in other faiths. All people of goodwill who love and who serve and who seek to do good are upheld by the God of us all.

At the Church of Christ the Eternal in Binger, Oklahoma, beyond Cherry Dale Creek, there was a Romans 6:23 sign board. The creek was a sight to see, and beyond it lay contrasting and well-manicured farm fields of brown and green. The missive was not at all unlike the one received back in Tennessee, "For the wages of sin is death, but the gift of God is eternal life in Christ Jesus our Lord."

There in Binger, in the Malt Shop Cafe, we were swallowed up by a bunch of young teens, most of whom were wearing Kids in Christ tees. On the back of one was Psalm 23, the ever and always appropriate, good for any journey, so special Psalm 23, penned by none other than King David himself.

"The LORD is my shepherd; I shall not want. He maketh me to lie down in green pastures: He leadeth me beside the still waters. He restoreth my soul: He leadeth me in the paths of righteousness for His name's sake. Yea, though I

walk through the valley of the shadow of death, I will fear no evil: for Thou art with me; Thy rod and Thy staff they comfort me. Thou preparest a table before me in the presence of mine enemies: Thou annointest my head with oil; my cup runneth over. Surely goodness and mercy shall follow me all the days of my life: and I will dwell in the house of the LORD forever."

There are many prayers, beautiful prayers, but few like Psalm 23.

On February 11, we visited the Oklahoma City National Memorial & Museum and participated in a moving presentation. It is the kind of moving site that invites prayer. So pray we did.

Not more than five days after visiting Oklahoma City, we walked past Sawyer Lake, a pretty little lake where there was a Camp Conference and Retreat Center. That was Camp as in a "Camp Meeting" or religious revival. Its sign carried the words of Isaiah 58:11 – "The Lord will guide you always; he will satisfy your needs in a sun-scorched land and will strengthen your frame. You will be like a well-watered garden, like a spring whose waters never fail."

Finally, a biblical reference that was entirely *a Journey for 9/11* appropriate or specific! A much-needed one, I might add, for little did I know just how sun-scorched we were soon going to be in the deserts of New Mexico and Arizona. A well-watered garden, we would most certainly need to be.

Just past the camp, there was a quaint little church, The Church of the Nazarene. The sign in front, the kind that could truly get my attention, read simply, "Come Home."

Wherever we may be, we're not done yet and we are always on our way back to or in search of home.

Later that February, in a forgotten spot in the loneliness of Oklahoma, in the most desolate of places, miles from and miles to nowhere, I was stunned to see a sign rising in the distance. Closer and closer I walked until I could make it out. "God Bless America," it read. As I approached it grew bigger and bigger still.

God Bless America! In red, white, and blue!

A most familiar but always welcome prayer that resonated all the more and all the louder because of its seeming isolation!

In late March, deep into New Mexico, we passed the white adobe Kenna Community Church. Now, we passed many churches, but what made this one unusual is that with all the motorcycles out front it looked like the Hells Angels or the *Sons of Anarchy* themselves had stopped in to visit. When we saw them exit they sure looked the part, but I like to think they had stopped at this little church to pray or to offer something up or maybe to thank God, rather than as a cynic among us suggested: to shake down the local pastor for a share of the Sunday collections.

There on the side of the Kenna Community Church was a small board with John 4:14, which says "But whoever drinks of the water that I will give him will never be thirsty again. The water that I will give him will become in him a spring of water welling unto eternal life."

I love the idea of the waters that usher in eternal life, but my thoughts, having just entered the desert, were much more parochial and mundane, as I kept daily crying out ""Water, water, water!" – as in Poland Spring or Dasani or Great Bear. The higher-order implications, however wonderful, had to be put on hold.

"But whoever drinks of the water that I will give him will never be thirsty again. The water that I will give him will become in him a spring of water welling up to eternal life."

Amidst the low-lying hills and water-starved earth of southern New Mexico, there was a small, nondescript, little home in what was the Hondo Valley. Upon approach, what made it unique was a sign that read, "God Bless this Place." But what made it even more interesting was the simple sign directly in front of the front door - John 3:16. That was it and nothing more!

Now John 3:16 I knew by heart, the ringing and stirring, "For God so loved the world that He gave his only begotten son, that whosoever believes in Him shall not perish but have eternal life." That is for Christians, a precious and certain truth, a cornerstone of faith. But it is, for all, I believe, a promise of the extraordinary measures that God will go to in order to bring us home.

As we entered Las Cruces, New Mexico, roughly around April 14, the sign that welcomed us to town read, "The Faith Chapel welcomes you to Las Cruces – Just Follow the Ten Commandments."

By the way, Las Cruces sat on a low-lying New Mexico mesa, flat as a pancake, so flat that it was hard to imagine all that much sin taking place there in the first place.

One of the primary reasons that the spiritual aspect of *Journey* resonates so profoundly is the quiet solitude and meditative repose the open road provides. But other events on the road cause your thoughts to reach heavenward as well. In New Mexico an incident occurred that I have never shared with my wife Dianne for fear that she would then be able to crystallize the inherent danger of the open highway. One afternoon Lee and I were traversing along a road cut into a tall mesa with steep hillsides flanking the two-lane highway, as we had done hundreds of times to this point. Suddenly, a rather large panel truck happened upon us as we were walking against the flow of traffic, as we occasionally did. Normally, we would never allow ourselves to be positioned between oncoming traffic and an unclimbable hillside with absolutely no viable outlet should the unthinkable ever happen, as it seemed to be happening right then.

The truck's driver must have been momentarily distracted as he entered into the curve and he was actually riding the outer white line, which allowed absolutely no margin to maneuver for Lee and me. We both froze as we had immediately realized that we had nowhere to go. At the very last second, the driver looked up and saw us in his path and corrected the truck's trajectory, causing it to fishtail back and forth across the road divider.

Talk about having your life flash before your eyes! Lee and I knew that we had dodged an enormous bullet, and thankfully realized that divine intervention must have interceded. Events such as those only serve to reaffirm one's faith in a higher power.

Just a couple of days later, on April 16, we entered the little town of Akela Flats, which well could have served as the set of an old western movie. There on the main street stood the Akela Flats Pistol Shop. The signs upon it, signs that definitely come National Rifle Association-approved, read, "Guns," then "Big Guns," and then "Bigger Guns." But what made their straightforward, we-don't-beat-around-the-bush-here appeal to gun lovers everywhere was the guy exiting the shop in one of Lee's pictures with his "God Loves You" T-shirt. Only in America!

We are, whatever the contrasts and the knock-down, drag-out ironies, a nation of believers indeed, in both guns and God. Sadly in guns!

In the heart of nowhere in an Arizona desert and in the Arizona heat, again miles to and from nowhere, we stumbled upon one of those memorable and powerful people's memorials. On a huge rock, the number of American soldiers killed in the Iraq War was tabulated. At the crest of the rock, there was a small American flag and a cross.

The cross again reminded me that out of suffering, we; and that out of sacrifice, we; and that out of the deaths of our innocents, we; and that out of this all too harsh and bitter service, we; and that out of the richness of our faith, we approach the great leveler in our lives and reach for deliverance and peace.

We walked, or rather, baked, in the deserts of New Mexico and Arizona for some time, feeling the 113-degree heat and calling out again and again for more water, but only four days after we came across the Iraq memorial, we encountered another lost-in-nowhere, lonely celebration of faith. Here, there was a semi-circle of large rocks. Atop each rock was a white cross. There were no words, just the stunning white crosses.

We are, whatever the contrasts and the knock-down, drag-out ironies, a nation of believers indeed, sadly in both guns and God.

Coming upon monuments like this, the making of which took brawn and strength and time and faith in the cross, never got old.

We also came across oh so many makeshift memorials on the road where people had obviously died. Of course, we didn't know their names, but we felt the love of those who left the now-dry flowers and worn cards and small mementos that lay on the ground. Each roadside memorial gave us pause, for as John Donne long ago reminded us, "Ask not for whom the bell tolls – it tolls for thee." Lee took a picture of one such forgotten memorial with a discarded Coke can lying upon it – or rather, I thought, desecrating that which was sacred about it. We removed the Coke can. It was the least we could do.

I remember that in the last 5 miles of the *Journey*, we passed quite a few churches, one of which had Acts 2:12 posted in a 4-inch by 12-inch message board on a front door. I wouldn't look it up until long after, but when I did, I laughed to read what was but one component of a depiction of Pentecost when the Holy Spirit descended upon the Apostles.

It read, "Amazed and perplexed, they asked one another, 'What does this mean?'"

For indeed, we asked that about the *Journey* from time to time, and people of faith ask it always.

For we are not and nor have we ever been a perfect people. We are not, and sometimes we find our beliefs and our answers only in our doubting.

Yet, while not perfect, we are capable of doing perfect things and I believe *a Journey for 9/11* was one of them.

It was rooted in faith and manifested in faith!

Interestingly, the tall steeple and cross from the Acts 2:12 church hovered in the background in dozens upon dozens of pictures as we walked our final miles.

I never doubted but that God was there to see us through and to bring us home.

Each step along the way, we had been uniquely blessed and upheld.

For we are not and nor have we ever been a perfect people. We are not and sometimes, we find our beliefs and our answers only in our doubting.

10 – *THE HEART (AND COLD) OF THE COUNTRY*

Three Dollars and Seventy-Eight Cents

After a Christmas reprieve with our families, we rambled through Arkansas in what was little more than two weeks, in what was a stark contrast to the near two months spent in the Volunteer State. In the dead of winter, our roadside visits slowed down and there were fewer school visits planned, so we made great time. I do, however, have a great memory of being accosted by 30 to 40 middle school children when a bus pulled over one afternoon. I made a mental note at that time of the abundance of patriotic sweatshirts worn by them, emblazoned as they were with "Semper Fi" and American flags and the U.S. Army advertising slogan, "Be All That You Can Be." a reflection of the prevalence of military families in Arkansas.

There were sacrifices that had to be made as we crossed into Arkansas. Maybe the one and only thing that we knew of the history of Arkansas going in was that President Bill Clinton had served as governor there before winning the presidency. We had hoped to visit the William J. Clinton Presidential Library and Museum, but it was well removed from our route in Little Rock and our schedule was tight; in retrospect, a painful and regretful decision that I harbor to this day.

The one day of great ceremony was, I believe, January 12, 2008, when we visited the Arkansas State House, Little Rock City Hall, the Little Rock Central High School, where the fierce battle over school integration ended in victory, and the Arkansas Fallen Firefighters Memorial. Mayor Mark Stodola of Little Rock read a proclamation, gave us the key to his city, and then spent time showing us around, while Mark Knowles of the Little Rock Fraternal Order of Police presented us with a check for $1,000. The *Journey* itself presented a check to the Fallen Firefighters Memorial fund. Stand-up people, the "salt of the earth," it was an honor to be with them on a memorable and busy day.

Additionally, our masterful and award winning PR guru Jay Winuk had arranged for *Journey* to participate in a travelling 9/11 memorial, the "Tree of Life" exhibit of the National EMS Memorial Service Organization. It was an elaborate network of intertwined branches, with each bronze leaf bearing the name of fallen EMS worker nationwide who died in the line of duty, including four Arkansans and those who perished on 9/11. The exhibit was coincidentally being displayed in the magnificent Arkansas State House. Lee took a picture of me with the leaf honoring Glenn Winuk, the late brother of Jay Winuk. Glenn was a volunteer firefighter and was doing what came naturally to him and his brother firefighters on that fateful day, as he rushed "to serve and protect." I later came to realize that this was not merely a fitting national theme of police officers and firefighters, but rather a literal doctrine of fervent belief that all in uniform have pledged to do – protect and safeguard the everyday freedoms that you and I enjoy freely. This exhibit spoke so clearly and movingly to the fact that 9/11, like our *Journey*, and like our history, belongs to all of us. I and the entire *Journey* team were honored to attend and pay tribute to such heroes. After all, that was the very essence of *Journey*.

We also got to see up close and personal the remarkable and moving National Historical Site dedicated to the Little Rock Nine with their bronze statues in a monument directly across from the state capitol in Little Rock, in what was perhaps our most stirring engagement with history. What I embraced and absorbed there was a gut punch and a reckoning with a personal history that uniquely belongs to me – and of which, I am, in many ways, so very proud.

It played out in September of 1957, when nine brave African-American students agreed to be the first to be integrated into the segregated, all-white Little Rock Central High School. The mere fact that this was to occur was the result of the famous and monumental 1954 Supreme Court decision in Brown v. Board of Education, which found the longstanding Jim Crow segregationist policy of "separate but equal" to be "inherently unequal." The Little Rock Nine first attempted to enter the school on September 4, 1957, when I was but 4 years old, but were blocked by the Arkansas National Guard, which had been ordered there by Governor Orval Faubus to deny their entry.

Can you even imagine that?

President Dwight D. Eisenhower – ironically my namesake, my middle name is Dwight – responded by sending in the 101st Airborne Division of the United States Army to see to it that the students were admitted and to provide for their safety. Eisenhower also nationalized the Arkansas National Guard to take control of it away from the governor.

What an extraordinary moment in history. Under death threats and in the face of horrific racist demonstrations, nine brave, innocent African-American children agreed to enter a high school where they were not wanted and where they would encounter hateful and spiteful treatment for years, to move this nation forward and change history. According to the obituary of Jefferson Thomas, one of the nine, on September 25, 1957, they "marched up the steps of Little Rock Central High School and into the history books," in the company of the 101st Airborne.

Imagine the need to have soldiers accompany children to school.

I walked through the bronze statues memorializing each of them and I read their powerful quotes reflecting upon what they achieved together. And no, the ill treatment they suffered did not end on September 25th of that year, or anytime soon thereafter. These nine would literally be tormented for years, in bathroom stalls and quiet corridors and empty classrooms and cafeterias, wherever they could be cornered. The school would close a year later, when a vile, segregationist governor pulled out all the stops in an attempt to turn back history. His attempt to replace the public schools with private ones that could deny African-American children entry ultimately failed.

Under death threats and in the face of horrific racist demonstrations, nine brave African-American children agreed to enter a high school where they were not wanted and where they would encounter hateful and spiteful treatment for years, in order to move this nation forward and change history.

But they led and others everywhere followed, and change was effected and our nation grew for the better on the backs of the Little Rock Nine. I think of Jackie Robinson and of what he suffered and I take some comfort in the fact that at least he had a team of men who largely had his back. But not these kids! They were essentially out there on their own, facing all that bigotry and the hatred it evokes.

Melba Pattillo Beals, one of the Nine, wrote a book, "Warriors Don't Cry," for warriors they were, and President Bill Clinton presented them each with Congressional Gold Medals after both houses of Congress voted to give them the accolade in 1999.

To say that I was moved is an understatement. For that was the same world in which I grew up. Even when my family left the Deep South and Jim Crow for sunny, liberal California, we rode into our new town, past a welcome sign that read, "Let's keep Fairfield White." The first thing – the very first thing – I learned about my new town is that they didn't want me there.

On the very next day, Nick Lane and Andrew McMahon of AXA Equitable flew in and joined us for a day of walking and champagne dousing at the 1,290th mile. I think we focused on 1,290 because we wanted to record a celebratory moment with my AXA employers, whose corporate address was 1290 Avenue of the Americas, New York, N.Y. Additionally, Kim Jones, a sports announcer with the New York Yankees' YES Network at the time, walked along with us as she would later film and broadcast the entire festive occasion.

I was struck by the Arkansas' wetlands and its relentless sea of brown dirt and muddy creeks, and by the fact that I once got lost there in a sea of mini Grand Canyons. There I came across an old, long-abandoned windmill on a late afternoon as the sun toyed with it in a way that rendered it magnificent. Darkness and light fought for their place and the beauty to be found in black and white was made known to me.

It was there that I indeed discovered the excellence that Oklahoma promised me, an array of small towns in which neighbors took responsibility for one another, an array of small towns where community was actively manifested.

They quite literally raised the barns for one another. They fed, clothed, housed, and supported as needed.

*****

No-man's land, by the way, is real. It does exist.

We walked through it in the extreme western part of the state of Arkansas. As the state trooper who accompanied me said, "This is truly unchartered, unclaimed land in that it falls into no municipality whatsoever. There is nothing for miles around here," he added. "There are no stray dogs and no birds here either – at least, I've never seen any. Nobody wants a part of this." You can include Lee and myself in the club as well.

Yet there, beautifully and wonderfully, waiting for me at a barren intersection that was bounded everywhere by dirt and choppy clumps of green weeds for as far as the eye could see, was a young boy. No more than 9 years old, he had ridden out on his bicycle to meet me with his treasure, the savings from his piggy bank – all of $3.78 in a brown velvet Crown Royal bag, or as great a gift as one can imagine. It was truly a fortune.

Moments as great as this virtually paralyzed me, for I wondered where they came from – how did our message get to this boy and why did he respond?

In truth, he didn't even know all the details. He told me that his teacher had told him that our country was attacked and that people were hurt and that other people were walking across the country to get money to pay the doctors to help them. His parents apparently told him that it was OK to take off from school to meet us. Walking alone with a state trooper that day, I decided to forget the day's mileage objective and stay with this young boy who would be a man. I also made a larger contribution in order to save his, carefully preserved as it remains today in the original brown velvet bag. God bless him and his goodness.

Oh, how he touched my heart. That young boy had the power to keep me smiling for days.

Goodness gives way to goodness. The next day that boy's Dad, a trucker, found me in his 18 wheeler to thank me for being so kind to his son. He also handed me a $20 contribution.

Yes, goodness always gives way to goodness. Incidentally, this was not an isolated act; such selfless encounters permeated our *Journey*. And we were always duly careful to log and issue receipts during each and every such encounter. Professionally executed, always professional!

For instance, "Mr. Smokey," a rather vagabond character who drove an old beat-up Caddy that sounded like the remnants of a World War II Sherman tank, and was filled with, you guessed it, cigarette smoke. During the pleasant roadside exchange, at which time Smokey generously contributed to our cause, my eyes teared up as we spoke. The staff thought I had become emotional as a result of Smokey's generosity, but instead it was from the barrage of smoke that I was suffering as I leaned towards the open window of his automobile. After a brief encounter, Mr. Smokey apologized for the amount of his contribution then abruptly drove off. Believe it or not, about 30 minutes later, here comes Smokey once again and presented us with a larger contribution. He said that he had gone back into town to the bank because he was ashamed of the original amount that he had given. What a guy.

Then there was "Florence Nightingale," another nickname that we conjured up for lack of a better or official description. She was a beautiful anonymous donor, who, as we passed one another while I was exiting the hotel one morning, shook my hand and acknowledged our mission, and placed $200 cash in my palm, and quietly walked away. When I inquired as to her name, as was our practice, she simply turned and flashed a warm benevolent smile and said "God Bless" and continued walking. You just can't make these stories up.

Such improbable encounters were actually commonplace throughout the course of the *Journey*, and will forever remain pleasant memories.

*****

By January 15, 2008, we found ourselves standing under the bright blue "*Discover the Excellence* – Welcome to Oklahoma" sign, and not a day went by in Oklahoma in which I failed to meet great people.

On January 31st, I simply stopped for a water break in the vicinity of DJ' s Burger Barn, where a gentleman, John Clark of the *Spiro Graphic* in Spiro, Oklahoma, also stopped and introduced himself. He kindly invited me in for a glass of iced tea and there went any further progress on that very cold winter's day.

I had been looking for an excuse and talking football and life with him and other patrons for the next few hours was certainly a preferred alternative to 10 degrees and 50 mph headwinds. The place struck me as a genuine slice of down-home Americana, as locals gathered there, I was told, almost daily, to shoot the breeze, and as my new Burger Barn acquaintance T.J. Adams said, "Stay in touch with our neighbors so as to be sure of being there for those in need. Here, we place a lot of value upon being there for one another and picking each other up when any of us are down. To us, community is much more than a word."

The locals from Spiro told me that they were impressed with my intimate knowledge of local Oklahoma football (What can I say – once a football junkie, always a football junkie), in that I was aware of some of the boys from Oklahoma, playing on the collegiate level, who had a genuine shot at making the pros. But I was much more impressed with the folks I was speaking with. I had the honor of meeting a band of brothers and sisters at a nondescript local eatery in what most Americans would look upon as the middle of nowhere, who considered being a good neighbor absolutely essential. It was there that I indeed discovered the excellence that Oklahoma promised me, an array of small towns in which neighbors took responsibility for one another, where community was actively manifested. That's middle America, where everybody knows everybody else by their first name. It still exists.

They quite literally raised the barns for one another. They fed, clothed, housed and supported one another as needed.

At the Burger Barn, they actually apologized to me, because cash flow was then an issue for them and there was no ready money to contribute to our cause – but, they said, "We can damn well feed you and your crew for as long as you're in the neighborhood." After one of the most enlightening and endearing afternoons and early evenings on the *Journey*, not to mention some of the most delicious burgers that we had tasted so far. I presented a Giants football to T.J. Adams, Lisa Akins and David Todd, patrons of the Burger Barn, residents of Spiro, and shining examples to all who long to lead selfless lives.

The ebbs and flow of conversations were always delightfully simple. After the usual inquiries into the origin of the *Journey* and perhaps delving briefly into my NFL experience, the conversations would take a normal course and we would respectfully discuss various common aspects of our everyday lives. There was no magic potion or standardized backgrounds needed to initiate meaningful dialog, just two or more people, who once we were partially unmasked, pleasantly discovered that we'd have far more in common than we did differences. I sincerely wish that more people would take a chance to know one another in this manner.

Now T.J., you have to understand, was no ordinary Joe. T.J. was in his late 80's, still drove his old pickup truck throughout the state and thoroughly enjoyed horseback riding. I took an instant liking to him and I dare say that the feeling was mutual. T.J. was a man of fierce independence and became an immediate inspiration. Even though he was slightly built, weighing all of perhaps 145 lbs., he seem to always wear a pleasant smile that instantly welcomed strangers, and a personality such that one would swear we had met in friendship in a prior life. It's strangely odd that when people, regardless of preconceived notions, snap judgments or other negative predilections, simply accept others at simple face value, the results can be astonishing. T.J. and I instantly hit it off and I felt as comfortable talking to him as I would my own father. That's rather remarkable.

While visiting the Oklahoma Oil Museum the following week – a simple, one-floor, white building, filled with old fire engines, the earliest and crudest of drills, and pictures of "black gold" or "Oklahoma tea" rising into the air – I had an informal *a Journey for 9/11* gathering with folks from Tecumseh and Seminole, places bearing witness to our Native

American roots. There, I was pleased to present pairs of worn Nike sneakers to Seminole residents Ed Herber and his young granddaughter, Kaylyn.

*****

I might note at this point that I went through 27 pairs of MBT and Nike shoes on the *Journey* – two pairs for each state, on average. They were still in pretty good shape for casual wear, but under the rigors of my walk and my defensive end's size and weight, their structure tended to go a little soft when I needed full support.

I also used 413 Nike socks, drank 1,860 bottles of water and sports drinks, and found roadside coins totaling $196.36. As the saying goes, it pays to keep your head down.

I walked for 171 days, covering 3,003 miles in 5,206,082 steps. We calculated that by me actually counting each step in a linear mile in Tennessee using a GPS. The length of my stride is dependably the same with each step, and when plowing ahead without distractions I did a mile every 15 minutes. Once we had the actual number of steps per mile, Fairleigh Dickinson University students did the final calculation after *Journey* was completed.

As testimony to the benefits of regular exercise, I lost 41 pounds on the *Journey*, usually eating a bowl of Raisin Bran and a banana in the morning, soup and a turkey or chicken sandwich for lunch and energy bars throughout the day for nutritional snacks on the road. I had to keep my energy up.

We walked until dusk, but not in the dark because of the safety factor. Often, the team drove the route the night before to check on the location of sidewalks, which unpredictably would disappear on us, and potential hazards and difficult terrain. The route was planned to avoid high-range mountain walking, though there were plenty of hills and lots of adverse weather.

Somewhere southeast of Oklahoma City in February, the temperature was 13 degrees and we were walking into 50 mile-per-hour headwinds, as the prevailing winds in the Sooner State generally flow from west to east. As a means of combating the extreme elements we put the trailer car out front in an effort to "draft" or create a vortex that might make it easier to walk. It just didn't work. Our goal each day was to walk a minimum of 20 miles and we'd generally average 4 miles per hour, distractions aside, but on this bitterly cold day, we netted only 1.4 miles during the first hour, way off our usual pace.

Highly frustrated, I wisely called it a day and we took a welcome break at a Denny's Restaurant, always a pleasant oasis for me. As it was, we were going to lose the day, so we gathered the team to discuss the situation and see if there were any options to consider, as the weather pattern was to be unchanging for the next few days. There, in an inspiring moment, I recalled an old story about a tractor-trailer that once got stuck in an underpass along the highway. Having exhausted every idea to free it, the adults who gathered there at the scene were at a loss, until a young boy curiously surmised the situation and suggested taking the air out of the tires. It was that simple. Just a little thing called wisdom!

We, too, needed to figuratively take the air out, so why not work with the elements rather than against them. The preference for cyclists who routinely bike across the country, is always to travel from west to east, thus allowing the constant westerly wind to serve as an ally as opposed to an adversary. What I determined was to ride westward out the 20 miles and walk back in an easterly direction toward that day's starting position, with the bitter wind and the bright sun at our backs rather than in our face. We called it "Reverse Progression," and it was what became the solution for us on days that demanded extraordinary measures. We would cover the exact same route, but only from west to east rather than east to west. "Reverse Progression" saved us on a lot of windy days, as well as severe days when the setting sunlight was intolerable as we neared the scorching desert.

God's television set, you see, never shuts off and, for me, a simple country boy from Greenville, South Carolina, what i was to see of our land, up close and personal, quite literally and daily, blew me away.

*****

I detoured briefly to Phoenix, Arizona, to watch my New York Football Giants defeat the New England Patriots in one of the most exciting and stunning Super Bowls ever. There, I had the pleasure of gathering with Giants executives and enjoying a mini reunion with quite a few of my old teammates, but the greater pleasure was escaping to the stands in the second half, where I got to enjoy the company of and to catch up with the youngest of my three sons, Aaron. I have always enjoyed spending time with my children, and especially Aaron, better known as Mac.

However brief, it was an escape for the ages and we appreciated Giants' President John Mara's recognition of and pitch for *Journey* in the midst of one exciting locker room celebration. Part of the Giants' family, he noted what we were trying to accomplish for the 9/11 rescue and recovery workers. John, who is cut from the same humanitarian swath as his father, Wellington, before him, was simply a saint of an ally for the entire *Journey* excursion. Additionally, Giants' longtime employee Joann Lamneck, the Community and Alumni Relations Manager, was allowed to assist *Journey,* serving as the only female board member of our organization. She along with the long-time Giants' employees Allison Stangeby, Vice President of Community and Corporate Relations were simply invaluable to our mission.

*****

In Oklahoma, history was to be discovered in the fading Coca Cola signs behind the rusted gas tanks on byways that the interstate had passed by. In a town like Fort Coffee, it lived in the memory of Colonel John Coffee and the Seminole War, and in Choctaw Indian legend and lore, and in a minor Civil War passion play that played out there. But in a place like Binger, Oklahoma, history lay explicitly in the fact that one Johnny Bench, the great Cincinnati Reds Hall of Fame catcher, had been born there. Every welcome sign, every water tower proudly proclaimed, "Home of Johnny Bench."

It is important to note that along our entire route west, we regularly witnessed the dying of a once flourishing rural America, where small farming trades gave way to corporate farming; and as we were not walking on the interstate, we also bore witness to the death of local industries that chased the interstates, from gas stations to restaurants to small retail shops. We passed by so many dead gas stations, rusted and peeling and crying out for their own time and place in history.

Wednesday, April 19, 1995, witnessed the destruction of the Alfred E. Murrah Federal Building in Oklahoma City by domestic terrorists Timothy McVay and Terry Nichols, which was the forerunner to New York's 9/11 tragedy. Modern history in Oklahoma largely settles upon the Oklahoma City National Memorial & Museum, which again can't help but leave you shaken and numb. The long brick steps, the one tall tree, the cropped circle, the bronzed arched chairs – large ones for adults, and the smaller ones denoting the children that perished, the serene vanishing pool, the wall that so reminded me of Jerusalem's Wailing Wall (at least from the multitude of photos and videos I that have observed), all masterfully blended together to give you a sense of and appreciation for all that happened there. Artfully, poignantly memorialized and remembered, it connects you and all to that act of domestic terrorism and extraordinary tragedy and force in our recent history.

We always knew from the very the outset that *Journey's* sister city regarding domestic terrorism was to be Oklahoma City. I remember the first responders there showing appreciation for what we were doing, and an immediate level of mutual respect and admiration between Bill Markowski, our retired New York City Police security officer, and his fellow Oklahoma lawmen in uniform. I put my hands upon the wall and looked at the benches representing those who had died, and someone told me that the smaller benches were for the children. At that point I teared up for those kids, and I felt so much appreciation for my own children. I don't know how someone can survive the loss of a child, except that God gives them the strength.

It was a highly moving and poignant experience. The Memorial is the kind of place that can't help but bring you to your knees and to prayer as I solemnly did out of respect for those that were lost, and in honor of all whom survived, a place where you so palpably feel the spirits of those who were lost.

Billed as a place of comfort, strength, and peace, it invites you "to remember those killed, those who survived, and those changed forever."

It was all the more striking to us, given the obvious connections that link this sacred place to our own Ground Zero. Another inscription says, "We come here to remember those who were killed, those who survived and those changed forever. May all who leave here know the impact of violence. May this memorial offer comfort, strength, peace, hope and serenity."

Indeed, it did and does. The dead and the living alike truly come to life for you as you pray there.

The emotion of the press conference that we held immediately after our visit there rendered it, I believe, one of the seminal moments of the entire experience for all on the *Journey*.

After visiting the site and recognizing the strong and tangible bond that linked our own cause to this place, we made a presentation and were commended and thanked by Mayor Mick Cornett of Oklahoma City, as we humbly honored Oklahoma City and expressed our appreciation for what it had accomplished in so beautifully memorializing such a tragic day.

I'm not suggesting that the skinheads or Neo-Nazis are non-existent, but I am suggesting that they are not at all representative of who we are. And I am further suggesting that goodness and decency prevails.

Later, Lee and I enjoyed an audience at the State House with Oklahoma Governor Brad Henry, to whom we presented a signed Giants helmet. Henry had just barely defeated former Republican Congressman Steve Largent, my former opponent from the Seattle Seahawks and an NFL Hall of Famer, in the election.

We were especially touched upon meeting Reggie Cervantes, a resident of Oklahoma City who was "us." Reggie had been a 9/11 first responder in New York. He was what we were walking for, a gentleman who gave his all in the wake of 9/11 and who was now suffering mightily with an array of life-threatening maladies. Like so many who withstood the muck and mire of that toxic disaster, cancer was but one of the threats to his health and to his life. Reggie also spoke to the fact that ours was, as we always maintained, a national and not a local issue.

Reggie Cervantes, Oklahoma City, and *a Journey for 9/11*, one in spirit and one in fact!

On February 18, we were, after enjoying the company of alpacas on the broad brown fields with mini-mountains of green clumps in the western part of Oklahoma, visiting Binger, the birthplace of Johnny Bench, the great, Hall of Fame, All-Century Team, Cincinnati Reds catcher. In what was a kind of local convenience store/malt shop, we were just inundated with visitors. Somehow, the word had gotten out and people kept pouring into that store to see us – young and old, male and female, old ladies and young babies, teenagers and the entire local basketball team, and working men. We may have run into more people at that store than we did at the high school that we enjoyed visiting the next day.

Simply put, Binger was fantastic to *a Journey for 9/11*; their interest and enthusiasm sublime motivation for tired bodies and sore feet.

Interestingly, upon reaching the Texas State line and its lone star on February 28th, we looked back upon the rear view "*Welcome to Oklahoma*" sign. From the east, it had read "*Discover the Excellence*" but from the west, it was "*Discover Native America.*" Maybe it's as simple as one sign being of newer vintage, but still, it left me wandering if there was an east-west differential, as we ventured into the Texas panhandle and its warning that littering could cost us $2,000.

Where I traversed Oklahoma and Texas, the landscape was dominated by rocky outcroppings. My looming six-foot-four frame was often rendered insignificant when contrasted with these stunning and intricate formations, which often stopped us in our tracks. And, by the way, if I felt small, can you imagine how Lee must have felt. It often seemed as if we were walking in the center of the Earth on a road to nowhere or forever; and there, where the Earth celebrated its formidability and strength, there was such beauty to be found in the sight of one lone tree or the smallest stand of scrub pines. There, seemingly lost in space, I looked up and learned the meaning of "Big Sky over Texas."

11 – OH, THE PEOPLE, 'GOOD LORD, THE PEOPLE'

In Texas and New Mexico

Out of what had been Oklahoma's early February bitter cold, we discovered Texas' early March heat and humidity. Texas, or at least the Panhandle, was for the most part wide open range and flat rural fields, but we'd find the occasional cluster of homes and the periodic rustic looking eatery.

One such place gave way to a don't-judge-a-book-by-its-cover experience.

Though hungry, I decided to bypass a place billed as "Burgers Only." because its lot was filled with pickup trucks with large shotgun racks, Confederate flags and the like, suggesting to me that it might be redneck personified. But just a little bit down the road, an attractive young African-American woman who had not long ago relocated from New York City pulled her pickup over to say hello. In the course of conversation, upon our betraying our hunger, she wondered aloud why we didn't stop at her restaurant, which we had only recently passed – Burgers Only.

Go figure!

So to there we returned to discover that we had much in common with the "good ol' Southern boys" who patronized Burgers Only, and that the flag with the stars and bars often has ever so much more to do with heritage and identity than it does with race or the vestiges of bigotry. For at Burgers Only, the respect and affection that these rustic and gruff patrons had for a young, African-American proprietor was strong and palpable. Yes, that young African-American woman who greeted us on the highway owned what we had quite mistakenly perceived as a redneck establishment – and, even more, she was the second-generation owner.

We ate there for the next two days in enjoyable conversation with these truly good ol' boys from Texas, as well as extended family members of the wonderful proprietor.

*****

I look back upon Texas, where schools were few and far between in the Panhandle, and I recall the Malt Shop Café and Burgers Only and pecan cobbler and a few laughs with Texas emergency personnel and this kind fan who arrived with a complete collection of all my Giants football cards – proving that I had at least one fan in Texas. There was also a man named Kenny and his *a Journey for 9/11* cardboard cut-out of the state of Texas – and my knock-down, drag-out with Lee. This was a very unfortunate confrontation between brothers-in-arms, which although we didn't realize at the time, would eventually make our fraternal bond even stronger.

It happened when I overheard Lee talking to his "Wizard Behind the Curtain," Jennifer Skor, about airplane ticket prices back home for him. I was taken aback, for though I was well aware of what Lee had contributed and of his right to take a leave and go see his fiancée, I also was ultimately responsible for the expenditure of all finances and any such trip, or even the exploration of the same, had to be discussed with me first. That's all!

Good, bad or indifferent, I was from the Bill Parcells school of executive leadership.

When I confronted Lee about this, I may not have communicated my concerns very well and our conversation rapidly deteriorated to a point where, as Lee later became fond of saying, "It was on like popcorn." Lee went off the charts with F-bombs and it was World War III and nuclear annihilation for all. We both unloaded with everything that we had in our verbal arsenals.

We worked up a great sweat and finally it was concluded with Lee making this clear and salient declaration: "George, I'm a grown-ass man and you can kiss my ass." With that, we simply parted. The escalation was as heated as I have ever been involved in – however, never was there a single thought that the situation would become physical. I had far too much respect for Lee, and I suppose he had far too much appreciation for pain and common sense, to ever consider crossing that pathway of Mutually Assured Self-Destruction!

What we later discerned was that such confrontations are in many cases unavoidable and even necessary to cleanse the buildup of frustration and hostility that naturally surfaces when two people work so intimately together for so long. Having been baptized in the NFL school of hard knocks, I was used to such confrontations, but Lee, on the other hand, was completely unfamiliar with having such frank discussions with a 265-pound Neanderthal.

I would never have allowed it to become physical, but I'm not so sure Lee knew that. The overarching respect I had for the man who had been covering for and protecting me since Day One simply ran much deeper than any imminent frustration or anger. We would later look back on this incident and have a great laugh about it, especially when we watched a similar incident unfold on screen in the movie, "Welcome Home, Roscoe Jenkins," starring Martin Lawrence and Cedric the Entertainer and the now deceased Michael Clark Duncan, in which love conquered all, except Martin Lawrence found out the hard way that the bigger they are, the harder they hit. Lee must have remembered that scene as he later told me that he didn't want our encounter to serve as a sequel to that movie. Life truly imitating art. It did with us, too. Crisis averted, and more importantly, lesson learned!

*****

Like Sylvia, like Magic, like the grandmother, and like the proprietors of the Pig & Chick and Burger Barn restaurants, the characters of Texas took their place among the most memorable, gentle, loving souls we met along our *Journey* across the United States of America.

Texas was an ongoing encounter with rodeo riders and scraggly-haired, mustache-laden cowboys in dark black hats. There also were plenty of former GIs and United States Marines and people of limited means who sacrificed what little they had, young men who liked to talk of their "Friday Night Lights" heroics, and classic, tattooed bikers, who liked to hang out at rustic bars like the Branding Iron Café.

Everything indeed is big in Texas and everything in the "off the beaten path" of it that we walked reminded me of yesteryear and the Wild West and the Saturday-morning, after-the-cartoons westerns that children of my generation watched.

In the literal middle of nowhere, we would come across stone memorials. One was dedicated to William E. Schott, Briscoe County Pioneer. Now, I'm certain that he did good, but from our perch there, we were left to wonder what on Earth he pioneered – there was nothing to be seen but dirt and rock. (A website about road markers reveals that Mr. Schott developed the first cattle road in the region and was "a strong supporter of local education.")

I did love the Branding Iron Café and the antiques within it, including old stagecoaches, windmills, whisky barrels and branding irons, each with untold stories of its own to tell.

*****

My good friend Ken Vehrkens joined us for our march into New Mexico, and he came with far more than the ceremonial in mind – he was ready to walk. He did present us with a ceremonial check for $17,000 that he personally raised from his Fairleigh Dickinson University colleagues, but he also set the record for miles walked by a Board member or guest as we moved on into the Land of Enchantment, past the welcome sign with the bright orange glow of the Zia sun.

We started off walking with a huge crowd of locals, plus my nephew, Daniel Graham, son of my college colleague Mr. Tom Graham and an NFL tight end himself, had also kindly joined us, along with twin brother Josh and their Aunt Yaya. What a raucous, fun-loving band of adventuring misfits we were that day. But at the end, after 23 miles in scorching heat and blinding sun, it was Ken alone who was still standing with me. Ken had trained diligently for this welcomed visitation, and had lost considerable weight in the process. His dedication truly paid off as he was a warrior among warriors on this grand occasion. At the end of that day all I could think about was grabbing a nap, while Ken had to drive 70 miles to the airport to catch a red-eye flight back home. Impressively, it was he who pushed the pace that day, on one of those days where the elements were crying out that this day was theirs and not yours.

However, Daniel, a member of the New England Patriots, at one point said, "Uncle George, I have to go to training camp soon, but I don't know if it's going to be as hard as this. I don't know how you have done this every day for this long." I considered that quite a compliment at the time.

*****

The next day, March 20, 2008, we celebrated our 2,000th mile in the Portales High School gym, where the bleachers were packed close together and their occupants as tight as sardines in a can.

Nicole Wilkening, the Portales coordinator of community affairs, had actually heard me speak earlier in Texas and said they would love to pull out all the stops in Portales, which worked out perfectly for us, given the *Journey* milestone we celebrated there. A parade of military officials, local police and firefighters, emergency services staff and town dignitaries led us into the gym, where we were met by the entire student body of Portales High School and many of their parents and siblings. Entering that gym, the ovation and enthusiasm seemed as great as if we had just turned back a first and goal at Giants Stadium.

I remember being hugged and kissed on my way into that gym by the mother of a severely disabled child and thinking that it was all backwards – that these people deserved this adulation and outpouring of affection, not us.

I certainly spoke to that and to the extraordinary job that Nancy had done for us. There was a "George Martin Day in Portales" proclamation and there were press releases that captured the thrust of my message about heroism and the duty that we owed to our 9/11 rescue and recovery workers, and there was an audience that had been so prepped and so turned on to both our message and our mission.

And the students holding up the "2,000 miles" banner were as diligent as the honor guard at the Tomb of the Unknowns at Arlington National Cemetery.

If every town on the way to the Pacific were even half as enthusiastic for us as was Portales, New Mexico, we would have walked on air to Embarcadero Park in San Diego.

Thank you, Nancy Wilkening.

However, this does not nearly complete of Portales experience, not by a long shot. After the grandeur of the high school festivities had concluded, Lee, I and the *Journey* team blissfully resumed our merry march westward along Highway 70. As the memory of the last occasion was fresh in our minds though the site of the event was rapidly fading in our rearview mirrors, a patrol car came alongside and its occupant began conversing with Lee. As I continued marching ever onward, Lee asked if I could hold up as he wanted to introduce me to our new police escort, which in and of itself was not unusual. As I reversed field and started back toward Lee and the officer, out stepped the most impressive image of law enforcement that I had ever seen.

"George," Lee said, "meet Officer Glenn Russ," and out steps a vision of impeccable law enforcement locked in a Marine-like poster image. Broad shoulders, uniformed pressed to the nines and an attitude that seemed to shine with patriotism, and every response finished off with a snappy "Sir." A patrol officer for Curry County, New Mexico, Deputy Sheriff Russ was spit and polish to the max, and enthusiastic as hell to be escorting our caravan. Believe it or not, this was the beginning of a wonderful friendship that has endured to this day.

Glenn is the type of individual who was totally sold on our mission from the word go. A devoted husband and family man and a former United States Marine who bleeds red, white and blue. So devoted was Glenn, that even on his day off,which he normally spent with his family, he was willing to split the time with *Journey* in order to safeguard our passage. I never felt as safe and secure as I did when I was with the American hero. The Glenn Russes of the world are who this book is in tribute to, and I will never forget him.

Our trek through New Mexico and Arizona was perfect, as we trekked into the desert and passed right by a major slice of modern American history. We walked by San Augustin Pass and Roswell and its secrets and mysteries, whether real or imagined. We pushed on by the Cold War-era Nike Hercules Missile site and White Sands Missile Range, the early home of America's missile and space activity. We paused at the White Sands Monument, by the "Birthplace of the Race to Space," and by the sad Trinity Site, where they first exploded and unleashed the horror of the atom bomb.

"We come here to remember those who were killed – those who survived and those changed forever – may all who leave here know the impact of violence –may this memorial offer comfort –strength, peace, hope, and serenity."

Our New Mexico transit took us past the Billy the Kid National Scenic Byway Visitor Center and Blazer's Mill, where Billy was involved in the Lincoln County War and among the 15 men who hunted down poor Buckshot Roberts, who eventually went to his death in one of the best documented gunfights in the Wild West.

History gets written in so many different ways and in such crooked lines. Born William Henry McCarty in 1859, Billy the Kid had many aliases, most notably William Bonney, and he was dead by the age of 21 in 1881. He was troubled and criminal and just destined for the same. He contributed nothing to society outside of the legend of his youthful exploits, and yet you walk by his name, over and over again, when you journey in the southwestern United States.

We crossed the Rio Grande, realizing that General Sam Houston and General Antonio Lopez de Santa Anna and our sad mid-19th century war with Mexico rendered it larger and mightier in lore and legend than it is in reality. A bit farther on, in Bylas, Arizona, on the San Carlos

Apache Indian Reservation, and at the city of Apache Junction, it was Geronimo who was celebrated there.

In New Mexico, we also enjoyed an endless array of local fire department escorts, and members of those fire departments and local police kept signing our American flag, which is now proudly displayed along with many other precious keepsakes of *Journey* in my office. We made stops at Red Cross centers and local post offices and court houses and, despite our personal aversion to the buying and selling of guns, at the Akela Flats Pistol Shop, where there was a community gathering. The faces were increasingly Hispanic and bright and the children we met far outnumbered the adults. The people of New Mexico were, as advertised, enchanting, and they took us almost as high as did the Continental Divide that we crossed there at an elevation of 4,585 feet.

The people greeted me always with amazement, and always with spectacular smiles. People who don't know me are often a bit intimidated by my size and color, but in these remarkable instances it was refreshingly different and embracing. Their smiles in Portales made me feel so good.

One woman, a Mrs. Chavez in New Mexico, touched me to my very soul. "I'd like you to do a favor for me," she said, giving me a picture and a rosary. The picture was of her son, a soldier who had died in the war following 9/11. She said, "Would you carry these for the rest of your *Journey*?" Naturally, I was honored and agreed, and I still have the picture of Lance Cpl. Steven Chavez, 1986-2007 United States Marine, positioned front and center of my *Journey* memorabilia case to this day, a haunting reminder of a young life cut tragically short because of the terrorism of 9/11. Thank you ever so much for that remarkable honor Mrs. Chavez, along with the exceptional sacrifice that your son and many others gave on behalf of our nation.

In New Mexico and Arizona, there were, early evening after early evening, clouds of burnt red with spectacular rays of cascading sunlight. Mountains forever loomed in the distance and there were white sands underfoot and sprawling seas of cactus and rarified fields of pine and a single prodigious climbing tree on Don Pablo Lane and an out-of-place yellow bush in a patch of scrub pine. In Apache Junction, palm trees suddenly appeared and we continued to be mesmerized by sunsets over every sierra that took one's breath away.

Then, there was Devil's Canyon and jagged, red rock outcroppings that took on faces and personalities and a surprising sea of desert wetlands. Nature never fails to surprise and amaze.

Walking along The Old West Highway in Arizona, I was struck by the fact we, on our *Journey*, had indeed "Gone West" as Horace Greeley had urged Americans to do in the mid-19th century, west where one "could grow up with the country."

We had gone west and into the future and into time, and in those rarest of moments of introspection, I was paralyzed momentarily, uncertain as to whether I was the man of the world looking and ingesting this splendor in an awestruck moment of amazement, or that impressionable young boy from the South enjoying the euphoria of my inevitable quest as simply destiny. I have often pondered the paradox, and even today I remain satisfactorily perplexed.

*****

A Living History

The tragedy of 9/11 is an American tale, a bitter one that speaks to how complicated and absurd our way of being in the world today is, but also *to our capacity for greatness and to our resounding hope and faith in a better tomorrow.*

Early on, I realized that we were going to quite literally walk through the American story. We were heading west just as our history did, past the sacred vestiges of the American Revolution and the Civil War and the arduous, tortured struggle for equality and civil rights ,and vestiges of the Wild West and the tortured legacy of Native Americans and the remnants of economies lost and the missile launch sites that first took us into space. Right by Fredericksburg and Little Rock and Oklahoma City, we inevitably walked west into time and into the future, just as our America did over the course of some 240 years.

In the end, we saw the yearning of a people to produce and prosper, by the very birth and the full flowering of the American Dream, and all of the heroism and the epic rumblings of human advance. History was in the places we passed, in the very air we breathed, and in the souls of the people we met. Our history, our remarkable, tortured, tragic, sometimes sordid, yet modern and great American story – yours and mine – unfolded before us. Among so many other gifts, *a Journey for 9/11* enabled us to discover, up close and personal, the stirring legacy that has been passed down to all of us.

So there was the window of natural beauty and then the window of living history staring us in the face. But there was more. More than any book or documentary or video or classroom, the *Journey* bore witness to the heritage that should live deep in the hearts of all Americans.

9/11 is an American tale, a bitter one that speaks to how complicated and absurd our way of being in the world today can be, but also to our capacity for greatness and to our resounding hope and faith in a better tomorrow.

*****

The Witness of the Press

The *Journey* was also a story that was well chronicled by others, by the members of the press who regularly informed people all across America of our mission, our progress, and our whereabouts. Indeed, the press fashioned another perspective and in the end produced an incredible body of work that gives us much to reflect upon. For it is good to know how both you and what you did were perceived.

From Day One, Jay Winuk, his right-hand man John Mooney and the rest of Winuk Communications' *Journey* team, driving our publicity machine, stayed a step ahead of my fellow road warriors and me, keeping print and broadcast journalists in New York and San Diego and all through the hinterlands informed about our mission, efforts and plans as we made our way across the nation.

From ESPN to Fox Sports to NFL Films to local affiliates of ABC and NBC and CBS, and from The (Newark) Star-Ledger and the New York Post and The New York Times to the San Diego Union-Tribune and the hundreds of newspapers in between them, and Sports Illustrated Senior Writer Peter King, and the press in Phoenix and southern

Early on *a Journey for 9/11*, I pause for a TV interview in Menlo Park, N.J., one of hundreds along the way.

WNBC Sportscaster Bruce Beck covers the *Journey* launch at Giants Stadium in the Meadowlands, N.J., on September 16, 2007.

Roadside interviews were a common occurrence along *a Journey for 9/11*. This reporter chased me down in Tennessee.

Dianne and I answer a reporter's questions as we happily near the finish line in San Diego.

California and in venues as distant as Toronto and Vancouver, they covered *Journey* and urged citizens to embrace our mission.

On the whole, *Journey* had reason to be very pleased, as Jay did a fantastic job with both the national and the local media. Wherever we walked, they knew we were coming.

In a year in which the New York Football Giants would win one of the most compelling and dramatic Super Bowls in history, it is important to remember that *Journey* began with a halftime celebration at the Stadium, just as the Giants were in the midst of being soundly pummeled by the Green Bay Packers on opening day of that very season. In one of my favorite eat-crow pieces, Steve Serby's column in the New York Post the following day brutally condemned the team, suggesting that they might as well "pack it in" for the season. Ending his column with a welcome pitch for *a Journey for 9/11*, he closed by suggesting that, "The shame of it was that Martin didn't take the entire Giants defense with him." That is the very same defense that rattled Tom Brady's mind, body and spirit and the 18 and 0 Patriots in Phoenix in late January. So much for "packing it in," Steve.

That's the first in a series of media pieces on *Journey* that I want to share with you, just a small and telling sampling of articles and media events arranged by Jay that either touched me or made a difference. In New Jersey there was a literal avalanche of pictures of me with local fire departments in an array of weeklies. You might well have thought that I had joined the force.

On September 21, 2007, on SNY-TV Sports Net, Joey Wahler was kind enough to plug *a Journey for 9/11*, but I don't know what wonder he saw in it, given that he said I would be driving across America.

On October 12 we had a great interview with Bruce Murray and Pat Kirwan of Sirius NFL Radio. I reported that I had lost 19 pounds, that I was meeting wonderful people every day, that my convictions about *Journey* were only growing stronger, and that I remained in a state of "euphoria."

Peter King of Sports Illustrated walked a full 18 miles with me on a blustery December 5th for what became a major HBO *Inside the NFL* production on *Journey*. He was very gracious to us and his compelling report reflected the true spirit of our efforts.

Accompanying Wendy Isom's December 18 article in the Jackson Sun, there was a great picture of us encircled by firefighters as Jackson, Tennessee, Mayor Jerry Gist presented me the key to the city. While Wendy caught the essence of what we were about and treated us so very kindly, it was her take-away tribute that moved me the most: "Their walk is a labor of love."

In the January/February 2008 edition of *Philanthropy World*, the one with a smiling actor Gary Sinise on the cover, there was a spotlight on *Gridiron Giving* that profiled *Journey* as well as other NFL-related charitable initiatives. While it focused upon me and my love of the outdoors and my love of the cause that drove us forward, it also featured Joseph Reich, our primary donor. Reich graciously said, "Both George and I were upset at the way the federal and local government treated real American heroes. I told George that what he was doing was extraordinary and I wanted to be a part of it."

Kevin Manahan of The Star-Ledger, New Jersey's biggest daily, was kind enough to walk with me for a couple of days. His first-hand experience contributed to a February 2 story and what was, in all likelihood, the best article ever written about *a Journey for 9/11*, one that was crafted through the lens of an artist.

His lead was this:

"This is God's work of art. I'm seeing this land the way most people will never see it. It is breathtaking even when there's nothing out there. Oh, the magnificent sunsets!" Later he wrote, "Out on U.S. Highway 271, somewhere between Oblivion and Forgotten, George Martin is being escorted by Oklahoma state troopers on a two-lane road that roller coasters through a dusty brown patch of the world. Scorched by the sun, dried by winds, and barely touched by man, this place looks more like the moon than the earth. Martin wonders what town he is in. You're not in any town, Trooper Mike Stafford tells him. He wasn't kidding, as we were 15 miles from Eufaula and 948 from Glendale, Arizona, where tonight's Super Bowl would be played."

In what was a mosaic of a feature story on a two-page spread, Manahan continued, "In Jersey, Martin saw the rich in their McMansions, in the rolling valleys of Virginia, he saw the rural beauty of America, in Tennessee and Arkansas, he met the rural, impoverished of America, people in shacks, and here, nothing but rusted oil lights in decaying barns......but suddenly, there is Tammy Horton, a grandmother from Seminole, Oklahoma." Crying, she didn't want an autograph, a picture, or a hug, she wanted the opportunity to show her grandchildren what real heroism is, and wanted them to feel as though they were a living part of history. Then, in the middle of nowhere, "There is the deaf young boy, Tommy Rogers, who waited with the bag of $3.78 that he collected. Martin hangs with him, thanks him, and hugs him. I didn't want to leave him or his goodness."

Out on U.S. Highway 271, somewhere between Oblivion and Forgotten, George Martin is being escorted by Oklahoma state troopers on a two lane road that roller coasters through a dusty brown patch of the world. Scorched by the sun, dried by winds, and barely touched by man, this place looks more like the moon than the earth.

In a Brian Sargent story in The Oklahoman on February 12, I must have been feeling particularly good, because I was quoted as saying, "It's like walking across the street, only a bit further." In a March 14 production of ESPN's *The Magazine*, they treated the subject of *Journey* much more seriously, even poignantly. They said that I was compelled as a Giant to do it. They said that the "Maras taught us about family and to treat the fans as family. Sports can help the athlete to forget," it was said, "but it also gives the athlete the opportunity to remember." They mentioned that Dick Lynch, who had been in the Giants broadcast booth for 40 years, lost his son, Richard, who worked on the 84th floor of the South Tower. They said, "George Martin thinks of that and so he walks."

On April 11, I spent some time with Michael Waltrip, the great NASCAR driver at the Phoenix International Speedway, before returning to Las Cruces, New Mexico, to continue the walk. There I was interviewed by Paola Boivin of the Arizona Republic. In the article published on April 12, Paola kindly suggested that "Martin is a man driven by other people's heartbreak. We should all be in awe of him." Then, the above hyperbole notwithstanding, I also was quoted as saying, "Every day on *Journey* is like Christmas Day." Looking back on it, I never felt that it was about me, so awe wasn't in the equation, but there was such truth in the line about Christmas, for every day on *Journey* was indeed a gift.

They said that I was compelled as a Giant to do it. They said that the "Maras taught us about family and to treat the fans as family. Sports can help the athlete to forget," it was said, "but it also presents the athlete the opportunity to remember."

On May 1, there was a great piece in Phoenix Magazine. The article highlighted what they looked upon as my "Three Life's Lessons." As to the first, given that I was an 11th round draft pick, it is wise to develop tunnel vision and to freely pursue one's goals without waiting to be told to do so. The second was, "To get involved," as each of us has a duty and an obligation to serve our brothers and sisters in need. The third was to "always lead by example," to go first, and "to point the finger at yourself first." There's nothing above that I don't continue to lay claim to.

In a May 19 piece, Peter King of Sports Illustrated focused on the question of the money raised. He suggested that I had to be "a little disillusioned" because the response had not been as "overwhelming as we had hoped." He observed that I was in the home stretch. And then, in a powerful closing and empathetic pitch, he noted, "Martin has given nine months of his life for those who need help to breathe. Help him help them now." The same subject was picked up in a great May 20 *Gorilla News Radio* segment in which they discussed the fact that the fundraising goal seemed to be a far reach. It was said that the fact that I, rather than official America, had to do this was a shame, for "In our rush to get back to business, we ignored the flip side of the 9/11 story. I thank

George and I have a message for him. When the subject of coming up short enters the equation, you're nowhere to be found. Not in my book. Thank you for showing all of us what was really lost and what is still being lost."

"It's just like walking across the street, only a bit further."

They then memorialized James Zadroga, Felix Hernandez, and Tim Keller, the heroes. They spoke about those lost on 9/11 and today's suffering and dying for whom we walked. They closed by noting, "Like *Mr. Smith Goes to Washington*, Martin recognizes that the only causes worth fighting for are the lost causes. He is walking on heart alone now."

While the above is at issue, we did, however indirectly, meet our goal of $10 million, in that the $3 million raised was matched in free services for the rescue and recovery workers at three major hospitals in the New York region. Suffice it to say that our greatest contribution was in helping to raise the national consciousness and helping to win the battle for the responders in Congress.

In a great Apache Junction News piece by Jill Jones, the fantastic May 22 Hall of Flame ceremony in Phoenix, Arizona, the May 23 5K Walk in Tempe Beach Park, and the May 23 Barbecue with Super Bowl Heroes were all highlighted. As to the Hall of Flame, she noted that no one among us could go untouched by a poignant program that brought our collective ownership of the events of 9/11 to light. It called upon all of us to respond by dedicating ourselves to building a better world.

'Like Mr. Smith Goes to Washington, Martin recognizes that the only causes worth fighting for are the lost causes. He is walking on heart alone now.'

And so, to the windows of natural beauty and living history, we add the one fashioned by the press. Still, there is an even more compelling perspective for me.

Many retrospective and highly positive articles about *Journey* continued to be written long after we crossed the finish line, and in fact continue today – as, in many spiritual and practical ways, does the *Journey*. The following handful capture their essence.

On June 22nd, Kirk Bey, a self-proclaimed cynic who produced *The Sideline* column for the La Crosse (Wisconsin) Tribune, wrote, "These are troubling times in our country and it is so easy to dwell on the negative, but Martin's selfless journey can make even a cynic like me believe in the goodness of humanity." On June 23, the Pennsylvania's Titusville Herald wrote an editorial recounting the *Journey* story, highlighting that beloved grandmother who so wanted her grandchildren to see heroism. Matt Goldberg of the Quincy Herald-Whig in Illinois wrote a major feature for the July 10 edition. In an offbeat fashion, he related the heroism of *Journey* to that of the Giants for having knocked off the Patriots. He wrote of my having "left my cushy job" and "having hopefully forgiven those who thought that I sustained too many hits to the head" – a matter upon which the jury is still out. But it was his conclusion that humbled and mattered most to me: "Normal athletes host golf outings or dinners, but Martin wanted to make a 'Giant' contribution so he set his sights higher. It's one thing to write a check, but to do what he did is the stuff of real heroism. Other athletes should take a page out of his book."

"These are troubling times in our country and it is so easy to dwell on the negative, but Martin's selfless journey can make even a cynic like me believe in the goodness of humanity."

In a July 28 feature in the Athens (Georgia) Banner Herald, a McClatchy Newspapers story recounted the inspirers like the grandmothers in Rogersville and Seminole, the proprietors of the Pig & Chick, and none other than Bill Parcells, my Hall of Fame coach and cheerleader. "You've done good, Martin.....Hey, Martin, you have got to get moving.....The weather is going to get bad out there, Martin, move ..... and ..... Hey, you have got a national treasure here." Let me say, with all humility, that it takes one to know one.

In a Vallejo (California) Times Herald piece by Tim Scott on August 3, my local roots at Armijo High School were noted, as well as my Oregon and New York Football Giants days. And before Mr. Scott got into the *Journey*, he wanted the world to know that I sacked John Elway. He recounted all of the great *Journey* stories, but more than any other writer, with the exception of Kevin Manahan of The Star Ledger, he focused upon the beauty of America. "Martin," he wrote, "was taken aback by the beauty of our land, by the glorious mountains of Virginia and Tennessee, by the magnificence of autumn in Virginia and Tennessee, by the splendor of New Mexico, and by the breathtaking sunsets."

In the August 19 edition of *Light One Candle*, Dennis Heaney, the president of The Christophers, a Catholic inspirational group, wrote about *Journey*. "So Martin kept his promise and some say 'big deal,' but this was a big promise and a really big deal. Maryknoll Father James Keller, our founder, said just one person, acting on his own, for all of the right reasons, can make a tremendous difference in the world – one person like George Martin."

Finally, there was a great piece by Deborah Viola on September 8 in Gannett's Journal News in Westchester County, New York. She wrote powerfully of 9/11 and of our collective ownership of it. "It is all of ours. It belongs to the entire nation. So as we prepare to memorialize this coming 9/11, consider those who survived and then follow in George Martin's footsteps and write to your representatives in support of H.R. 6594 and then let us harness our collective will and consider what we need to do for all of the rest."

To this day, the mentions of *Journey* in the media are all positive! And we keep the spirit of it all alive with annual walks and periodic events.

But let me be very clear about one thing regarding the accolades thrown my way along the way in the press. Repeatedly, I was referred to as a hero. Over and over again, a hero! I personally lay claim to nothing of the kind. Not for walking, nor for being of service to my fellow human beings, nor for doing what we all should do. What I did was not heroic, while what the rescue and recovery workers did was, and what those on the line in Afghanistan do is, and what the police and firefighters do for us every day is. They are the real heroes.

So you might reasonably wonder why I referenced all those articles that did so. Why? Because they all were indirectly pointing the finger at and honoring *the cause*, a cause that was ever so much bigger than Lee and me and ever so much bigger than *Journey*. All along the way, to crowd after crowd, I kept saying that it's not about me. All along the way, I kept reminding people that the cause was never meant to be overshadowed by the event.

So it was then and so it is now. So, thanks for the accolades, which I respectfully defer to the real heroes.

12 – 'WELCOME TO CALIFORNIA, GEORGE MARTIN – *A JOURNEY FOR 9/11'*

Arizona and the Sunshine State

One month in New Mexico and we were suddenly celebrating underneath the inviting red, orange and blue "*Welcome to Arizona – The Grand Canyon State*" sign. We were greeted by a Safford Fire Department truck, small palm trees, the mountains of the sierra on the western horizon, and a state law that precluded us from walking on highways – a law that we had to break, as there were no byways to accompany their highways.

Lee's standard joke was that in Arizona even the snakes had the right of way.

Only about a mile in, we met the five Menendez children, between the ages of 5 and 14, who like Man Mountain Mike had tracked us on the Internet. Alone and waiting in the hot sun, we scurried through our belongings and found one remaining Giants football to autograph and reward them with. Just beyond where we met them, there was an entrance to a Martin Ranch, but well knowing that there were no ranchers in my family, we didn't pause to investigate.

Firefighters, firefighters and more firefighters, that was the story of sunny and sandy Arizona, as we seemed to be escorted daily by local fire departments. There was the Tolleson Fire Department and the

Goodyear Fire Department and the Globe Fire Department and the Buckeye Fire Department and the Tempe Fire Department, and they wore safari hats and they mocked me with soft Dallas Cowboys hats, and the local police kept signing our memorial flag and there were crowds of children walking with us in every town.

Tumbleweed, sand and a burning hot sun, and walking phalanxes of firemen, police and locals, were with us constantly.

Here, Lee and I no longer walked alone.

We had enjoyable local receptions at both the Dollar General store and the Visitors Center in Buckeye, where local citizens printed their own "Buckeye Journey for 9/11" posters for us to autograph. Globe Fire Chief Al Gameros kindly presented me with a check for $200 and Teresa and Stosh Hatch, Ashley Denton, Scott Cameron and Haydee Valdepena of Globe and Buckeye took up a collection that netted another $200. Simple and small, but so very personal and genuine, heartfelt and real!

Lee's standard joke was that in Arizona even the snakes had the right of way.

Other than the Reichs, the NFL, the New York Football Giants, the NFL Players Association, Bill Parcells, Phil Sims, Ken Vehrkens, AXA Equitable and a handful of others, most of the revenue raised, totaling three million dollars, came from the pocket change and valuable $10s and $20s of people along the way who could ill afford to let go of even a dollar of disposable income.

It came from the poverty of thousands of Americans who cared and wanted to help the rescue and recovery workers who had responded for all Americans. They saw and appreciated the connections. Day after day after day, I had the honor and privilege of meeting people who connected these dots and embraced me in the name of those I served.

They were a people who believed in redemption and they were, without question, instruments of grace.

In what they did, they unquestionably elevated Lee and me.

It was Tom Brock, a retired, disabled-in-the-line-of-duty policeman from Rutherford, New Jersey – which bordered East Rutherford, the home of Giants Stadium – and now a Phoenix, Arizona, resident, who pleaded with and urged *a Journey for 9/11* fathers to change our original Arizona route to a southerly direction to come through Phoenix. He argued that it made sense weather-wise, people-wise and publicity-wise. He further insisted that I needed, on behalf of the 9/11 responders who we were serving, to get to the Hall of Flame Fire Museum and National Firefighting Hall of Heroes in Phoenix, where the service of those we served was forever memorialized.

His voice and impact were felt and *Journey* responded to him, ultimately redirecting south through Phoenix and on to the finish in San Diego rather than San Francisco, our original final destination.

We are forever grateful to Tom Brock for his pushing and prodding and for his role in engineering *Journey*'s most memorable of all welcomes.

We also had been in touch with Joe Brodsky, a former New York City police officer who had likewise retired to Phoenix prior to 9/11. But he had ironically returned to New York City during that beautiful, early September of 2001 to attend the U.S. Open Tennis Championship in Forest Hills, Queens. In New York City when it all came down, he did what instinct demanded and he joined his former colleagues immediately. Among the very first responders, he served at Ground Zero for weeks, extending his trip again and again. Like so many of them, he paid an inordinate price, for he no longer plays his beloved tennis as he did and he no longer gets around easily or lives a normal life, because simply breathing is always an issue.

He does continue to come back to New York, but only because he is being treated without cost at Mount Sinai, one of our *Journey* beneficiaries.

My dear friend Harry Carson described what Joe Brodsky did as "one of the most unselfish acts I have ever witnessed."

Like Reggie Cervantes, his counterpart in Oklahoma City, Joe Brodsky's life has been forever impaired because he dared to serve. Sadly, we are powerless to heal or to restore the vitality and vibrancy of their lives, but it was our clear duty at that time to, at the very least, take away the burden of paying for their own care.

That was our clear and simple mission – to remove that wholly callous and unnecessary burden.

And oh, how the meaning of our mission was celebrated in Phoenix on May 20, at a place I didn't know even existed prior to our *Journey*. Given the advance billing, I even put a jacket and tie back on for the first time in nearly eight months. We were escorted to the Hall of Flame Fire Museum by a Phoenix police honor guard and the Chandler, Daisy Mountain, Tempe, Mesa and Phoenix Fire Departments, and a memorable troop of Irish and Scottish pipers. It was a long, elegant and moving escort that led us into that phenomenal Hall of Flame, where I was immediately blown away by the huge and stunning mural of the lost towers, depicted within an American Flag, with the majesty of an eagle swooping overhead.

The only words, near the bottom, were, "Lest We Forget."

But there are no words to describe it or to do this mural justice. Yes, eye-catching and beautiful and powerful and stunning, but it was all of that and more. Everywhere we looked, we were surrounded by the historic tools and the earliest vehicles of the firefighter's trade, but the mural stole all attention and we sat on a stage in front of it.

The place was packed with firefighters and police and military and locals and dignitaries.

My former teammates Harry Carson and Stacy Robinson and Maurice Carthon had flown in for this event, as did my generous employer representative and *Journey* board member Andrew McMahon, and we also were joined by NFL Hall of Famer Mike Haynes, a local Phoenix celebrity. Along with Harry and myself, speakers and presenters included Hugh Hallman, the mayor of Tempe; Peggy Neely, the vice mayor of Phoenix; and Philip Gordon, the mayor of Phoenix; Tom Brock; and Hall of Flame Fire Museum Director Peter Molloy. They all spoke of the connections that bind us to 9/11 and to our cause.

What is more, they noted that both Tempe and Phoenix are greatly populated by transplanted New Yorkers in search of perpetual sun, creating a particularly special bond between the two cities.

Residual activities over the next couple of days included a celebration in a local park where an incredibly large National Flag of Unity, composed of the flags of all states in the union, was raised by fire truck cranes. Arranged by an array of local fire departments, including Phoenix, Globe, Tempe and Buckeye, it was a breathtaking sight, unlike anything I had ever seen, symbolically bringing our nation together in the context of addressing our 9/11 rescue and recovery workers cause.

There was a Memorial 5K walk in Phoenix, with literally thousands of participants, and what was billed as a *Barbecue with the Champs.* Harry and Stacey hung in with me for days and we met so many great people, young and old, and I was literally numbed by the ongoing effort of leaders and locals in Phoenix and its surrounding municipalities. They went above and beyond any call to both welcome and celebrate *a Journey for 9/11.*

We then walked through the desert, wholly buoyed by goodness, so much so that the Arizona heat that beat the Oklahoma cold hardly bothered us at all. The elements just don't seem to be a problem when you're walking on air, raised up as we were by a neighborly goodness of monumental proportions. And while fire departments in western Arizona continued to join us, Lee and I actually were left to our own devices for a few days as we approached California, the 13th and final state of the *Journey.*

On our last day in Arizona, we had a tremendous Yuma County and City of Yuma escort leading us to the bridge over the Colorado River. Yuma Mayor Lawrence Nelson presented me with the Yuma city medallion, and there, at what was our 2827th mile, he noted that "This *Journey*, which will soon be coming to a close, pales in comparison to those of our first responders, whose journeys will comprise the all of their lives." With the mayor's blessing, accompanied by both Arizona and California Highway Patrol officers, we proceeded to cross the bridge into California and the Fort Yuma Indian Reservation, home of the Quechan tribe.

We then walked through the desert, wholly numbed by goodness, so much so that the Arizona heat that beat the Oklahoma cold hardly bothered us at all.

The "Welcome to California" sign was accompanied by a "Welcome to California, George Martin – *a Journey for 9/11*" sign. Leave it to Lee, my compadre, my Man Friday, my Sancho, my best friend, my leader, to do the subtle little things to accent our accomplishment.

For "California, Here We Come," and California, there we were, knocking on the door of fulfillment.

On that same June 5, Christopher "Kip" Condron, AXA's chairman and chief executive officer, back on the other side of the country, announced that I would be receiving AXA's 2008 Darwin Davis Award for Community Service. While you already know how I feel about being personally raised up, I do celebrate the good that it does for our mission and this came with a $10,000 stipend that would, of course, go to the *Journey*.

Throughout California, Mitch Mendler, a firefighter, sought to assure us that we would be escorted everywhere. While we appreciated his interest and concern, his zealousness for us turned our *Journey* into a new and modern version of the Keystone Cops from time to time, as he literally had escort units tripping over each other and teams ready and waiting for us down the road when we were nowhere in sight. The truth is where we needed one, Mitch usually called upon three or four or more just to be sure.

He loved us that much and he "doth protested" a tad too much on our behalf.

Oh, how we loved the sun and the low-lying mountains and the Calexico sunsets and the warmth of California and its 109 miles to San Diego signs, and then 79 miles and 35 miles signs. Excited, exhausted, about all we noticed were the miles left and the good firefighters and police who accompanied us. Before long, it was the Alpine and La Mesa Fire Departments and motorcycle patrols and conversations with an array of women's groups and what I refer to as the "boys in the hood."

California also marked a reunion of sorts between Lee and his eldest son, Octavius, a former U.S. Marine and now marketing executive who at the time lived in San Diego. "OCT," as I referred to him, decided to come out on the road and show the older generation a thing or two about fitness, a miscalculation that he regrets to this very day. After nearly 3,000 miles of relentless daily rigor, OCT's challenge to Lee and myself proved to be no contest, and like the infamous Roberto Duran vs. Sugar Ray Leonard fight, OCT's "No Mas, No Mas" came a mere three miles into the contest.

Every conversation with anyone on the road started to take on higher and deeper meaning as we inched closer to the finish.

Everything, and the slightest of things, took on greater intensity.

In California, we met desert lizards and inviting lavender skies and sunsets that never disappointed. We met green fields of palm trees and scrub pine and fields of beautiful wild flowers. Then in Embarcadero Marina Park, we met the Pacific and sails and a day with blue skies and a bright sun that was made in Heaven to honor our finish.

Yes, nature never disappoints and God speaks to us through all of it. In sunshine and in shadow, on the mountaintops or in the wetlands, in the lush green forests and rich rock outcroppings, and in the most spectacular of sunrises and sunsets. He speaks to us.

Tired as I was and as much as I wanted to finish, there were component pieces of the *Journey* that I longed to hold onto. I wanted to hold onto these chance gatherings that I had been blessed to have with thousands upon thousands of Americans.

In the end, it had not been about fulfilling the dream of walking across America; having met America loomed as ever so much more important.

In bits and pieces, along the way, I had indeed met the problems and the struggles, the hopes and the faith, and the visions and dreams of the American people, who showed me that what they believe and live and value is ever so much more open and honest and hopeful than is our politics.

*****

It was a lighter-than-air, exciting, and brilliant morning for the end of our *Journey*.

Just 5 miles left to the Pacific shore in beautiful San Diego, America's city of St. James, and while I did not walk The Way of St. James – Spain's El Camino de Santiago – *Journey* had been my Way, my pilgrimage, my personal reckoning.

Suddenly, as if in a dream, we were walking with a mob of people along the crowded San Diego Boulevard, past the churches and the banks and the shops and the hotels and the pandemonium, past the corner of Georgia Street and El Cajon Boulevard, past 3 and 2 and 1 mile signs, past the 9-and-a-half months and the fragility of expectations and all of the "*what ifs*" and *"wonderings"* and *"what may yet come to passes*."

There I was, again as if in a dream, with my arms raised high in Embarcadero Park in the company of a crowd that seemed so very similar to the one that had been with me back at the George Washington Bridge, in what now seemed a lifetime ago.

The faces of the fire and police and local officials were indeed different, and this time, rather remarkably, my Mom was with us. I'm not a teary guy, and the only time my eyes moistened on the *Journey* was in Oklahoma City remembering the children lost in the domestic terrorism there. The only time, that is, until I was able to push my mother across the finish line in her wheelchair. When she sees her children having such an impact on society, it overwhelms her. That was probably one of the proudest moments of her life.

As to the rest, there were Dianne and my children and their spouses, and there was Ken Vehrkens and Dave and Alice Jurist and John Kirksey, Ed Mullins and other board members, and friends and our "Wizard Behind the Curtain" Jennifer Skor, and Jay Winuk and Tom Brock and Lee's beautiful bride to be, and Phil McConkey, another former teammate and the day's master of ceremonies.

It was a crowd that seemed familiar to me after all the supportive crowds on the *Journey*, and the simple summer celebration that we enjoyed in that park was just perfect. In the midst of it, I reflected upon

My Mom, Janie, launched me on life's journey on February 16, 1953. And she helped me complete *a Journey for 9/11* on June 21, 2008. Here we are together, approaching the finish line, in San Diego, California.

all those who gave the *Journey* life and made it happen, upon all those who worked for nine and a half months to fulfill it, and upon the endless array of good people who contributed, cheered, and/or inspired us along the way.

Each and every one had been a blessing and a gift outright.

What a sight was the marina beyond Embarcadero Park – welcome, inviting and beautiful. There was a collage of *a Journey for 9/11* tees and warm-up suits and "*We Will Never Forget*" patches. There were giant American flags and patriotic hats and "Worn with pride in the memory of our fallen brothers" patches and shirts. In the final mile, I was surrounded by people carrying "Thanks, George Martin" signs, and by bagpipers and motorcycle escorts. I leaped across the finish into the arms of my Mom and Dianne and my children and great supporters and friends like Ken and David and Phil. The first responders, fire companies and police, and friends looked very much like they did at the beginning at the George Washington Bridge in New York. Of beginnings and ends, there were stark similarities and the same celebratory aura, separated by some 3,003 miles and 5 million steps and many a pair of sneakers and socks.

From the nation's largest city to its 8th largest, from the waters of the Atlantic to the Pacific, from the retired aircraft carrier Intrepid on the Hudson to the retired USS Midway at San Diego, from New York to the City of Saint James and a phalanx of recreational vehicles celebrating *Journey* and loudly proclaiming "Thanks," the physical journey was complete.

*****

a Journey for 9/11 had been blessed. I had been blessed. A difference had been made and I was at peace.

The very next day, the 22nd, Lee and his beautiful bride would be married and I would have the distinct honor of being his best man. Not bad for my first post-*Journey* duty.

The *Journey*, of course, continued as John Ferguson and then Robert Garrett of Hackensack University Medical Center, and Michael Dowling of North Shore LIJ, and Wayne E. Deathly of Mount Sinai proceeded to fulfill their generous commitments.

On September 24, sportscaster Len Berman presented me with a "Sports Angels Inspiration Award," and our own *a Journey for 9/11* fundraising gala at the (now unfortunately closed) Sports Museum of America in New York City, which recognized Frank Gifford and my old teammates Harry Carson, Sean Landeetta and Mark Bavaro. Finally, on September 29, I was again honored at the Sergeant's Benevolent Association's 101st Annual Heroism Awards event. Me, I was merely the pass-through for the accolades to the *Journey* and to its mission, and so to the better America and the better world that people of goodwill everywhere long for.

We are all in it together, as the people who crossed our path on this extraordinary *Journey* seemed to understand.

*****

Our goal, of course, was first to raise awareness, to make America cognizant of what was happening to the 9/11 rescue and recovery workers and to place a spotlight on the effort to pass the Zadroga bill progressing in Washington, D.C., to come to their aid. There we no doubt succeeded.

Secondly, we also aimed to raise $10 million for healthcare monitoring and treatment of the rescue and recovery workers, and whether or not we succeeded becomes a matter of interpretation. Hard dollar-wise, we fell short as we raised just under $2.5 million, but we got three hospitals each to match that in services delivered, so there's the $10 million. Then too, there's the Dietl contribution and the Fuchs contribution and the Reeves contribution and the AXA Equitable contribution and the Best Western contribution, and the list goes on and on.

We would have liked to have raised more, but we certainly moved a paradigm, and honestly, while I believe that I'm good at a number of things, professional fundraiser wouldn't be anywhere near the top of my list. We did have one great day in Tennessee where we raised $26,000 at Casey Jones Village, and we had just as great a day when that young boy of no more than 9 sat out in the middle of nowhere in Oklahoma with a brown bag full of the $3.78 that he extracted from his piggy bank. I'm serious in telling you that we must have been 10 miles or more away from the nearest human being or building. It was just that beautiful boy and his bike and his bag full of $3.78, and a young heart that was bigger than the whole state of Oklahoma.

By the way, I kept that brown bag and the $3.78, just as I kept the jug with the 911 pennies. In lieu of giving these pieces of young hearts up, I made a personal donation of $1,000.

A steal, I know, for their value is priceless!

It is my firm belief that our real contribution was not in dollars and cents, but rather in raising awareness about the plight of the Ground Zero workers, in changing and then reinforcing a public mindset, and in helping to get the national legislation passed that finally addressed this critical issue. There was always this overarching desire on our part to impact the public perception of whose responsibility this was. With the great help of the press and the expressions of concern from a limitless array of average Americans, I can confidently say that *a Journey for 9/11* succeeded in doing that; and we have the thank-you letters from the congressional delegation that finally won the day attesting to our help.

For the all of this, we were blessed and fulfilled, and are so very, very grateful.

THE FINAL CHAPTER

After a rather euphoric conclusion to the *Journey* in San Diego, along with the customary pomp and circumstance that comes with triumphant endeavors, I was indeed ready for a long and secluded respite of anonymity and social withdrawal, far away from the glaring public spotlight. Unfortunately, to whom much is given, much is expected, and there was an extensive list of invaluable associates, supporters and sponsors who wanted – and in some cases – insisted on my presence as they paid appropriate tribute to a remarkable milestone accomplishment of *a Journey for 9/11.*

The *Journey's* West Coast celebration had concluded with the spectacular wedding ceremony of my road manager, Lee Reeves, and his fiancé, Flora DeJesus, aboard the decommissioned and iconic aircraft carrier the USS Midway, now a floating museum prominently anchored in San Diego Bay. This was an extremely fitting moment for a man who had sacrificially partnered with a rather deranged colleague, while also leaving his family behind over the previous eight and a half months to positively impact society's unsung heroes.

The actual finish line of *Journey* during the Embarcadero Marina Park festivities best resembled a condensed version of New Orleans' annual Mardi Gras extravaganza. Huge San Diego fire trucks with a gigantic American flag draped around them served as the ceremonial backdrop for our festive assembly. The ever-present Irish bagpipes, playing with such orchestrated, rhythmic precision in this final parade added patriotic flavor and exceptional pageantry to the occasion. Hundreds of local and regional first responders, many of whom were adorned in their departmental uniforms, filled out the lengthy precession. My very good friend, Sue Atchison, Community Relations executive for WWE, had also assembled a grand formation of West Coast "Superstar" wrestling talent to participate in the event as well. Friends, relatives, board members and NFL teammates all enthusiastically assembled to bring a fitting conclusion for this remarkable, and yet improbable, *Journey* finale.

After being out on the road and in the hinterlands of America for nearly nine months, and having endured weather conditions of every sort imaginable, along with erratic terrain that was as unpredictable and challenging as any NFL training camp, to say that I was mentally drained and physically exhausted would have been a dramatic understatement. However, the surging adrenaline rush that I was experiencing during the closing celebration was palpable and more than enough to sustain me indefinitely, or so it seemed.

Along with the grandeur of that festive occasion, the entire Journey team had one more rather fitting celebration to undertake. As founder and executive director of *a Journey for 9/11*, I personally felt it a fitting tribute to assemble and acknowledge the wealth of extremely talented and dedicated associates who had banded together to make *Journey* a success. As such, I issued Lee his final official order, and instructed him to convene a gathering of these indispensable souls for a final private West Coast appreciation gala later that evening.

Just off the main boulevard in San Diego's marina district, directly adjacent to the old Spanish adobe courthouse, sits a landmark establishment of Ruth's Chris Steak House. It was there that we decided to break up the band as it were, and just like the nearby USS Midway, to officially decommission this remarkable endeavor, while paying appropriate tribute to all of its stellar mates. Of course, there were many *Journey* participants and enablers who unfortunately could not attend the closing gala, but for those able to attend it was an evening of honor and recognition.

In a private and secluded room, nestled away from the mainstream restaurant patrons, I humbly officiated over an impromptu program of appreciation toward our team. Jay Winuk was naturally recognized for having arranged a hero's welcome of media opportunities for *Journey* throughout its 3,003 miles, and San Diego was certainly no exception. Then there was my great friend, Dean Kenneth T. Vehrkens, lauded for his ever-present contributions representing Fairleigh Dickinson University (FDU), along with an unsung hero in the person of Joseph Thomas from FDU's School of Administrative Science. Joseph was our invaluable back-office IT professor, who continually kept *Journey* front and center with his able students and whose work mapped and measured the progress of the *Journey* from beginning to end.

Our behind-the-scenes guardian angel in the person of Ms. Jennifer Skor, affectionately referred to as our "Wizard Behind the Curtain," had been called upon day and night to keep us on course and on schedule. She was simply remarkable at crisis management, as whenever we needed a lifeline, a remote hotel arrangement, a media contact or restaurant reservation, or even an emergency course correction, she was there. Without Jennifer's constant oversight and guidance, we might still be out wandering about aimlessly in the wilderness, and I was thrilled honor her for her efforts.

In addition to Ken, several other *Journey* board members also made the trip to San Diego. Our treasurer, Dave Jurist, and his wife, Alice, were in attendance, and John Kirksey, a colleague at AXA Equitable at the time, was kind enough to once again join us in tribute to our collective success. Finally, my good pal Ed Mullins, president of the Sergeants Benevolent Association, arrived with an awesome contingent of New York's Finest to cap off the celebration in grand fashion. It was a tremendously emotionally event for all in attendance, as the culmination of a dream had come to marvelous fruition.

Regrettably, other *Journey* standouts such as Brie Ingrid O'Neal, whose organizational genius almost solely launched *Journey* from its

a Journey for 9/11 was a success by any measure. Between donations and in-kind contributions, we raised $5 million to benefit Ground Zero rescue and recovery workers and other emergency responders.

And today I remain especially proud that *a Journey for 9/11* focused attention on the plight of ailing rescue and recovery workers, and helped pass the Zadroga Bill to pay for their ongoing care and treatment. Here, U.S. Rep. Pete King of New York and several other members of Congress endorse the legislation at a *Journey* event in D.C.

Many honors and accolades came my way as a result of *a Journey for 9/11*, including the second-ever Heisman Humanitarian Award. But it was *my* honor to be of service to those who gave so much of themselves as America reeled and then recovered from the national tragedy of September 11, 2001. The first responders, and the rescue and recovery workers, deserve our deepest gratitude.

inception, couldn't be there to take her appropriate and well-deserved bow. Neither could our board's MVP, Andrew Giangola of NASCAR, who constantly garnered respectful praise from everyone for his creativity and exceptionally strong sense of mission. Then there was of course Beau Dietl, who singularly contributed the most by far of actual out-of-pocket costs, supplying all of the security for the entire *Journey* crossing. Thanks Beau. And of course, last but by no means least, Carol and Joe Reich, who not only contributed the initial million dollars, but were absolutely instrumental in connecting *Journey* with a number of exceptional charter schools along the way. These remarkable individuals represented the rule rather than the exception of all who were associated with the success of *a Journey for 911.*

Although the final tally of funds raised by *Journey* would not be concluded for several more weeks, it was clear to all of us that several million dollars had been raised through our collective efforts. Add to that the fact that all moneys would eventually be matched by the three participating hospitals of Mount Sinai, North Shore-LIJ, and Hackensack University Medical Center, there was an undeniable collective sense of pride that completely permeated the entire a *Journey for 911* family. Kudos on an outstanding job well-done one and all.

But to be fair, monies raised really do not tell the entire *Journey* story of overall contributions to our success.

Lee and I were always dismayed that numerous contributions under the "goods and services" category were never entered into the equation. For instance, hotel accommodations were unquestionably one of our largest line-item expenses to contend with. However, when Best Western International came aboard and provided rooms for more than three quarters of the *Journey*, it had a tremendous positive impact on our bottom line. Secondly, there was 24/7 security provided by Beau Dietl & Associates for the entirety of the *Journey*, which was huge to say the least. General Motors, which graciously contributed a brand new recreational vehicle, was a very important contributor as well. Companies such as Nike generously supplied sneakers and sports apparel. MBT donated Mesi Barefoot Technology shoes for rugged terrain. Local family eateries and shops fed and clothed us. These and countless others who made *Journey* the eventual success that it was are all to be saluted. Inevitably, when attempting to list all of the important contributors there will be one or two unintentional omissions. For any such oversights, I want to apologize.

Now that the arduous task of walking more than 3,000 miles across the width of the United States of America had been accomplished and the attendant ceremonies observed, the unenviable process of collecting, packing, labeling, cataloging, identifying and shipping the remnants of our nomadic caravan had unceremoniously descended upon us. Clearly having to marshal all of the accumulation of maps, charts, receipts, sneakers, medical gear, road apparel, awards, memorabilia etc., was a daunting task to say the least. The responsibility of closure was upon us, and we needed all hands on deck to finalize things accordingly.

When we first arrived into San Diego, the *Journey* team had established base-camp and we had all settled into the local-yet-trendy Porto Vista Hotel overlooking the picturesque San Diego Bay. The amount of gear we had accumulated over the past months was simply staggering. Nevertheless, we began sorting by dividing the stuff we wanted to keep versus the items that none of us ever wanted to see again. For example, we had out of necessity accumulated a wide variety of energy bars in order to maintain our stamina. Not the tastiest of treats, eating them was a daily ritual that became nearly unbearable by the end of the trip. As a result, ALL energy bars were deep-sixed into a local food shelter, and I dare say that I have not eaten one such item since that day.

The *Journey* officially ended on June 21, 2008, and the return flight for Dianne and myself, along with our four adult children, all of whom had come out to join in the celebration, on a Continental Airlines non-stop to Newark Airport area was scheduled for June 24. The newly minted Mr. and Mrs. Reeves and various members of their immediate family were also on board. Additionally, final security guard, a gentleman by the name of Bill Crosson and a rather affable individual with a middle-of-the-road, somewhat easygoing personality, joined us. Like all of our team members, Bill was the butt of many pranks and jokes, but always seem to take things in stride. What was unique about

Bill was that he was engaged to a beautiful Latina who read Bill the riot act at every possible occasion. It was indeed hilarious to see our representative of safety and security being reprimanded by this 5-foot, 5-inch beauty at every turn. Bill would go from a pillar of strength to a pillar of salt the moment she walked into the room. Needless to say, we all took great delight in mocking Bill, as it was all in good fun.

We were without a doubt a rather elated and jovial caravan as we boarded that eastbound flight homeward. And yet, I am absolutely certain that each and every one of us gave serious thought to the irony that on September 11 just seven years earlier many airplane journeys began in the same fashion, but would end with the most unimaginable consequences. Those faithful flights of September 11, 2001, would serve as the unfortunate catalyst for our unification as a country in the days and years that followed, a postscript that I am certain none of us will ever forget.

After we all got settled in it was a pleasant and enjoyable flight home. The *Journey* miles taking their toll, I quickly fell into a deep slumber for most of the flight and awakened just before landing. While I was sleeping, Lee had secretly spoken to the flight attendants and alerted the captain of our presence as well as our accomplishments. And so the captain came on the P.A. as we docked at the terminal and regaled the passengers with the story of our milestone feat, and asked if they would please join in acknowledging our triumphant return home. I was totally caught off guard, as Lee knew that I would never have agreed to such a call to attention. But it was an extremely warm and gracious ovation, and many of the passengers came to me to express their personal appreciation for our sacrifice. And it was my naive conclusion then that this was to be the finale of public displays and appearances for quite some time. Wow, was I ever in a fog.

After getting over my initial anger at Lee's well-meaning stunt, I gratefully proceeded through the crowd toward baggage claim in an attempt to retrieve my belongings and get home as fast as possible. But then another round of applause erupted as I was making my way toward the exit. Apparently local TV news had gotten wind of my arrival and dispatched a team to cover the returning Giant. Despite having played for the Giants for 14 NFL seasons, and having done so in the media capital of the world, this was never my particular cup of tea. I would have been perfectly content to fade off into obscurity and remain there for the foreseeable duration.

By now Lee could sense my uneasiness, as he knew very well my displeasure with being spot-lighted, and he quietly interceded and circumvented the remainder of the interview. After a barrage of autographs and pats on the back I was finally safe and secure in the car we had arranged and homeward bound at last.

Or so I thought. Before we could get moving, Lee came running over to me in his usual excitable manner and blurted, "GUESS WHAT!? George you've been nominated for an ESPY!"

"WHAT?" I replied.

"Yes, I just spoke to Jay and he confirmed that you were nominated for an ESPY!"

For those unfamiliar with the ESPYs, it represents ESPN's version of the Academy Awards for sports figures. WOW, what an honor, and very much a stellar surprise. Lee went on to say, yeah, well, that's the good news, to which I replied, "And the bad news is what?"

"It's being filmed in LA and we have to return to California in a couple of days in order to take part in the televised ceremony," he said.

Let's see, I've just spend eight and a half months *walking* across the entire width of the United States of America, I'm suffering from every iniquitous malady known to man, including sleep deprivation, homesickness, fatigue, swollen joints and will probably need a full time podiatrist for the rest of my life, I don't want to go back to California in any way shape or form on the off chance that I might win this award, however prestigious. Not walking, riding, driving, flying or even in Captain James Tiberius Kirk's warp-driven Starship Enterprise. Do the math yourself, Lee!

But wouldn't you know it, turns out that I actually won the category that I was nominated for. DAMN Lee, he should have talked me into it. And little did I know that this was merely to be a sneak preview of many such things to come.

Ahhhh, home, sweet home. Our house of more than 20 years in Ringwood never felt so good. It was sheer delight to be able to wake up in one's own domicile and not be faced with the perpetual question of "Where the hell am I today?", a recurring nightmare that plagued me while out on the road so long. In reflection, I had set out to accomplish something unique and tangibly poignant.

As I had done all of my adult life, I quickly begin to assess the efforts and results of my *Journey* goals, and after a cursory examination, I was totally satisfied with the results. I intended to raise both money and awareness for a sector of heroes who I admired and appreciated. And with the prospect of the Zadroga bill pending in Congress and glaring brightly, it would be merely a matter of time before it would receive the necessary approvals and be voted into law.

Once firmly back on New York soil, a grand celebration as we had done in San Diego was understandably in order. The very capable *Journey* dignitaries began the coordinated effort of assembling a royal reception fit for a king, and it was appropriately scheduled at the now-unfortunately closed Sports Museum of America, which was located in lower Manhattan's financial district.

a Journey for 911's closing ceremony was an exceptionally stunning affair to say the least. The "Who's Who" in the annals of the New York Football Giants were front and center, and I was absolutely astonished at the caliber of well-known attendees that graced the evening's soiree. The entire Mara family was present and well represented, including who could be considered the quintessential royalty of the NFL, Mrs. Ann Mara herself, wife of the late Wellington Mara. Naturally, her son John, president of the New York Football Giants, was also in attendance along with his wife, Denise, and presented me with a very flattering acknowledgement for *Journey.*

Scores of former Giants' teammates, current players, owners and alumni from across the NFL adorned the hallways of the Sports Museum, which lent itself to an enormously successful evening. Longtime Giants' employee and *Journey*'s only female board member, Joanne Lamneck, did a simply fantastic job at getting so many notable Giants alumni to be a part of this historic occasion. Tiki Barber, former all-pro running back; along with fellow running back Lee Rouson; former Giants team Captain Doug Van Horn; Sean Landetta, who played 20 years in the NFL as an outstanding All-Pro punter; phenomenal tight-end Mark Bavaro; two-time Super Bowl champion offensive lineman William Roberts; and my very good pal and Super Bowl 25 MVP O.J. Anderson rounding out the cast.

Several new-found associates whom we had befriended out on the road during the *Journey* were also in attendance. Deputy Sheriff Glenn Russ of the Curry County Sheriff's Office in New Mexico was such a dedicated believer that he and his wife made the journey to New York to present me with his shield, which humbled me to my very core and still does to this day. In addition, 4-foot 8-inch Arizona paramedic Erica Waters, whom we all absolutely fell in love with, also braved the journey along with her new husband, and presented me with her paramedic's badge as well.

9/11 rescue and recovery workers and the hospitals caring for them also helped make this a remarkable gathering, a true convergence of all the people who made *Journey* happen.

The entire evening was hosted by the noted and rather dashing TV anchorman Maurice Dubois of WCBS-TV, Channel 2 in New York. Maurice, along with nearly all of the local televisions stations, had completely embraced the *Journey* and I had appeared on his show on several occasions during the cross-country event.

Additionally, there were the not-so-usual suspects who lent themselves to the elegant and star-studded evening. Giants' Hall of Famer and former General Manager Andy Robustelli was there along with his beautiful bride, as well as Hall of Famer Harry Carson, out front and center, naturally. The vast majority of the *Journey* Board of Directors were present and accounted for, including Ken Vehrkens, Dave Jurist, John Kirksey, Andrew Giangola, Ed Mullins, Joe and Carol Reich, of course, and the ubiquitous Beau Dietl was also among the illustrious faithful.

After a litany of extremely impressive awards, speeches and presentations, the evening fittingly concluded with a check presentation in the amount of $250,000, which was made directly to Executives of

Hackensack University Medical Center. This was to be merely the first of several installments that the three designated hospitals would eventually receive, however not under such lavish circumstances. In all, it was an event that literally saw me brought to tears; I was humbled, stunned and speechless over the outpouring of appreciation that the City of New York and its many diverse friends and representatives, forged together by the 9/11 tragedy, displayed toward this son of a South Carolinian sharecropper.

As I earnestly attempted to retreat back into the quiet repose of being George Martin, it quickly became evident that the terms "quiet" and"repose" were not going to be an option. Shortly after declining to attend and yet winning the ESPY Hummer "Like Nothing Else" award, I received a call from, of all interested parties, *Dancing With The Stars*. This to me was pretty funny, as anyone who has ever seen me attempting to dance will tell you that those two concepts simply don't go together. In my estimation, I was the only African-American male in the world who was completely deficient in the dancing department. Of course, I would eventually be proven horribly wrong when former NFL wide receiver Jerry Rice, my Giants' teammate Lawrence Taylor, and comedian D.L. Hughley proceeded to lower the bar somewhere beneath Antarctica on the global dancing scale. In 20/20 hindsight, next to those three, who at times seemed to have shared six left feet between them, I might have been the black Fred Astaire. Of course we'll never know, now will we?

Shortly thereafter the proverbial floodgates began to open. During the course of *Journey* and well prior, too, I had accumulated quite a few IOU markers in order to assure success of the mission, and now a multitude of organizations were calling in their chips for an understandable quid pro quo. Please understand that embarking upon *Journey* was never intended to result into an act of self-aggrandizement, rather quite the opposite. It was always intended to highlight and elevate heroic acts of first responders and rescue and recovery personnel. However, I quickly came to realize that my appearance at many other charitable affairs was indeed another act of contributing to the success of *a Journey for 9/11.*

The number of post-*Journey* accolades and requests were simply staggering, and at times, I was in total disbelief. Jay Winuk was more than a bit preoccupied fielding all of the incoming requests, while acting as my official agent and still retaining the position of my PR guru. Many of the truly remarkable honors were beyond my wildest imagination and to this day are prominently displayed in my home and office. For example, in 2007 I was awarded only the second Heisman Humanitarian award in history during the annual trophy ceremony in New York City. This also included a $5,000 check, which naturally I donated to *a Journey for 9/11*. The illustrious Tim Tebow was the recipient of the Heisman Trophy that year and this was simply a spine-tingling affair.

In the fall of 2007, I was awarded an Ellis Island Medal of Honor, in company with a host of mega-star recipients including singer Gloria Estefan. What an indescribable honor. Additionally, I was truly blessed to have been the recipient of The New York Sergeants Benevolent Association's Humanitarian of the Year award as well. However, the award that I received as a result of my *Journey* of which I am proudest was given away in similar fashion as my Super Bowl Championship Ring, which I had immediately bequeathed to my eldest son, George II. Fairleigh Dickinson University bestowed upon me an honorary Doctor of Humane Letters degree during its 2008 graduation ceremony. On that occasion I was nearly in tears, and paused for a moment to allow that humbling recognition to sink in and to be thoroughly enjoyed. At the conclusion of the event, I shipped the award out to my mother in Seattle, Washington, as she was my sole inspiration for every molecule of that award. "Common sense is an uncommon virtue" – Mother proved to be absolutely correct.

Of course there were many more awards and accolades forthcoming as a result of my *Journey*'s accomplishment. The Arthur Ashe Humanitarian Award, The Boys and Girls Clubs of America, The New York Football Giants Wellington T. Mara Award, named after the owner of the Giants. Also The New York City Fire Fighters Humanitarian Award, The Bill Walsh Champion of Change Award, The NFL Players Association Award, and many, many more. Even the World Wrestling Entertainment WWE presented me with "The

Peoples Champ's" belt, which incidentally I have hung proudly as a centerpiece in my office to this day. But I always attempted to maintain a staunch sense of humility and tried diligently to keep things in proper perspective. Once again, as a professional athlete, which is the equivalent of entertainer, I have never been asked to sacrifice my life in the line of duty. That, my friends, should serve as the definitive standard for true and genuine heroes in our society.

I had begun my improbable *Journey* at the rather mature age of 54 years old. I had played in the National Football League for 14 years, and upon my voluntary retirement in 1988, I went on to complete nearly 20 years as an executive in corporate America. In 2007 the nation's economy was experiencing a dramatic economic decline and beginning its worse recession since the 1930s. Of course, this was brought on by the toxic assets in the housing market, and quickly exacerbated by Wall Street's "too big to fail" multibillion dollar federal bailout. The country was also embroiled in a presidential election process, and as I recall, there was a highly contested Democratic primary race between veteran politician Hillary Rodham Clinton and a young African-American congressional upstart by the name of Barack Hussein Obama.

During the *Journey* itself, I recall rushing to the hotel room or lobby TV after the day's tasks were completed and becoming totally mesmerized by the series of heated debates between the two Democratic contenders. It was, of course, history in the making – a contest between the first female with a real chance of winning the presidency and the first African-American in the same position, who would eventually go on after the primaries to challenge Republican John McCain. Needless to say, we were gripped by every aspect of that election, certainly one for the record books. Nevertheless, as we progressed westward, the political debates, presidential primaries and election to come weren't the only concerns on our minds, there was of course the overall state of the economy, and what was to be in the aftermath of our concluded mission.

As fortune would have it, AXA Equitable was experiencing its own economic challenges during my charitable excursion and an internal reorganization was fully underway during my absence, resulting in me being offered a generous corporate buyout of my executive position. After consulting with Dianne, we decided that perhaps my nearly 35 years of non-stop travel could be put on a well-deserved sabbatical. So I gladly opted for the buyout and proceeded to seek a new challenge in life. As fate would have it, I wouldn't have to wait very long for my next opportunity.

With prodding from friends and colleagues who believed in my abilities, after AXA I took on the challenge of being the first president and executive director of the NFL Alumni Association. I saw it as an extension of what I had done previously as an NFL Player Representative, and felt it would be a natural move from advocating on the national front for 9/11 rescue and recovery workers to advocating once again for my former colleagues. I am proud that I was able to help increase retirement benefits substantially for NFL Alumni, and likewise assist those alumni and their families who suffer the lingering effects of their years on the field in this "collision" sport. Many former NFL players suffer from disabling joint and skeletal problems, as well as psychological and cognitive issues from the non-stop blows to the head, and resulting concussions, that are part of the game. Though the NFL has recognized the concussion problem and reached a settlement with former players, much remains to be done to protect current and future athletes – not just football players, but ice hockey, lacrosse and soccer, as well – from the depression and dementia of chronic traumatic encephalopathy.

However, the overall NFLAA job, after the spiritual and emotional triumph of *Journey*, was a major letdown, and perhaps one of the few risks in my life that I regret taking. But that's another story for another time.

*****

Many years have now passed since my father's unfortunate departure. However, hardly a day goes by that I don't integrate some of his immutable wisdom into my life. "Son," he often said, "as long as you live, please try and leave this world a better place than how you found it." With that indelible imperative in mind, I proudly became the first in my family to obtain a college degree. I was invited to the White House on two separate occasions to be honored by two sitting presidents – once by Ronald Reagan for our Super Bowl victory, and second by George W. Bush for my charitable accomplishments. I became a professional athlete for 14 seasons, along with team captainship, team Chapel Leader, and eventually President of the NFL Players Association. By the way, we also happened to have won a Super Bowl Championship as well.

The civic awards themselves are far too numerous to recite individually, but suffice to say that among my proudest professional accomplishments was when I was presented with Byron "Whizzer" White NFL Man of the Year Award – named for the man who was both a Supreme Court justice and a pro football halfback. As the single NFL athlete to win the award in 1987 for exceptional accomplishments, it was indeed validation that I had somehow distinguished myself among my nearly 2,000 NFL peers at the time.

As for *a Journey for 9/11*, it hasn't really ended - not yet. The Zadroga Bill, which I believe my *Journey* helped to gain passage in Congress, continues to care for 9/11 responders who become ill as a result of their work. The three hospitals remain on the case, and have used some of the money we raised to prepare for future emergencies with essential services such as an Emergency Medical Response Unit, complete with mobile diagnostics and operating rooms, that can be set up and functioning quickly at the site of future catastrophes.

Though the 501(c)(3) today is inactive, we haven't closed it down, and every once in a while another $100 contribution comes in the mail. In fact, in 2013, we were able to make an additional $50,000 donation to Mount Sinai Hospital. We also continued with commemorative walks from the George Washington Bridge to Fairleigh Dickinson University and Hackensack University Medical Center, and it is very meaningful to me that people I meet remember me not only as No. 75 of the New York Football Giants, but the guy who walked across America and helped a vital cause.

Today, my main cause is Minority Athletes Networking Etc., Inc., which I co-founded more than 25 years ago. As Executive Director, I work toward the success of its many programs, including youth basketball and football, SAT prep, mentoring and a scholarship fund. MAN is a unique conglomerate of former professional athletes, corporate executives, attorneys, entrepreneurs and performing artists with a deep, abiding social commitment.

And I cherish my family, including my four kids – all of whom played sports, and the youngest of whom had his own NFL tryout – my six grandchildren, and of course, my Dianne. We just celebrated our 40th wedding anniversary.

Like *a Journey for 9/11*, my life has been a collection of far-reaching goals. I'm not certain if I have accomplished all that needs to be done, as my journey is as yet incomplete, but God only knows that I have certainly given it one hell of a try.

EPILOGUE

Everyone over the age of 19 remembers exactly where they were when the towers fell. We remember just where we were and what we were doing when we first heard that a plane pierced the World Trade Center. Even before racing to the TV, to view it all up close and personal, we heard and we remember. It is one of those moments in a life that is forever frozen in time.

It's almost hard to believe that it was 13 years ago, for it was only yesterday or so it seems, just yesterday and memories of it still stun and numb and devastate.

Maybe you were in the playground at Holy Trinity Grammar School or walking to your office on 43rd Street or in your kitchen sipping coffee in Ringwood, New Jersey, or at a committee meeting in a conference room in an office complex in Rutherford. You were there, on your cell phone or with your hands on the steering wheel of your new Honda, or before the computer that you had just opened up, or maybe you were getting the news from passersby on the corner of 59th and 5th.

And even if you were but being born, it is a story that you have been told about again and again.

Others, of course, were in an elevator in the North Tower on their way up to the 96th floor, or on the ferry or PATH train on their way to a meeting at the Port Authority offices, or in the subway beneath the World Trade Center Plaza. Or maybe they were members of the NYPD or the New York City Fire Department in nearby precincts or garages who had just listened to the morning roll call or wet down their prized rigs.

All those police and firefighters, lawyers, accountants, brokers, advertising agents, marketing gurus, adjusters, consultants and priests – stunned and murdered out of a clear blue sky – they were our friends, our husbands and our wives, and our parents and our children. They were loved and cherished. They belonged and they believed and they dreamed. They were ours. They were America's.

Oh, we remember all right, that stark, horrific, so very vulnerable moment. We remember thinking, who, what, how, why? We remember the questions surging within, the "Oh my God" questions that we asked of each other and the answers that did not come – at least not then.

But in the moment, it was enough to know that whoever it was had the capacity to hit us with a gut punch in the heartland and lifeblood of American commerce, as they reduced the most iconic commercial center in the greatest city in the world to rubble.

Oh so suddenly, we were bleeding and broken, and there most of us found ourselves, silent and numb before the TV, as we cried when we watched some poor souls who would rather jump out of a 95th floor window than burn to death. And when the towers fell, we imagined the firemen and police who were climbing up the steps and the thousands who had been unable to escape and were desperately trying to reach their families to say "I love you" one last time. Human beings were, right before our eyes and oh so suddenly, reduced to bone fragments and black ash.

And then there were the tens of thousands in the vicinity who were bathed in black soot and grime and toxic dust, frightened-looking, alien-like creatures caught in this vortex of madness. As most so understandably ran from, there were others who kept running into the heart of the black cloud, toward the destruction, in the hope that defied reason that there would still be some left there to save. Yes, there were many who kept rushing into the fire and the black cloud and the darkness.

Human beings were, right before our eyes and oh so suddenly, reduced to bone fragments and black ash.

They were EMTs and firefighters and police officers largely, but private citizens as well, people desperate to help, to dare to try to do anything other than simply stand by and watch.

It was for them and their health and their care-giving needs that I walked some six years later across an America for which September 11, 2001, remained a gaping wound, into a nation of people who remembered exactly where they were when they first got the news and where they were when the towers fell, and where they were when the black cloud and darkness enveloped downtown New York.

As most so understandably ran from, there were others who kept running into the heart of the black cloud, towards the destruction in the hope that defied reason that there would still be some left there to save.

So, I have often been taken by this thought, by the thought that this is ultimately a book about redemption, for both in this story and in our daily comings and goings in life, we work to save each other. In both simple and profound ways, we do this.

We save each other in this life, and with God by our side we also redeem each other. I am forever moved by the story of the firefighters who struggled to take one disabled woman down the steps of the second tower after the first had fallen. Aware of their grave danger, they refused to abandon her and in the end found themselves in that reinforced structural cavity on the 8th floor, which stayed intact during the collapse. Ironically, it was she who saved her would-be saviors. Yes, indeed, we save each other and with grace, we redeem each other.

*****

Every day, on my *Journey for 9/11* into the heartland of America, we remembered and prayed for those who passed that bleak morning, and for the many in our dominion who remained victimized by the toxins that had made their home in that black cloud - our *Journey for 9/11* responder family!

I have in the preceding pages tried to do justice to my story and the story of *a Journey for 9/11* … and, in the telling, to do justice to our rescue and recovery workers as well. I focused upon all of the critical moments, experiences, people, perceptions and reflections. And I am satisfied with both the story and our telling of it.

In a very real way, 9/11 forced America into a new and turbulent age, and into a nebulous future. Our response to it and its impact is still being felt and men and women from every state in our land have given their "last full measure of devotion" in places like Iraq and Afghanistan. In fact, more have died in 9/11's wake than on that infamous day itself. And so many of those I sought to serve also have fallen to a phalanx of cancers and lung ailments.

They are, each and every one of them, ours. And America, you and I, we owe a solemn duty to all the dead, the dying, and the living. I have spent years working with good congressmen and women in an ongoing effort to wake up Washington, so that we as a nation might finally and fully embrace that duty.

I forever remain a New York Football Giant, proud of having been a captain and of having played a role in winning a Super Bowl championship for the greatest football fans in the world. Oh, that was a moment all right. Just to be on that field being embraced by one tear-stained teammate after another was beyond any imagining.

But my greatest experience and the apex of my life, beyond my marriage to Dianne and the birth of our children, was *a Journey for 9/11.* Those nine months, replete with extraordinary moments on an almost mystical sojourn across this beautiful land on behalf of first responders, were the ultimate.

Yes, I am George Martin, Football Giant. That I spent more time working with Tanagraphics and AXA Equitable does not change that, nor did my recent stint as president of the National Football League Alumni Association, and nor will any other endeavor of mine in this lifetime. I am, forever, a student of Bill Parcells and so proud to have been in his company and to have been worthy of playing on a his team.

On *a Journey for 9/11,* my almost mystical sojourn into the heart of America, I would be received always as a Giant who just happened to have the good fortune of sacking John Elway in a late January Super Bowl and swimming in a sea of confetti.

Yes, there was the occasional question about playing for Bill Parcells or with Harry Carson or Phil Simms or Lawrence Taylor, but in truth and in large measure, those I met rarely talked football. It was 9/11 experiences and memories and stories that they wanted to share. We talked about what made us proud to be Americans and how we came together as one people in the wake of that day, and why it was that we could not sustain that sense of belonging and common purpose. We shared what it was about the promise of America that we hung onto, and about hopes and aspirations and dreams, and about putting food on the table and dodging bullets and running the good race and making it work.

But my greatest experience and the apex of my life, beyond my marriage to Dianne and the birth of our children, was* a Journey for 9/11*. Those nine months, replete with extraordinary moments on an almost mystical sojourn across this beautiful land on behalf of first responders, were the ultimate.

Some talked about their love of family and others about their heroes or their troubled children, or keeping a tractor running or their spouse's cancer, or where the best fishing holes in the vicinity were. And while there was no time for fishing in the running rivers or muddy creeks or mystic lakes that we passed, we fished all right, for a broken, tattered and worn, yet resilient American Dream, for that is what we unmasked on *Journey.*

In the hardworking, persevering, courageous, generous people I met day after day, I discovered an America that still believes in tomorrow and in better days to come, and in beating the odds and in damning the gods above to take their best shots. Up close and personal, day after day, I met goodness and grace and belief and that old fire in the belly and the faith that gave rise to an American Dream to begin with.

So pay no attention to the polls, cynics or disgruntled commentators on the state of contemporary America who want to lay the darkness upon you, for in the most intimate of ways, I read the pulse of this land. And we remain a people of hope and optimism who are still willing to lay it all on the line in order to grow and achieve. Great or small, your fellow Americans in the 13 states I walked through hold onto dreams – a home, a car, beating back the cancer or addiction, owning a restaurant, getting a better job, helping a son through rehab, returning to college, becoming a minister, seeing the Grand Canyon or the waves of the Pacific and Atlantic. Measured and reasonable, they look first to feed and to clothe and to house and then to advance and to cure and to be part of the answer. They hold on tight to their dreams, and they do not let go.

Up close and personal, day after day, I met goodness and grace and belief and that old fire in the belly and faith that gave rise to an American Dream to begin with.

In the final analysis, while *Journey* fulfilled its mission for 9/11 Ground Zero workers as best it could, and even more importantly, helped to fashion a paradigm shift on their behalf in Washington D.C., it also was, in its own unique and powerful way, a reaffirmation of faith in the promise of America.

I know, because I had the privilege of talking to America and what I heard lifted and inspired. Believers still, dreamers still, and proud to be American, we remain a nation of "whalers and explorers" with "promises to keep."

And keep them, we will!

A POST-MORTEM

Having read this work, you already know this – Lee Reeves is as extraordinary a friend as one can have. Volunteering to join me on this *Journey*, he gave his all to our mission and quite literally helped carry me when either the tedium or problems that we confronted threatened to break us – problems that he tried his best to buffer me from.

His inherent humility and generosity grounded me always and enabled me to keep my eye on the prize. And whether it was 10 degrees with 50 miles per hour headwinds in Oklahoma or 110 degrees in an Arizona desert, he laughed and smiled and found the joy in each moment, as well as in each other.

And to Flora, then his bride to be, who gave Lee to me for 9 months and put off their wedding until the day after – the very day after – we completed our *Journey*.

Lee and Flora are my heroes, the heroes of *a Journey for 9/11*. Their sacrifice forever humbles me.

ABOUT THE AUTHOR

George Martin was born on February 16, 1953, grew up in South Carolina, Georgia and California, and went to college on a football/basketball scholarship. Drafted by the New York Football Giants, he scored a quarterback sack on his first set of downs in his first professional game, and went on to become captain of the team and make history in the NFL.

Martin later graduated from Fairleigh Dickinson University through a program he helped create for Pro Footballers who wanted to finish their degrees. He has been president of both the NFL Players Association and the NFL Alumni Association. George Martin also co-founded and is Executive Director of Minority Athletes Networking Etc., Inc., dedicated to making a difference in the lives of inner-city and "at-risk" children.

A resident of New Jersey, George Martin has been married to his high-school sweetheart, Dianne, for more than 40 years. They have four adult children and six adorable grandchildren.

24523498R00189

Made in the USA
Middletown, DE
27 September 2015